Praise for *Human Leadership*

"Through honesty, humility, and hard-earned wisdom, Kristen Hadeed demonstrates that lasting leadership growth begins with the courage to face who we are and who we can become. A valuable read for leaders at every stage of their journey."

—Marshall Goldsmith
Thinkers50 #1 Leadership Thinker and
New York Times bestselling author

"We spend so much of our lives becoming who we think we *should* be. Not without tenderness and fierce compassion does Kristen Hadeed remind us that the real work of our lives is remembering who we've been all along. This book is generous, courageous, and what's most meaningful to me: deeply human."

—Jennifer Pastiloff
best-selling author of *On Being Human* and *Proof of Life*

"*Human Leadership* shows that to lead others well you must lead yourself well. You can't give from an empty bucket. You must fill yourself up to fill others up. I highly recommend this book!"

—Jon Gordon
19× bestselling author of *The Carpenter* and *The One Truth*

"Kristen Hadeed's *Human Leadership* shows us all how to lead with heart through the ups and downs of the entrepreneurship journey. In the book she shares the authentic personal story of how she became a Great Human Leader by practicing empathy, experimentation, and, especially, vulnerability. If you're a leader who wants permission to be human, grab a copy of this book today."

—Erica Keswin
bestselling author and workplace strategist

"If you've ever looked successful on the outside while privately wondering why it doesn't feel that way on the inside, this book is for you. Kristen Hadeed gives language to an experience countless leaders share but rarely admit, and in doing so, reminds us that achievement means little if it comes at the cost of ourselves."

—Morra Aarons-Mele
podcast host and author of *The Anxious Achiever*

"Trust grows when our words, actions, and values align. Kristen Hadeed's *Human Leadership* is a powerful reminder that the most effective leaders don't strive for perfection. They strive for authenticity. This book will challenge you to lead with greater honesty, humility, and purpose."

—Frances Frei
Harvard Business School professor and coauthor of *Unleashed: The Unapologetic Leader's Guide to Empowering Everyone Around You*

Human
LEADERSHIP

KRISTEN HADEED
Author of *Permission to Screw Up*

Human LEADERSHIP

The Courage to Face Ourselves and Each Other

WILEY

Published by John Wiley & Sons, Inc., Hoboken, New Jersey.

For general information on our other products and services or for technical support, please contact our Customer Care Department within the United States at (800) 762-2974, outside the United States at (317) 572-3993 or fax (317) 572-4002.

Wiley also publishes its books in a variety of electronic formats. Some content that appears in print may not be available in electronic formats. For more information about Wiley products, visit our web site at www.wiley.com.

Library of Congress Cataloging-in-Publication Data is Available:

ISBN 9781394398249 (Cloth)
ISBN 9781394398256 (ePub)
ISBN 9781394398263 (ePDF)

Cover Design and Image: Isabel Urbina Peña Author Photos: Ling Wang Photography
Printed and bound by CPI Group (UK) Ltd, Croydon, CR0 4YY

C9781394398249_300826

For you, friend—
May these pages help you find the courage
to face yourself and others with an open heart.

Contents

A Note on the Humans and Stories in This Book

One of the hardest parts about sharing your story with the world is that it doesn't belong only to you. So much of what we experience in our lives involves other people.

I am in awe of those who have trusted me to write about our shared history and publish it here for all to see. Can you imagine the kind of courage it takes to let someone else tell a story that is also yours? Their bravery and trust humbles me.

My hope is that as you read, you'll celebrate the remarkable people who have allowed me to illustrate their humanity alongside my own. They are the heartbeat of every page.

A Check-In Before We Begin

On my team, we start every meeting with something called a "check-in."

It's a time for us to connect personally and share anything on our hearts that needs to be said in order to be fully present for our time together. It's our reminder that before we dive into the work we're there to discuss, we are human, and that comes first, always.

It didn't feel right to start this conversation with you any differently. So, before we get into the pages ahead, I want to check in with you: How are you? How is your heart? What's weighing on you?

(I know I can't hear your answers, but I really wish I could.)

As for me, I have a few things on my own heart that I want to share with you before we go on this journey together.

Here's my check-in: I want you to know that while you may have picked up this book for leadership advice, I didn't write it to teach you how to lead. You won't find any quick fixes, step-by-step action plans, or guidance that fits neatly into boxes or formulas.

Instead, you'll find a story. *My* story.

At its core, it's a story about something we all share: our humanity. It's about the places inside of us we're afraid to look, the difficult emotions we bury, the inner truths we ignore, and the freedom we can unlock in our lives and relationships when we have the courage to face who and what we'd rather avoid.

This is the book I wish I'd found on my worst days. It holds the words I longed to hear other leaders say out loud because hearing them would have made me feel so much less alone. I wrote it to tell the truth about what leadership has asked of me, what it's taken from me, and what it gave back to me when I stopped abandoning myself. It's the unfiltered story of how I once completely lost who I was and what it took for me to find my way back.

My path was far from linear. I learned, unlearned, and relearned again and again. Instead of presenting you with a neat and polished version—which was tempting, by the way—I made a promise to myself that I wouldn't sugarcoat a single part of it. To do so would have taken away my journey's meaning and set an unrealistic expectation for your own path.

And can I be *really* vulnerable with you?

It felt absolutely terrifying to write a book so honest. You reading these words means that my story is out in the world, and that makes me feel totally exposed. My deepest, darkest truths now live outside of me, and I can't take them back.

There were many times throughout the writing process that I questioned whether to publish these pages at all. At one point, I even considered writing this book, printing it out, and putting it in a locked drawer for my eyes only. (I even have a fear that by the time you finish reading, you'll think the drawer idea would have been the wiser choice.) On some of my hardest writing days, I'd go for a long walk and ask myself, *Why am I putting myself through this if it feels so scary?*

Inevitably, I'd come to the same realization: I'm writing this book for *you*, friend.

I hope this book found you when you needed it most. Maybe you're feeling lost. Stuck. Far apart from the person you once were or want to be. My greatest wish is that my words will make you feel seen and lead you back to yourself.

I'm not here to give you the answers. You already have them inside of you. If you're open to it, the pages ahead may help you see yourself a little more clearly. And seeing yourself more clearly could change your whole life.

If there's even the smallest chance that this book can do that for someone—for you, I hope—then choosing to publish it instead of stuffing it in a drawer was so very worth the risk.

So now, let's imagine that you and I are meeting for coffee. (Or tea. Or whatever you love most.)

I'm sitting across from you, and you lean in and say, "Tell me everything."

Here it goes.

Part I

Avoiding

Chapter 1

Stranger

It's 10 p.m.

I'm sitting in the living room of my new apartment in Houston, high up on the 32nd floor.

I'm on my second (okay, maybe third?) glass of cabernet as I watch the city lights shine through the floor-to-ceiling windows surrounding me. That's when I see her: a stranger staring back at me through the glass.

She stops me cold.

I'm struck by her weary brown eyes that look tired in a way that sleep can't fix.

Strands of her long, wavy hair fall across her face, partially hiding a blank expression that feels so . . . empty.

My heart breaks for her. She seems so *sad*. Like she's given up trying to carry the weight on her shoulders, and now it's slowly crushing her.

For a second, neither of us moves as I study her.

This is no stranger, of course. I know this woman—or at least, I used to.

As I look at a reflection I hardly recognize, I think:

I can't live like this anymore.

Chapter 2

Someone Else's Life

That night in my living room happened a couple of months after my 30th birthday, in the spring of 2018.

On paper, I had a lot to celebrate.

My first book, *Permission to Screw Up*, had been on shelves for six months, and I was flying across the country doing book signings. Student Maid—the cleaning company I started in college—had been in business for a decade, and we'd made headlines for our ability to engage the next generation while they cleaned toilets. Business leaders were paying five figures for me to stand on stages and share our cultural secrets.

And on the personal front, things weren't too shabby, either. I shared that high-rise apartment with Spiros, the love of my life (and a neurosurgeon, no less). A friend set us up when I was 26. Little did I know that he'd recently bought an engagement ring, which was tucked away in a dresser drawer in our bedroom. Later that year, Spiros would propose at one of the most romantic hotels in Washington, DC, with his six-year-old daughter by his side.

I had everything I'd always hoped I would—and more.

So why did I feel like a stranger to myself?

Each day, I was growing farther apart from the Kristen I used to be. The Kristen I *wanted* to be.

It was as if the tiny spark of life within me was being slowly suffocated. My misery came with me everywhere I went. It was there when I opened my eyes in the morning, it was the reason I hit snooze (multiple times), it consumed my thoughts in the shower, it followed me to work and then to dinner with Spiros, and it was still with me as I tossed and turned on my pillow at night.

There were days when the weight of my responsibilities felt like too much to bear. I suspect it would have felt differently if they were responsibilities I *wanted* to have.

But I didn't want them. Not all of them, anyway. And it felt like there was nothing I could do about that fact.

It was as if, somewhere along the way, I'd started living someone else's life instead of the one that was supposed to belong to me. And now that I knew that, I couldn't unknow it. I moved through the motions of a life that looked wonderful from the outside with a deep knowing that it was no longer the one that lit up my heart.

I wasn't the only one who noticed a change in me. I was becoming a stranger to my family, too.

They will tell you that at that time, they usually got one of two versions of me: On-edge Kristen, who was stressed, intense, and glued to her laptop, or Withdrawn Kristen, who rarely contributed to the conversation because her mind was somewhere else. My sister, Lauren, was usually the one with the guts to call me out on it, and when she did, I'd snap and tell her to leave me alone, moments before my guilt pushed me to apologize.

That was my cycle. It was becoming more of a struggle to be the loving, patient, and present person I'd always prided myself on being at home.

Even my grandma, who was nearing the end of her journey with Alzheimer's, could tell that something in me was off. During one of my visits before she passed, the first thing she said to me was, "Why are you so sad?" She couldn't remember my name or who I was, and yet, somehow, she could sense the weight of what I was carrying.

The thing is, I knew exactly what was causing my despair. I just didn't want to admit it—not to myself, and certainly not to anyone else.

The source of my too-heavy responsibilities, my unhappiness, my regretful behavior at home?

It was my company, Student Maid.

Yep, *that* Student Maid. The business I'd started in college. The one that launched my speaking career. The one I'd just published a book about.

The one that used to make me the happiest girl in the world.

That one.

Chapter 3

My Everything

Student Maid was the first great love of my life.

I know it's crazy to describe a business that way, but it's true.

Our relationship began when I was a 19-year-old sophomore at the University of Florida, in Gainesville. It was 2007, and I was studying finance and dreaming of moving to New York to become a banker. But that all changed when I needed a way to make extra money as a full-time student. I could've gone out and applied for a part-time job, but for some reason that wasn't my first idea. Instead, I put an ad on Craigslist to clean a stranger's house.

I was lucky I didn't get murdered.

The first person to respond to my ad was a kind working mom with two kids, two dogs, a traveling husband, and a sprawling, 4,000-square-foot house. When I showed up on her doorstep with a single bottle of cleaning solution and a sponge, the look on her face told me she thought she'd made a mistake in hiring me. And even though she was probably right (she eventually had to teach me how to clean because I was that bad), she made me an offer I couldn't resist: She wanted to pay me to clean her home every week.

So that's how it started. The better I got at cleaning, the more she told her friends about me. Between that and the other responses to my Craigslist ad, I had a nice little side business going. I cleaned houses between my classes and hired a couple of students who were also looking for flexible jobs.

The real turning point came right before I graduated, when I bid on a contract to clean hundreds of empty student apartments and got it. I had just three weeks to get every single filthy unit move-in ready for the new school year. I hired a team of 60 students to help and saw it as my last side-hustle hurrah before I moved to New York.

At first, it all went according to plan. But a few days into the contract, things took a turn when 75% of my team walked off the job. (You read that right: *Forty-five* of the 60 people I hired just quit.)

Looking back, it's obvious why: Cleaning apartments in the Florida summer heat was no joke, and I was nowhere to be found. I cringe when I think about my leadership back then. I didn't know anyone's names; I didn't give anyone breaks (I assumed they'd just take one when they needed one); and instead of being in the trenches with them, I sat with my feet propped up in the air-conditioned apartment clubhouse, convinced that was what being "the boss" was supposed to look like.

While that was certainly a terrible day, it changed my path forever.

I had to get those apartments cleaned, and I didn't have time to hire a new team. I called an emergency meeting that came with the promise of pizza and early paychecks and invited the 45 who quit and the 15 who hadn't. Unsure of what to say as I stood in front of my peers, I figured an apology would be a good place to start. I owned up to the fact that I had never led a team before, and I told them I needed their help. I promised that if they gave me another chance, I'd be there cleaning right next to them.

Every last person agreed to give it to me.

That was the summer I fell in love with Student Maid and decided it would be my forever.

It was also the summer I fell in love with leadership. Losing my team, earning back their trust, and finishing that contract together stirred something deep within me. I became obsessed—and I mean *obsessed*—with figuring out how to make a cleaning company the most incredible place to work. It was an easy choice to give up my dream of moving to New York and stay in Gainesville to grow the company instead.

In those early days, my passion for the business was all-consuming in the best way. A fire burned inside me that I couldn't put out—and didn't want to.

I traded late nights at dive bars and frat parties for evenings at bookstores and read every book about business and leadership I could get my hands on. I drove past tailgate parties and football games at one of the biggest college stadiums in the country on my way to the local business incubator, where I learned how to run a company alongside other entrepreneurs.

It was normal for me to work most nights until 2 a.m. without even trying. My roommates would come home from the bars, and I'd still be at my desk, exactly where they'd left me. I'd get lost in brainstorming strategies to bring in new clients, researching competitors, or—my favorite—dreaming up all the ways I could surprise and delight my team.

Once, around the holidays, I decided to decorate the entry to our office with a "cleaning" tree. I cut sponges into tiny ornaments until the wee hours and hung each one on a fake Christmas tree. This memory is so clear to me because of what happened next: On my drive back home that night, my long-distance boyfriend called and abruptly broke up with me. It didn't even faze me because all I could think about were the smiles that would be on my team's faces when they walked in and saw the cleaning tree the next morning.

Another time, I rolled out a red "carpet" from our parking lot to our office door. It was really just a piece of red fabric, but I wanted to make my team feel special. I recruited a few people to help me cut out stars on shiny paper, and we wrote a team member's name on each one so they'd feel celebrated when they walked into work the next day.

That's the kind of leader I was. That's what Student Maid did to me.

All I could think about was my company, and more importantly, the people in it. My team was my reason. They were my everything.

Ever since I'd read about "servant leadership" in one of those business books I'd found, I knew that was the kind of leader I wanted to be.

My team came before me, always. I served *them*, not the other way around, and I never wanted to get that backwards. I didn't see them as numbers or as the vehicle to get me where I wanted to go. I saw them as humans with hearts and dreams. While most CEOs around me focused on growing profit, I focused on helping our team members grow into the people they aspired to be. The Why statement on our office wall read, "We empower people to try so that they can transcend their limits." It was never about the cleaning. It was about the people who did the cleaning.

I cared so much about my team's growth that I began hosting leadership workshops within the company. Just like they were paid to clean houses, they were paid to learn about leadership. I taught them what I was learning myself as a leader and covered everything from giving and receiving feedback, to building relationships, to having greater self-awareness. I didn't just want to help our team members succeed at Student Maid; I wanted to equip them with skills they could use forever. Many of them went on to start their own businesses, become educators, and take on leadership roles in other organizations. Some would even credit their time at Student Maid as the biggest influence on the trajectory of their lives.

If you had met me in those days and asked me about my vision for my life, I would have told you without hesitation that I wanted to open a Student Maid location in every college town in the country. I wanted to grow future leaders by making my cleaning company their classroom.

I had created my dream job. Nothing else could hold a candle to it.

But that was then . . . and this was now.

And now my love affair with Student Maid was no longer a fairytale.

Now I wanted to run as far away from my company as I possibly could.

Chapter 4

Is This Normal?

By 2018, Student Maid was still all I thought about—but for entirely different reasons.

My phone's ringtone almost exclusively signaled bad news. At this point, I had a leadership team in place to run the day-to-day operations, but I was still their safety net. When something serious happened (and something serious always seemed to happen), it didn't take long before the problem made its way to me.

In many ways, that was by design.

After more than a decade in business, I knew how tough leading Student Maid could be. A unique set of circumstances came together to make running the company especially challenging: We almost exclusively employed college students, and many of them had never held jobs before, let alone cleaned professionally. Despite that, we trusted them to manage themselves as they drove to different job sites all over town in teams of two.

I could count on one hand the number of days that went smoothly. There were always issues—keys that didn't work, vacuums that broke, chemicals that spilled, pets that escaped—and teams could rarely solve them alone. My phone rang so much with calls for help that just hearing my ringtone spiked my blood pressure. Combine all of that with the reality of running a 24/7 service business—inventory, client complaints, scheduling, last-minute call-outs, hiring and training, difficult performance conversations—and you had a recipe for burnout.

My leadership team was more than capable of handling many of the challenges that came up without me, and they often did. But I didn't want the weight of it all to crush them the way it had crushed me.

The memory of those 45 people quitting still lived in the back of my mind, and I worried that if the pressure of running Student Maid became too much, my leadership team would walk away, too. My fear of losing them pushed me to step in and resolve the issues myself. Over time, that meant I became immersed in the most exhausting areas of the business.

I didn't love those parts of my job, but I could handle them. I knew they came with the territory of owning a company. As Student Maid grew bigger and more complex, though, so did its problems. And eventually, they wore me down.

Once, a student altered a check left on a client's kitchen counter to add a hefty tip for herself that the client didn't authorize. She swore up and down she didn't do it, even though the handwriting on it matched hers perfectly. I spent an entire day with her and a police officer waiting for her to come clean.

Another time, a former team member threatened violence against me and insinuated they were going to come to our office and cause harm. I wasn't even there; I was out of state for a speech and, moments before I walked on stage, I had to frantically coordinate a safety plan to protect our team.

There was also the angry mother who threatened to sue us because she didn't like how we handled an incident with her daughter. Her call came moments after I arrived on a rare family vacation. I spent the first day and a half trying to deescalate the situation from my hotel room instead of exploring with my family, and we only had three days together to begin with.

These were the kinds of situations that left me in constant fight-or-flight. Just when I thought the worst was behind me and an issue couldn't possibly get more nightmarish, another one would pop up and prove me wrong. And *always* at the worst possible time.

It probably won't surprise you to learn that after a decade of feeling like I could never fully relax because I never knew when the next crisis was coming, I started to resent my business. I felt angry about how much Student Maid took from me and my life.

I didn't know what it felt like *not* to have to think about work. I'd go to a coffee shop or restaurant and find myself feeling jealous of the barista or server. I fantasized about how freeing it must feel to clock out after a shift and leave work *at work* instead of having it infiltrate every part of my being. I knew I had so much privilege and freedom as my own boss, and still, sometimes, I just wanted to change my name and phone number, move to another country, and start all over again.

I could never have done that, though: I *loved* my team. I loved them as much as I resented my business—and that's what confused me the most.

Investing in them still brought me incredible joy. I could be having the most stressful day filled with complicated HR issues galore, and then I'd go teach a leadership workshop to a group of our team members, and everything in my world would feel okay again. I loved catching up with them before and after their shifts and getting to know them as people. After our conversations, I'd walk away thinking, *How could I ever feel anything but love for my team?*

But I did feel other things.

The same people who brought purpose to my work also caused the stress I carried home with me each day. I didn't *want* to see it that way, but I couldn't help it. I could no longer ignore that the most meaningful part of my business was also often the hardest part.

I was stuck in an emotional tug-of-war: I'd go from feeling so much purpose in serving my team to wishing for a job where no one needed me for anything, often in the same breath.

Is this how leadership is supposed to feel? I would wonder. *Is this normal?*

It didn't seem normal to me.

But it wasn't just my misery that was making me question my path. I had found a new passion that lit me up and made me feel alive in ways Student Maid hadn't in years. I was avoiding an ugly truth: I was cheating on my company.

I had fallen out of love with Student Maid . . . and in love with something new.

Chapter 5

Everywhere and Nowhere

Just like I never intended to start a cleaning business, I didn't set out to be a professional speaker, either.

It all started at UF the year after I graduated, when Student Maid was still in its infancy. My former professors in the business school saw me as the perfect case study for their students. They wanted me to come to their classes and share my story of starting a company and everything I'd learned so far about being a leader.

The first time I gave a "speech," I was no good. I vividly remember when I realized this about myself. I was speaking to my former entrepreneurship professor's class, and I'd written out everything I wanted to say on a piece of paper. I stood there and read every line word for word without looking up once. When I was done, my professor asked me to come back and share my story the following semester, so I thought I'd done a wonderful job. But when I walked into his classroom with that same piece of paper, he took it from my clammy hands and kindly asked me not to read it again. Instead, he told me, "Speak from your heart."

So that's what I did. I looked out at a crowd of my peers and told them about my failures and the lessons I'd learned as if I were talking to my friends.

This time, instead of shuffling off to their next class, students lined up to talk to me afterward. They asked questions, shared their own stories and business ideas, and some even emailed me later that night to tell me how much my words had resonated with them.

That day was another defining moment. It was the second time in my life I felt something stir deep within me. And with every speech I gave after that, the feeling grew.

As Student Maid became more well known in Gainesville, local business leaders took notice. They wanted to know how a cleaning company—in an industry known for constant churn—could keep people happy enough to stay for years. We had our fair share of turnover, but more often than not, our team members didn't leave Student Maid because they wanted to; they left because they'd graduated and were moving on to the next chapter of their lives. It wasn't long before my calendar was stacked with local engagements where I was asked to share the story of how we built a culture that defied the odds.

All my speeches were unpaid until I got a request to speak at an event in Colorado. The client didn't have much of a budget, so I charged them $250. But that experience got my entrepreneurial wheels spinning: If I could charge for my speaking, it could open doors for Student Maid. Instead of relying solely on the slim profit margins of a cleaning business, I could fund bigger and more impactful cultural initiatives with speaking revenue.

I decided to apply at an agency that matched speakers with colleges across the country, and I got a spot on their roster. I traveled to dozens of campuses, and soon, my fees reached four figures, which was enough to cover my travel with profit left over. The speaking opportunities kept coming, so eventually we set up the speaking work as its own company.

The speaking revenue allowed us to do things like move into our dream office space and completely renovate it to make it feel like a home away from home: We added a library where our students could study, a kitchen where they could make meals, and a private office for every member of our leadership team so that they no longer had to be crammed into one room. It also really upped my surprise-and-delight game, allowing me to do things like hire a massage therapist every once in a while to give our team members chair massages after their shifts.

After a couple years, news of Student Maid's unique culture was making waves in the business world. My audiences were no longer college students; they were CEOs, HR directors, and leaders hungry for a new vision of what culture could be. My speaking fees climbed to five figures. It felt surreal.

Even though the extra money was nice, and even though it made Student Maid's culture even more special, I would have done the speaking for free. That's how much I loved it. It was never about having all eyes on me (and still isn't). It was about teaching. Empowering people. Holding space for them to grow. Leading them to their lightbulb moments. It was about doing the same thing I did in those leadership workshops with our students, only now I was doing it for audiences of hundreds. When I was onstage, I felt like I was making the kind of difference I wanted to make in the world.

And that was the problem.

The more love I felt for speaking, the less I felt for Student Maid. Onstage, I was *electric*. Speaking felt like the thing I was put on this earth to do. But as soon as I stepped off the stage, I'd check my phone and see another HR nightmare waiting for me. In those moments, every ounce of energy left my body.

Ping-ponging between speaking and Student Maid felt like going from the highest of highs to drowning in soul-crushing misery. I was both everywhere and nowhere—and it left me with so much guilt. I never intended to feel this way about Student Maid or to love it any less. It was supposed to be my forever, you know?

At this point, if I were you sitting across the table listening to this story, I'd be screaming at me, "Just sell Student Maid! Or make someone else the CEO! Go be a speaker full time! The answer is so obvious."

I know how it must look. But back then, I didn't allow myself to consider those options. I didn't think they *were* options.

Even as I was falling out of love with the business, there were parts of me that still loved it. Student Maid wasn't just a company I built; it was the place I belonged. My identity was so closely tied to the business that I couldn't imagine a life without it. It was an extension of me. I couldn't tell where Student Maid ended and I began. It felt like my *child*. It was something I'd created from nothing and watched grow up, and every ounce of my spirit was stitched into its story. How could I just walk away from something like that?

I also felt responsible for my team. Many of them depended on Student Maid for their livelihoods, which meant they also depended on me. So what if I was miserable sometimes? I couldn't rip that stability away from them just because I'd grown unhappy. This is what I signed up for when I started a company. This is what it meant to be a servant leader and put others first. I couldn't fathom hurting my team with a decision so selfish.

To top it all off, there was also the fact that everything I spoke about onstage came from Student Maid experiences. How could I remain credible as a speaker if I no longer led the business I spoke about? Who would take me seriously?

But as these things usually are, the situation was even more complicated than that.

Chapter 6

Human Calculator

Student Maid was in debt. A *lot* of debt.

Over the years we'd accrued nearly half a million dollars, and all of it was personally guaranteed by *me*.

Even though we chipped away at the crippling balance every month, we still had six digits to go. It felt like climbing a mountain with no summit in sight.

So how did *that* happen?

If you've read my first book, you already know that I've had my fair share of financial screwups. My most infamous one happened when I got that first major cleaning contract—the one where 45 people quit on me—and I needed a line of credit to buy cleaning supplies. As soon as the $10,000 hit my bank account, I spent $1,000 of it on sushi and sake bombs for my friends. (Could you imagine me as an investment banker?)

I'd grown wiser about money since those early days, but not wise enough to avoid taking on more debt than we could handle.

Long before my speaking career took off, I realized that Student Maid's profit margins alone would never allow me to pay people the wages I desired. Cleaning is physically demanding work, and I wanted my team to feel like they were getting paid generously for it. I also wanted to attract and retain a leadership team, which was made up of people I hoped would see Student Maid as a place worthy of their talents long-term. Convincing someone to build a career at a cleaning company was already a hard sell—even harder when you don't have a compelling salary offer to go with it.

But my options were capped: Student Maid was never a money-making machine, even if people on the outside assumed it was. The business had steady growth and many profitable years, but our margins hovered in the single digits.

In many ways, Student Maid operated more like a nonprofit than a traditional business. There are many things we could have stopped doing in order to improve our margins, like no longer paying our students to attend leadership workshops. But that wasn't an option to me. Things like that were the core of who we were, and I didn't want to lose that part of our culture. Not to mention that's often why our clients hired us: They believed in our mission of developing future leaders.

The way I saw it, the only way to grow our bottom line was to take on even more cleaning work, even though we were already doing a *ton*. Aside from being open seven days a week for commercial and residential jobs, every summer we cleaned thousands of recently vacated student apartments to get them move-in ready for the new school year. To manage a workload that huge, we'd hire hundreds of seasonal team members, and everyone—including me and every member of our leadership team—would work for days on end, most of us racking up overtime. The thought of trying to do even *more* work than that was overwhelming. Our summers became so stressful that people started strategically planning major events like weddings during that time so that they would have a valid reason to skip it. I wanted to find other ways to grow our revenue without increasing the burden on the team.

My speaking fees were starting to help, but they weren't yet enough to fuel our growth. I knew that if I wanted to keep giving raises and one day offer the leadership team the kind of salaries I dreamed of, we would need more revenue. So when the opportunity came along to launch two new ventures, I jumped on it, hoping they would give Student Maid the financial boost it needed.

The first venture was something we came up with ourselves when we realized how difficult it was to find a scheduling software that fit our needs. We decided to build our own and eventually sell it to other cleaning companies. When we learned about a grant for technology advancements in industries like ours, we saw it as our best chance to get started. I asked my friend Josh, who was an experienced tech entrepreneur, if he would partner with us, and together we applied for and were awarded the funding. We hired two developers, but by the time the money ran out, they were just getting started. To continue, we would need a *lot* more capital.

Around the same time, we seized an opportunity to open a second location of Student Maid in a city several hours away. A major resort in the area needed a new cleaning service and wanted to work with us, but launching in a new market meant we needed to cover the costs of getting that location up and running.

That's when I started taking on significant debt.

My banker—who believed in these new ventures and what they could mean for Student Maid's future as much as I did—helped me secure a loan that I was sure we'd pay back in no time.

But in the end, neither venture survived.

Tragically, Josh passed away unexpectedly in his sleep. We tried to continue the software company without him, but after a couple of years and inconsistent results, we shut it down. And at our second location, the client that recruited us treated our team so poorly that we chose to walk away. We were never able to replace the revenue we lost from that contract, and eventually we decided to close the location and sell our remaining client list and inventory to another cleaning company in the area.

Instead of fueling Student Maid's growth, the two new ventures left us with even more debt than we'd started with. Our six-figure balance had only increased.

Every time my banker called and asked me to prepare another report on the state of the business, I'd break out in a cold sweat. He still believed in Student Maid, but he also had a board to report to. He fought to get our line of credit renewed on more than one occasion, and if he hadn't, I don't know where we would have ended up.

My whole life, I'd been optimistic and carefree, always trusting that things would work out. But now I operated from fear, always worrying that we wouldn't have enough. I had hardened into a human calculator, constantly crunching numbers to figure out how much we'd need to bring in that week in order to pay the team, our bills, our debt payments, and, if I was lucky, myself. And then, whatever the gap was (and there was usually a gap) would torment me at night as I counted out in my head how many cleanings and speeches we'd need to book in order to keep everything—and everyone—afloat.

On top of the business debt, I had personal credit card debt, too. I wasn't taking a steady paycheck, and when I did pay myself, it usually wasn't enough to cover all of my bills. I was lucky to live in a home my parents owned in Gainesville, and I paid them rent when I could. Without their support, my circumstances would have been much more difficult. It didn't help that I also felt pressure to maintain a certain image: I was the CEO of a company as well as a professional speaker, and I told myself I needed to look the part. But beneath my tailored blazer, my chest always felt tight. I knew I was living beyond my means. I eventually moved to Houston, but my boyfriend was the only reason I could call that high-rise home. He paid most of our rent.

He also loaned me money.

At one point, Student Maid needed a quick influx of cash to help with upcoming expenses. I didn't want to ask our bank for help because we were already in a delicate spot with them, and Spiros knew the stress it was causing me. I asked if he'd be open to loaning me the money at an interest rate that would make it worthwhile for him.

It was my birthday, of all days. Spiros and I were away for one of his neurosurgery conferences at a resort. The second-to-last thing I wanted to be doing on my birthday was talking about Student Maid's financial problems. The first was asking my boyfriend for a loan. But it didn't matter what I wanted: Student Maid needed cash, and figuring out how to get it was my priority.

As we sat poolside, we agreed on an interest rate that worked for us both. Spiros took out his phone and wired me the money right then and there. Happy birthday to me. Now, in addition to the bank, I was indebted to him, too. I know how privileged I was to have that as an option, and yet it was an option I felt very ashamed of using.

I hated that Student Maid's problems were spilling into the lives of the people I loved most.

The growing financial pressure didn't just wear on me; it also played a part in driving my right hand to quit. If you read *Permission to Screw Up*, you may remember her as Abby. Before she left, she was Student Maid's general manager.

Abby is the one who helped me build the company into what it became. Though our relationship had become strained over the years because of our differing views on how to handle pretty much everything in the business, Abby was the one person I thought would never leave my side.

The week before she resigned, I flew to Gainesville just to take her to lunch on her birthday, so I was especially gutted when she asked me to FaceTime a few days later and told me that she had accepted another job. At the time it felt like the ultimate betrayal, but now I don't blame her one bit.

Abby oversaw the day-to-day operations of Student Maid, including keeping a close eye on our cash flow. It wasn't a job for the faint of heart. We'd already had a time or two where we couldn't make payroll, and the leadership team and I had chosen to delay our own paychecks to ensure that our students were paid on time.

Things remained tight after that, and there were many times I deferred my own pay. Abby did, too. Even though that was ultimately her decision—and a reflection of the ownership mentality she had for the business—I was still her leader. I can't *believe* I allowed her to put herself in that position. I paid her back, but it took time. That whole season remains one of my biggest regrets.

The financial pressure undoubtedly took a toll on Abby, but I think the bigger reason behind her decision to leave was that I wasn't there for her like I had once been. My demanding speaking schedule meant that I traveled constantly and spent less time in the office. Being away for a speech was easy to justify because that revenue went straight to the company and helped with our debt payments.

My move to Houston, though? That was less so.

Spiros and I had met and started dating in Gainesville, where we both lived at the time. When I got my first book deal, he got an opportunity to do his research at a prestigious Texas hospital—one that he couldn't pass up. I was devastated that he would be moving so far away, even though I wanted him to chase his dreams.

We did long-distance for a while, but I saw a future with him, and I didn't want our relationship to stay that way forever. I never made a formal decision to move to Houston; it just sort of . . . happened. Little by little, I brought more of my stuff with me on visits to see Spiros and stayed there longer and longer between speeches. At one point, Abby even came with me to drive my car from Gainesville to Houston because I needed it there more.

I was based in Houston for a long time before I ever admitted to myself that I was living there. I had trouble saying it out loud. I knew that moving there was the best choice for my life with Spiros, and I suspected it would be the worst one for Student Maid and my team. I couldn't stand the thought of my business costing me my relationship, but I didn't know how to choose between the two—so I pretended I didn't have to. I kept most of my things in Houston and left the basics in Gainesville, fooling myself into believing that I lived in both places. I came back to Gainesville often to spend time with the team, but if you counted the nights I slept in each city, there was no comparison.

It wasn't just the amount of time I was spending in Houston that made me feel so ashamed. It was also the unexpected feeling that washed over me every time I stepped off the plane at George Bush Intercontinental: relief.

I couldn't deny how freeing it felt to have physical distance between me and Student Maid. Being nine hundred miles away made it easier to ignore its problems. It also felt easier to have some space from Abby—which I hated admitting to myself.

Now that I can see it for what it was, I think my move to Houston was a subconscious attempt to distance myself from Student Maid and from Abby. By then, she was the one leading the operations, which meant she was also the one bringing me the toughest issues.

Nearly every conversation with her revolved around a money challenge or a serious HR incident—my least-favorite topics. I started to associate Abby with the stress of the business itself, and no matter how hard I tried, I couldn't separate the two.

We had always had such a strong relationship, but now our conversations were strained. There were even times when I raised my voice, which wasn't like me. I know I didn't always show up the way she needed me to: I avoided the hardest realities she brought up to me and deflected responsibility because I didn't want to face them. As her leader, I should have shouldered the weight so that she didn't have to, but I couldn't. Blaming it on the physical distance between us became a convenient excuse.

I wish I'd had the courage to end our working relationship before she had to do it. If I were Abby, I would have left me, too. I could tell how much stress the job was causing her, and she deserved to find one that didn't make her feel that way.

A year after Abby moved on, other leaders had stepped up and our culture was in pretty good shape, all things considered. But I was drowning. With Abby gone, I had lost the only real buffer I had between me and most of Student Maid's challenges. Even living in Houston couldn't keep them from reaching me. After she left, the pressure only intensified.

This was my moment to be the leader Student Maid needed, and I tried my best to be her—on the outside. But on the *inside*? Each passing day, it became harder to hold it all together. Running the company took everything out of me. It caused constant inner turmoil and anxiety, and some months, it actually cost me money to keep our doors open.

Most days, I wasn't sure I had it in me to keep going. And yet, somehow, I had to.

And I don't think anyone ever detected the amount of pain that lived within me.

Chapter 7

Sheets of Shame

In the months before I came face to face with myself in my high-rise window, I tried everything I could to find my spark for Student Maid again.

I wrote in gratitude journals every morning, became a collector of self-help books, got my chakras balanced, and even saw a psychic. (I should have predicted how that would turn out: She told me we had a lot of work to do and asked me to pay upfront for a package. But after a few sessions, she mysteriously dropped off the face of the earth.)

All of those things worked—until they didn't.

Eventually, I tried Adderall. A few friends told me it gave them energy, so I went to a psychiatrist and got a prescription, hoping it would reignite the drive I'd once had. I stopped taking it when I realized there wasn't a prescription strong enough to mask the lack of motivation I felt deep in my bones.

Some days, getting out of bed felt impossible. I'd stay there for hours—the whole day, even—wrapped tightly in my sheets of shame, watching Netflix and procrastinating on every work duty I had. My greatest surge of energy would come right before Spiros got home, when I would jump out of bed to get dressed and attempt to look like a normal, productive person.

I developed a habit that I knew wasn't good for me: I started drinking wine at night. It was a way to relax—just something to take the edge off. But soon I noticed that I ended most evenings with a glass in my hand. One often turned into two. Some mornings, I'd wake up with a headache. On bad days, a hangover.

Do I have a drinking problem? I'd ask myself.

I was escaping.

And eventually, it caught up with me. I began to feel a shift with Spiros, like something was changing in our relationship, and not for the better. When I brought it up, he said he'd noticed I wasn't taking care of myself like I used to, and he was struggling with that. I didn't seem to prioritize my health like I once did, and I had become . . . well, not fun to be around. I was almost always irritable.

His honesty crushed me. Part of me wished he'd lied. But the hurt I felt wasn't about him or what he said to me that night. It was that his words reflected how I felt about myself.

Shortly after our conversation, I worked up the courage to step on a scale. I couldn't believe the number I saw—I thought it was broken. Gaining weight isn't a bad thing. It's just that to me, it was undeniable evidence that something in my life had changed and I could no longer pretend I didn't see it. I promised myself I'd start working out for at least a few minutes every day and take pictures to document my progress, but there was no progress.

On my very worst days, I'd think about death.

Not about taking my own life, but to put my circumstances into perspective. Strangely, thinking about death helped me tolerate the stress and pain I carried. I felt trapped by the debt and by an identity so tightly bound to a company I didn't want anymore, but I found comfort in knowing that even though my circumstances were tough, they weren't as tough or final as death would be. My life might have felt hard at times, but I was alive, and I still had agency. And that was enough to keep me going.

So there you have it.

That's where I was in the spring of 2018, when I sat in my living room and found myself gazing back at a reflection I barely recognized in the window of my Houston apartment. It isn't pretty, but it's the truth.

I imagine that by this point—dozens of pages into my struggles—you may have caught yourself thinking, "Wow, this sounds pretty 'Woe is me.'"

I wouldn't blame you. I've thought that about myself plenty of times, too. I've thought things like:

- *Poor me, starting a company and finding success at such a young age.*
- *How rough, getting to be my own boss and only having to answer to myself.*
- *Toughen up, buttercup: You chose this. No one forced you to take this path. If you didn't want to walk it, you could have chosen another.*

And my favorite:

- *You should be grateful that you feel pressure. Pressure is a privilege.*

Except that, back then, it didn't feel like a privilege to me. All I could feel was the burden.

If you know me from my last book or knew me during this time in my life, you might wonder why I didn't share all of these things I felt back then.

I mean, people knew my life wasn't perfect. Onstage, I talked openly about many of my struggles as a leader. I wrote about our debt journey on my blog. I even called my first book *Permission to Screw Up* (and almost called this one *Permission to Keep Screwing Up*).

But the most difficult parts of what I was feeling? I didn't share that because I didn't have language for the complex and confusing emotions I felt. It's only now, nearly ten years later, that I can look back and clearly see what I felt and why.

I didn't trust my feelings. I thought that I shouldn't have them—and I desperately wished they would change. I thought that maybe I was just going through severe burnout. I hoped that one day I'd wake up and feel the way I used to about Student Maid. I hoped these were feelings that leaders had on bad days and that they weren't *really* representative of the person I'd become. If there's one thing I had learned to be as an entrepreneur, it was resilient. I thought this was just another bump in the road and that I would get through it, just like I'd gotten through everything else.

I was scared. From the stage, I was teaching people about the importance of vulnerability, but I was experiencing feelings I didn't think I could ever be vulnerable about. They were too sad. Too negative. Too "selfish." How could I, a champion of servant leadership, ever admit that I felt resentful of my company, and sometimes of my team? I feared that people might judge me. That knowing these things might change their perception of me. And what about my *team*? What would they think? How could I possibly look into the eyes of people I cared so much about and admit these awful truths?

What I didn't know was that writing *Permission to Screw Up* would be the beginning of everything changing for me. It's what finally caused me to confront my long, complicated relationship with Student Maid.

In so many ways, writing my first book was beautiful. It gave me a chance to remember the passion that started it all in the first place. But it was also painful in a way that I couldn't yet put my finger on. By the time I finished writing it, I could sense that my feelings about Student Maid weren't what they once were.

I imagine that when most people submit a manuscript they've been working on for years, they feel overjoyed. And I did—for a few moments. But then I got another one of those nightmare calls from my team. I can't remember what the issue was, but I was visiting my parents, and as soon as I hung up the phone, I leaned over their kitchen island and buried my face in my hands. Tears splashed down on the pages of the manuscript I had just finished scanning in to my publisher. When my mom and dad realized what was happening, they rushed over to hug me, and I fell apart in their arms. That's when I told them the thing I had never said out loud to anybody before: I wanted to give away my company.

They just held me while I cried. What else could they do? I think my parents resented Student Maid as much as I did by that point because of all the pain it had caused me, and, therefore, them.

But they knew—and I knew—that I couldn't just give it away. I was stuck—because of the debt, because of my identity, because of my responsibility as a leader, because of my team, and now, because of the book I'd just sent off to be published and shared with the world.

By the time the book had been out for six months, I knew I couldn't live like that anymore.

As I stared at my reflection in my 32nd-floor window, I knew that I didn't want to feel empty. I wanted my smile back. I wanted my radiance. My confidence. My peace.

I wanted to be the leader I used to be. The *person* I used to be.

I wanted to be me again.

Chapter 8

Hot-Air Balloon

There were plenty of people I could have turned to that night in my apartment when I felt like a shell of myself.

Spiros. My parents. My sister. My friends. Brilliant, caring mentors who would have happily walked alongside me as I found a way out of my mess. Even my team.

But I couldn't bring myself to reach out to a single one of them. It felt too hard, too embarrassing, and too vulnerable. I wanted help—just not from anyone I knew. That's what drove me to do what I did next.

I set down my wine glass, reached for my laptop on the coffee table, and Googled "life coaches in Houston."

A few minutes later, I was staring at a picture of a man named Paul.

His website was the first search result I clicked. He advertised himself as an "executive coach," but I didn't care what he was. What caught my attention was the image at the top of the homepage: a rainbow-colored hot-air balloon with bricks falling out of its wooden basket.

When I saw that hot-air balloon high in the sky among white, puffy clouds, basking in all of its rainbow glory, I imagined how light it must feel now that it had rid itself of those heavy bricks. I took a deep breath for the first time in a long time and saw what I wanted for my own life: to be free of my own bricks.

Without giving it another thought, I filled out the contact form on Paul's website—something I was sure my more sober self would regret in the morning.

Paul was quick to write me back, and we had a discovery call not too long after that. I learned that he used to live in Houston but was now based abroad. That meant if we worked together, our coaching sessions would be on the phone instead of in person. Aside from the fact that Paul seemed like a great guy and coach, that's actually what settled it.

Never having to face someone while doing this work?

Sold.

I hired him on the spot.

Chapter 9

Inner World

On the day of my first coaching session with Paul, I had the kind of stomach jitters that make you question if you're going to throw up. I think it was because I knew that taking this step meant I was deciding to change my life, and even though I didn't know what those changes would look like, there was no going back.

In that first call, Paul asked me to define my goals for our coaching journey.

Stop hating my business and my life, I thought.

If I'd had the guts, I would've said it out loud. But I wasn't able to be that honest in my life just yet.

Instead, I gave Paul a list of seven reasonable-sounding goals. Here they are, straight from my notes:

1. Clarity on personal goals
2. Clarity on goals for the business and scale
3. More effective in the way I work, more time spent "in flow" and avoiding procrastination
4. Financial coaching, both in the business and personally
5. Better leader and CEO and helping me identify critical weaknesses
6. How to take my team along with me as I grow
7. Be able to look back on this coaching relationship and say our time together was impactful and is the reason I am where I am

Sharing my goals out loud with Paul felt like an exhale. Like one little brick had fallen out of my hot-air balloon basket. Now someone else knew about my challenges, and even though I hadn't told Paul everything, that list gave him a hint that I was struggling. Lucky for me, it didn't scare him away. We got straight to work.

Paul suggested we start by identifying my personal core values.

I was familiar with the concept. Student Maid had a set of core values that we defined early on, and they guided every hiring decision we made. But I had never identified my own.

"Think of your values as your internal compass," Paul said. "They represent what matters most to you. When you're clear on them, they can help you stay true to your most authentic self."

That's when Paul gave me my first homework assignment: a worksheet filled with dozens and dozens of words. My instructions were to read through them and check the boxes next to the ones that resonated with me. Then I was supposed to take the ones I'd selected, group them by similarity, and choose my favorite word within each group. What remained would be my values.

The first time I looked at the worksheet, I froze.

There were so many words, I couldn't tell which ones stood out more than others. On my first pass, I checked nearly every box. But it wasn't just the number of choices that made the exercise difficult; it was what it was asking of me. I was supposed to identify what mattered most *to me*, and I realized I didn't have a clear answer. Even more unsettling, I didn't know where to begin looking for one. I wasn't used to asking myself questions like these. It had been a long time since I'd felt any real connection to myself at all.

Embarrassingly, my first instinct was to turn to Google (yet again): I thought about well-known people I admired and began searching for *their* values. At some point, I recognized that probably wasn't the purpose of the exercise. This wasn't a test or an assignment I needed to get an A+ on. This was my life.

Kristen, don't overthink it, I told myself. *You can do this. Just keep it simple: Which words do you like most?*

It took a few quiet sessions alone with my thoughts, but slowly answers started to come. As I spent time with the worksheet, I started to notice that certain words made my heart flutter, and paying attention to that subtle cue is what finally made the exercise click for me. Once I'd chosen my favorite words, Paul encouraged me to add verbs to make them my own, so I did that, too. When I looked at my final list, I felt it in my body before I could explain it in my mind. These were *my* values. Not something I found on the internet or borrowed from someone else . . . *mine!*

By the time I met with Paul again, I had my values list in hand and a tiny flicker of light back in my soul. I couldn't wait to share them with him. When the time came, I took a deep breath, smiled to myself, and then slowly and deliberately read each value aloud:

- Act with compassion
- Form deep and meaningful relationships
- Be authentic
- Seek opportunities to learn and grow
- Do work that makes a difference

As I read them, I noticed that they didn't feel like words on a page. They had weight. Meaning. Truth. Reading them to Paul gave me *chills*.

"Amazing work," Paul said warmly. I could hear the pride in his voice, and I knew he could hear it in mine, too. "And now, here's a really important question," he continued. "On a scale of 1 to 10, how well do you think you are living these values right now?"

Oof. That brought me right back down to earth.

I'm not even sure I answered his question. When I look back at my notes from that day, the only thing I captured was: "Realization that I'm living them well in my business but not my personal life."

I was partially right: I *wasn't* living them in my personal life. But I certainly wasn't living them in my business, either.

- **Act with compassion:** Was that the same thing as loving my team on the outside while resenting them on the inside?

- **Form deep and meaningful relationships:** Did that include distancing myself—literally *and* emotionally—from my right-hand person and leaving her to carry the weight of the business? So much so that it caused her to quit?
- **Be authentic:** Is that when you secretly don't love your company anymore but aren't brave enough to own up to it?
- **Seek opportunities to learn and grow:** Was that what it looked like to reach out to a stranger late at night, after several glasses of wine, because I was too afraid of being judged by anyone who actually knew me?
- **Do work that makes a difference:** I'll give myself that one. That was something I had always done.

Looking back, I think I answered a completely different question than the one Paul asked—one that was much more revealing.

Paul didn't ask me to think about my life in two different categories, but I did. Somewhere along the way, I had drawn a line between my outer and inner self. My outer self, the one that lived at work and cared so much about what other people thought of me, took almost all of my energy. I did everything I believed a servant leader was supposed to do to the best of my ability. And by most measures, I did it well: If you had asked my team back then, the majority would have told you I was a really good leader. I cared about them, and I showed it.

What I didn't show them was my inner world.

I never showed the pain. The exhaustion. The unraveling. No one knew how far I had drifted from myself. I kept it all hidden.

What I think I was trying to say with my answer was that I was doing my best to live my values—for my team, my company, and everyone on the outside. But the inside? The inner Kristen? The "real" me?

I had completely abandoned her.

That conversation with Paul was the first time I could clearly see the gap between how I was showing up and how I was actually feeling. It was the first time I had insight into that disconnect, even though it wasn't as clear as I've laid out here.

If I could revisit that conversation, here's what I would say: "Paul, I'm not really living my values at all. I'd give myself a 3 out of 10—and that's being generous."

Now I know what it feels like to live my values with no half-truths. When you are fully living your values, you always embody them. When you aren't sure how to handle something, you ask, "What do my values tell me to do?" and then you make that choice. You sleep peacefully because you know that you are staying true to yourself, and you wake up in alignment because you get to live another day where your insides match your outsides. And whenever you *don't* feel that—whenever you go to bed with discomfort in your chest or a lump in your throat, or you wake up feeling like something is off—you know that somewhere you've drifted from what matters most to you. And that means you also know exactly what you need to do to find your way back again.

One thing is for sure: When you are living your values, you don't mistake your reflection for a stranger.

Even though I didn't know any of this back then, identifying my values with Paul mattered. It was the first time in my life that I looked that far inward and really thought about what was important to me. Until then, the personal growth exercises I'd done were always connected to Student Maid or my role as a leader. This one was about *me*. And completing it was the first time I began to hear myself and trust what I heard.

I wish I could tell you that I immediately began to embody these values after discovering them and that doing so changed everything. But I think you can guess that it doesn't turn out that way (otherwise, there wouldn't be so many pages left in this book).

It would take me a long time to learn how to keep my values front and center in my life. Eventually, I would figure it out—and I'd realize I could boil down my list to just Courage and Compassion. But I wasn't there yet. I had only just taken my first step toward seeing myself differently.

When we lose ourselves, we have to start somewhere to find our way back.

And this was my start.

Chapter 10

Unconventional Assignments

Paul and I met every month, sometimes twice. It surprised me how quickly I grew close to someone I mostly knew as a voice on the other end of the phone.

My life wasn't magically better because I now had a coach. The six-figure debt still sent me spiraling at night. I still wasn't prioritizing my health. I still felt out of love with Student Maid, and I still kept that secret locked away and the key hidden. But I was showing up and putting in the work. My calls with Paul let me forget about the day-to-day for an hour and focus on my growth instead. It was more time than I'd spent on myself since I could remember.

It was progress.

Paul did what you'd expect an executive coach to do: He helped me understand my entrepreneurial style (through something called the BOSI assessment, which helps identify whether you're a Builder, Opportunist, Specialist, or Innovator), recommended books on procrastination (my favorite was *The Now Habit* by Neil Fiore), and even had me send an anonymous survey to a few members of my team to evaluate my leadership (the results were better than I expected).

While the books I read and the assessments I took helped me grow, it was the unconventional assignments he gave me that made the biggest difference. Like the time he asked me to write my own eulogy, for example.

"As in . . . the thing that someone reads at my funeral?" I asked him, hoping I'd misunderstood.

"That's right," he said. He explained that the point was to think about the legacy I wanted to leave behind and write about it as if it had already happened.

"And after you write it," he continued, "I want you to ask yourself if you are living your life in a way that will make that legacy come true. If you aren't, then you have some changes to make."

I didn't need the assignment to know I had changes to make, but I understood why Paul was asking me to do it: This was about setting a vision for my life. If I could get clear on the impact I wanted to have and who I wanted to become, I could work backwards and map out the steps I needed to take to become that person.

These weren't casual questions, though. I sat with them for days: What kind of difference did I want to make in the world? What did I want to be remembered for? What did I want my loved ones to say about me when I was gone?

At one point, I said to Paul, "This feels impossible." I still laugh when I think about his response: "It shouldn't be *that* hard—you're dead, remember?" I decided to stop taking myself so seriously.

What finally sparked my inspiration was a quote I found by speaker and author Wayne Dyer: "Don't die with your music still in you." I read it in one of his books and immediately reached for my highlighter.

Dyer's words gave me language for something I felt but couldn't articulate. The night that I caught my reflection in my apartment window, my sadness came from knowing this couldn't be it for my life. I *knew* I had so much more to offer the world. But it felt like my music was trapped inside of me, buried beneath the debt, the pressure, and a version of myself I had outgrown. And that was my ultimate heartbreak: that I might never get my music out and see what my life and impact could become.

Writing my eulogy helped me imagine what was possible. I thought about the friend, family member, and leader I wanted to be, and also about how I would show up in the roles I hoped to fill one day, like being a wife and a mom. I wrote about the difference I dreamed of making with my career, and before I knew it, I'd written three pages.

Here are some of my favorite things I wrote that day:

- "Kristen always made it clear that being a mom was more important to her than being a CEO."
- "It was no secret how madly Kristen loved Spiros and how madly he loved her. They grew together, never leaving the other behind."
- "She was always present and made you feel as if you were the most important person in the room."
- "She left nothing unsaid and lived without regrets."
- "She was the essence of humility, authenticity, and vulnerability."

I didn't realize this until I went back through my notes to write this book, but when I described the impact I hoped to make in my career, I didn't mention Student Maid. At *all*. I said I led companies. I said I developed leaders. I said I was a champion of better workplaces and cultures where people came first. I said I spoke on stages, helping people believe in themselves. But I never once wrote the words "Student Maid."

I see it now as another sign that things were changing within me. My accidental omission revealed what had been hiding in plain sight: I didn't see Student Maid in my future.

I wrote that Dyer quote on a Post-it and kept it on my desk. I promised myself that no matter what, I would get my music out.

But I couldn't yet imagine how I'd keep that promise. All I could see was Student Maid standing in my way.

Chapter 11

Seven Words

A few calls later, Paul introduced another exercise. He said he wanted to help me uncover my "limiting beliefs."

I'll admit, at first I was skeptical. It sounded a little "woo-woo" for an executive coaching call (and this is coming from the same person who paid a psychic upfront). But Paul had earned my trust, and I was willing to give anything he recommended a try.

"Okay, Kristen, this is what we're going to do," Paul said, likely sensing my hesitation. "I'm going to say a few statements out loud, and I want you to pay close attention to what happens inside your body as I say them. If the belief is active, you'll feel some kind of reaction. As soon as you notice something, tell me, even if the feeling is small."

He began with "I have to be in control."

I felt nothing.

"I have to be perfect," he continued.

Still nothing.

"Something bad is going to happen."

Nothing. Nada. Zilch.

I started to think I didn't have any of these so-called "limiting beliefs." But then Paul said the seven words that made my heart skip a beat.

"It's my job to keep people happy."

Wait a minute.

I felt something.

It wasn't a super obvious feeling; I just felt a twinge of anxiety. Like the hand that had been squeezing my chest for years was gripping me a tiny bit tighter.

I told Paul either I had heartburn, or we had a winner.

He didn't waste a second.

"Tell me, Kristen," he continued in the calm Paul voice I had come to love. "Why do you think this one spoke to you more than the others?"

Paul explained that because I reacted to it, it likely meant it was a deeply held, subconscious belief of mine. And the thing about our limiting beliefs? They usually start in childhood.

"You certainly weren't born with this belief," Paul went on. "Think about it: You weren't crawling around in a diaper thinking it's your job to keep everyone around you happy, right? This is something you learned from the people around you and from your early experiences. Where do you think it comes from?"

It was a difficult question. I sat there and tried to remember what it was like to be little Kristen.

"I think it comes from my parents," I said. "When they had disagreements, it really affected me."

I couldn't believe I was telling Paul something about my parents that wasn't purely positive. I love my mom and dad endlessly, and we have a wonderful relationship. I didn't want to say anything negative about them or their marriage, and at the same time, I'd hired Paul to help me dig deep. If I wasn't going to do that, then what was the point?

"It can be hard for a kid to see their parents argue," Paul said. "How do you think it affected you?" He was such a good listener, even over the phone.

"I guess I felt like it was my responsibility to fix things between them when they would have conflict." I had never admitted that before. "They both have strong personalities, and sometimes they just clashed."

I imagined Paul nodding as I continued.

"They didn't fight all the time, but when they did, I tried to become the peacemaker between them in my own kid way. I'd talk to each of them and do my best to help them see the other person's point of view. Sometimes I'd even grab their hands and bring them together to make up."

"Did it work?" Paul asked.

"I realize how crazy this sounds," I said, "but sometimes it did. I'm sure they worked things out on their own, too, but it seemed to help the tension."

He paused. "Why do you think you tried to play that role for them? Was there a fear that if you didn't, something would happen?"

I thought for another minute. "I think it's because I had a lot of friends whose parents got divorced," I said. "I was afraid that if my mom and dad were upset with each other, it meant they might get divorced, too."

Paul helped me see that as a kid, my parents were my entire world. The idea of them splitting up was the scariest thing I could imagine. To my childhood self, keeping the peace between them felt like the most important job in the world and a way to prevent my fear from coming true.

My parents have been married for more than 45 years. Now that I'm older (and married myself), I understand that conflict is a normal part of any relationship. But when I was a kid, their disagreements felt like life or death to me. I became hyper-aware of every mood, tone, look, and change in the air. Anytime I sensed a shift between them, I felt the urge to help prevent it from becoming something more.

My conversation with Paul that day opened a door I didn't know existed. I see now how my early experiences taught me a set of "rules" about emotions: what was safe to feel and express and what wasn't.

Growing up, when I had "negative" feelings—especially big ones, like anger—my parents didn't know how to handle them, likely because their parents didn't know how to handle theirs either. When my emotions were out of proportion to the situation, it's not like my mom and dad pulled up a chair and looked at me with interested eyes while saying, "Tell me more about that. . ." They didn't do that, just like most parents didn't do that. They told me to go to my room and calm down so we could talk about it, but only after I was calm. Or they became angry and upset because *I* was angry and upset.

Once I calmed down, they always wanted to hear what I had to say, and they were always there to comfort me. But I learned that not all feelings were treated equally: Positive emotions were okay to share and brought affirmation. Negative ones earned punishment and often came with rejection.

Through it all, my mom and dad were still my heroes—not just to me but to so many in our small town. They were known as people who freely gave their time, talents, and resources to help those around them, and they were cherished for it. They taught me what it looked like to be someone who *mattered*.

My dad built his legal career in public service, and while he could have made far more money working for a private law firm, he chose to fight for people who couldn't fight for themselves. He did things like shutting down a juvenile detention center after discovering that kids were being abused and closing down a puppy mill that led to the rescue of more than four hundred dogs. My dad was always working at night, on the weekends, and on our family vacations to help any person who needed it. His commitment to justice eventually led him to become the county attorney where my parents lived, a position he held until he retired at 77 years old. He made such a big impact on our community that the county declared his last day an official holiday to commemorate his years of service.

And my mom? She's the embodiment of selflessness. She left her career at a school to support my dad. Not only did she make his lunch and pick out his suit and tie each morning, but she also did legal research and watched every county commission meeting to give feedback on how he came across. She helped my dad so much that when he retired, our community honored *her*, too. Her generosity didn't stop with my dad: She was there for any person lucky enough to be in her orbit. When one of our neighbors got diagnosed with cancer, my mom took her to her chemo appointments and sat with her right until the end.

My parents made it clear what they stood for, and I loved watching them do it. Being a Hadeed meant being someone who gives. It meant putting others before yourself and acting in ways that would benefit the greater good. To me and my sister, *that's* what leadership looked like.

Once, when I was in kindergarten, my mom somehow learned that one of my classmates couldn't afford a Halloween costume. We were supposed to wear costumes to school the next day, so my mom grabbed an extra one we had at home so that I could give it to my classmate.

I walked into my classroom with that extra costume in my hands—it was a red Crayola crayon suit—and handed it to my friend. I will never forget her smile. It stayed on her face all day as she wore it. The best part was when I got to tell her she could keep it, and I saw how happy she was to wear it home on the bus. It's only now that I realize how much that moment meant to me. As if I wasn't already convinced from watching how my parents lived their lives, that was the day I knew I wanted to serve others.

When I look back at it now, all the dots connect. But even though I didn't have this depth of awareness then, I still gave Paul enough to help me understand how my childhood experiences shaped the way I saw myself.

When my parents argued, restoring the peace between them became my way of feeling safe. I learned that harmony was something I could create, and in my own way, I took on the responsibility of managing our household's emotions. When my negative feelings were rejected, I learned I could earn love and belonging by staying agreeable. And when I watched my mom and dad give so much of themselves to help people—and saw the praise and respect they earned because of it—I learned that success looked like putting others above yourself.

Over time, all of these lessons added up to a single guiding belief: I was responsible for keeping the people around me happy. And unbeknownst to me, up until my conversation with Paul, that belief had guided every choice I'd made and every action I'd taken as an adult.

I had no idea just how much it was costing me.

Chapter 12

Emotional Weight

I don't blame my parents for any of what I've shared with you, not even for a second. I know they did the best they could with what they knew at the time. They're as human as you and me.

Paul explained it better than I could.

"Your parents didn't intend to give you this belief," he reassured me during our call. "When we're young, we don't yet understand the world around us or our place in it. The way we learn to earn love and protect ourselves as kids becomes the strategy we rely on as adults, often without realizing it."

"We call them *limiting* beliefs because they're thoughts that can restrict our growth. And while they do eventually limit us, their first job and the reason they form is to protect us. Take yours," he continued. "Believing it's your job to keep people happy helped you succeed for a long time. It got you here, right? That's important to acknowledge—and to appreciate."

He paused. "So let's start there. In what ways has that belief positively influenced you? What strengths has it given you in your life and your leadership?"

"Well . . ." I let the silence stretch between us as I pondered his questions.

I thought about how driven I had always been when it came to my team and how important it was to me that they felt seen, heard, and cared for. I thought about my uncanny ability to read a room and how tuned in I had always been to people's feelings and needs. I thought about the moments I sensed tension before it boiled over and how I stepped in to help people see eye-to-eye. I thought about all the times I intentionally went out of my way to make someone's day better and put a smile on their face.

There was a *lot* to be thankful for. After sharing all of that with Paul, I summed it up simply: "It's made me someone who leads with my heart." I stopped and thought for another moment. "I always consider how my decisions affect others, and I try to approach every situation with empathy."

"Those are powerful strengths," Paul said. "It's clear how much you care about people."

I smiled. I had always been proud of that part of myself.

"And you wouldn't want to change any of that about yourself, right?" he asked.

"Definitely not," I said quickly, almost cutting him off. "I always want to be a caring person."

"Of course you do," he continued, "and it's wonderful to be grateful to your belief for inspiring those qualities. These aren't things you ever have to change about yourself."

I nodded to myself, letting it all sink in.

"There's also another side to this," Paul said gently. "Just like your belief has given you incredible strengths, it's also limited you. It's just as important to look at what this belief takes from you."

I could already feel where this was going.

"So," he went on, "when you think about it being your job to keep people happy, what are the costs that come along with that? How has this belief hurt you? Where does it hold you back?"

I didn't have to think for long before several examples came to mind.

"In meetings, when I can sense that someone is unhappy," I said, "I spend a lot of emotional energy trying to get that person back on board. I know it derails the meeting. My team has given me that feedback before."

"And what else?" Paul asked without the slightest hint of judgment in his voice. I felt safe to keep sharing.

"I also don't love giving feedback," I said. *More like I dread it with my entire being*, I thought. (If you read *Permission to Screw Up*, you may remember my "shit sandwiches" and how I buried critical feedback beneath so many layers of positive reinforcement, the message got lost.) "I've always struggled with it," I told Paul. "I focus on the positives instead of what the person needs to do better."

The answers kept coming.

"And I have a really hard time letting people go." I said. That was an understatement. Once, my leadership team asked me to let someone go because of their poor job performance. Instead of telling this person it was time to part ways, I gave them a *promotion* (to this day I don't know how that happened). Luckily, I had grown in these areas since then, but I still resisted these conversations.

"I just . . . *really* don't like hurting people," I admitted. Hurting others was my biggest fear.

"On a scale of 1 to 10, how important is it for you to be liked?" Paul asked.

"TEN!" I blurted out.

"And what do you want that number to be?"

"Ten?" I said softly. Probably not the answer he was looking for, but it was the truth.

Back then, if I knew (or even *suspected*) that someone was upset with me, I'd feel a pit in my stomach. I wouldn't be able to focus on anything else and would be consumed with anxiety until I knew that person and I were "okay."

If ever someone wanted to leave my company—even when it was clearly the right move for them—I struggled to accept it. I would try everything I could to convince them not to go. It was as if their wanting to leave was evidence that I had failed at my job of keeping them happy. If someone left, I thought it meant they didn't like me enough to stay.

Being so attuned to other people's moods and emotions was a strength, but somewhere along the way, the lines got blurred. Instead of simply feeling compassion for what people were going through, I felt responsible for fixing it. Once, a student team member was struggling with an addiction. I became the person she leaned on emotionally, and I even worked with a friend of hers to arrange for her to go to rehab. At the time, I believed I was helping her. But now I can see that I enabled her instead of empowering her to take responsibility for her own recovery. A couple of times I even let team members stay at my house when they were between places to live. There were no boundaries.

I meddled. If there was conflict between people on my team, my instinct was to insert myself and try to make things better, just like I used to do with my parents. But I often hurt people more than I helped them. Once, a few members of the leadership team were frustrated with one of their peers. Rather than encouraging them to talk directly with her, I passed their feedback along myself. Then I brought everyone together and attempted to mediate their conversation. Instead of building trust between them, I broke it. The leader wanted to know why she had heard about the feedback from *me* instead of her teammates. She was right.

Over time, people learned that if they mentioned an interpersonal issue to me, I would act on it. So, eventually, many stopped coming to me. Not because they didn't have conflict, but because they didn't want me to step in.

It was exhausting trying to carry the emotional weight of an entire company. And what stands out to me now is how I kept doing it, even when it was clear that my involvement wasn't always helpful.

It also led to people taking advantage of me.

I had earned a reputation in my company for being "soft." It became an inside joke: If you wanted something, all you had to do was tell Kristen you were upset. Want a raise? Hint that you might quit and you'll get one. Need a last-minute schedule change? Skip your direct leader and come straight to me because there's a 99.99% chance I'd say yes. Want a pay advance? Who cares if we need the cash for a debt payment—you got it.

It's also why I repeatedly took on the hardest part of the job: the worst of the HR issues. My leadership team could have handled them, but I rarely gave them the chance to try. "I'll just take one for the team" became my mantra, but over time, I came to resent it. In my attempt to shield my team from anything unpleasant and to keep their jobs as enjoyable as possible, I robbed them of the chance to grow and lead, and I made myself miserable in the process. Rinse and repeat.

One of the strangest things I told Paul was that I felt uncomfortable using the words "I," "me," and "my." When talking about the company, I always said "we" did this or that, described things as being "ours," even called the team "our team" instead of "my team." I used that language so much that people asked if I had a co-founder, assuming I must be talking about a business partner. To me, calling something mine meant stepping into the spotlight or taking credit in a way that might make someone else feel less-than. I feared it would harm our connection. It was a habit that started in my personal relationships: When I began building Student Maid, many of my friends were still figuring out their own paths, and the guys I dated often told me they felt intimidated by my success. I downplayed my accomplishments because I didn't want to create distance in my relationships, but it left me feeling unseen for who I really was and what I'd worked so hard to build.

As these words left my mouth, I suddenly saw how intricately my limiting belief had woven itself into my life and my leadership. (Turns out this exercise wasn't so woo-woo after all.)

"Good job," Paul said, after I shared as many costs as I could name. "And now it's time for the fun part." I could feel the excitement shining through in his voice.

"The most empowering thing about this work is that *you* get to decide which strengths of your belief you want to carry forward—and which costs you want to leave behind."

Paul then spent a few minutes introducing me to the work of spiritual teacher and author Byron Katie, which I've since come to love. Katie teaches that it's not a *thought* that hurts us; it's our attachment to it. We cling so tightly to the beliefs we carry that they start to feel like reality. But when a thought is causing us pain and limiting us, we have the power to question it and choose a different one.

I waited for Paul to lead me to my next big breakthrough.

But, of course, he didn't. Because that's Paul. Instead, he gave me another deceptively simple homework assignment—one that I'm still working on today.

"Kristen," he said as we wrapped up, "you are a kind and caring person, and you always will be. Those strengths are part of who you are. But you don't have to keep believing that it's your job to keep people happy in order to be that person. When you notice yourself thinking that way, pause and question it. Respond differently than you normally would. Give the feedback, even if it might not be what someone wants to hear. Resist inserting yourself, and let people face the challenges that belong to them. That's how you begin to grow beyond this belief."

Just before we ended our call, Paul left me with one last piece of wisdom: a question from Byron Katie's signature method of self-inquiry called *The Work*.

"The next time you catch yourself thinking it's your job to keep someone else happy, stop and ask yourself: Who would I be without this thought?"

After we hung up, I sat there and considered the question.

Who would I be if I no longer believed it was my job to keep people happy? I couldn't picture her.

But she was waiting for me—and she was more alive and free than anything I'd ever dreamed.

Chapter 13

Running the Show

What I shared with Paul that day was the tip of the iceberg. I was just beginning to see how much my limiting belief was costing me.

When I look back on that version of me now, my heart aches. I wish I could take one of those bricks from the hot-air balloon basket on Paul's website and toss it through the 32nd-floor window just to get my own attention. I wish I could hold my own hands and tell myself everything I know now. It would have saved me years of pain.

But I can't do that.

So instead, I want to tell you, friend—with the hope that it might save you from heartache of your own.

All that time, I thought Student Maid was the problem.

I blamed it for my exhaustion, my lack of joy, my financial struggles. I thought it was the only thing that stood between me and a life that felt beautiful again.

I blamed my team for my resentment. I told myself that they were the reason I could never relax or be fully present in my life. That they were the source of my stress.

But they didn't cause my pain. And neither did Student Maid.

The real source was inside of me all along.

If I had looked there, I would have found a belief that I never chose, never questioned, and didn't realize was running the show: that it was my job to keep everyone happy—no matter the cost.

Why did I take on all that debt? To keep growing my company and giving raises so that people would be . . . *happy*.

Why did I answer the phone on family vacations and handle every HR nightmare myself? Because I thought I had to protect the team from the hard stuff to keep them . . . *happy*.

Why did I keep doing work that didn't light me up anymore instead of choosing a different path? Because making a drastic change probably wouldn't make the team . . . *happy*.

Why did I hide how I really felt? Because when I was little, I learned that expressing difficult emotions never made anyone . . . *happy*.

After so many years of focusing on everyone else's happiness, I forgot to ask the most important question of all: What would make *me* happy?

When is the last time you asked yourself that same question?

We all have beliefs that weave themselves into the fabric of who we become, and usually without our permission, just like mine did. Our beliefs quite literally influence everything we do. They are the root of our behaviors, our decisions, our happiness (or *un*happiness), the way we show up in our relationships and our leadership. And yet so many people live their entire lives without ever understanding the unseen force behind it all.

For me, discovering my limiting belief was confusing. It contradicted so much of what I had always been certain was true. How could a desire to keep other people happy ever come with a cost? How could caring so much about other people's feelings lead me to a place of such anguish?

After all, isn't that what my mom and dad modeled for me? Wasn't it their selflessness that left me in awe as a kid? Isn't that what I admired most about them?

And it wasn't just my parents: This belief was reinforced by every servant-leadership book I ever read. I devoured pages that told me the best leaders put people first. They are *others*-focused, not *self*-focused. They prioritize their teams' needs, growth, and well-being—and how well they do all of that is the ultimate measure of their leadership. Servant leaders are *not* selfish. They build their legacy by serving others.

So, you see, confronting my limiting belief also meant confronting my identity. Because I *wanted* to be a servant leader. I *wanted* to be a caring person. I *wanted* to follow in my mom and dad's footsteps and devote my life to helping others. I *wanted* to measure my success by the number of lives I touched. To me, these things were central to who I was. They were the tenets of my life. They were the parts of myself that I was most proud of.

And clinging to that identity felt . . . *good.* Being the person who made others happy meant that people needed me. Relied on me. Noticed me. Praised me. Nothing lit me up more than being called "generous." Living and leading this way made me feel significant. Like I mattered in the world.

But now, here was Paul, telling me that something I'd always believed was purely good was also the very thing holding me back.

How was that possible? The answer is complicated.

It's not that what I learned from my parents or read in those servant-leadership books was *wrong*. The problem was the way I interpreted it all—through a perspective that was shaped by the survival strategies I used to earn love and acceptance as a kid.

Caring about other people and their happiness was never the problem. The issue was that when *my* needs conflicted with someone else's, mine were the ones that got sacrificed. When being honest with someone or choosing myself might've hurt the other person or risked the connection between us, I consistently chose their comfort over my truth. And I did that again and again.

The bigger problem was that I was abandoning myself and calling it leadership. But that wasn't leadership. Not the kind my parents modeled and definitely not the kind I'd read about. How could it be?

Leading that way cost me my health, my smile, and my peace. It stole precious moments with my family that I can't get back, connection with Spiros, and relationships that mattered to me. It made me resent my team and enabled stagnation in my business. It trapped us underneath six figures of debt. It kept me quiet about how I was really feeling inside. It caused me to make decisions I'm not proud of. It turned me into a shell of myself I couldn't even recognize. How could *that* ever be leadership?

If Paul hadn't held up the mirror for me that day, I might've never stopped to examine the way I was leading or who I had become in the process. He told me that it wasn't my job to keep everyone happy, and that left me with a burning question: Then what *was* my job?

Was it to manage other people's feelings, or to be honest about my own?

To avoid discomfort, or to act with courage and integrity?

To protect people from my truth, or to trust they could handle it?

To put others first, or to lead in a way that honored both them *and* myself?

Which leader would you follow? Which one would you trust? Which one would inspire you?

I know my answer. But it would take me a long time to learn how to become her.

Thank goodness for that night I didn't recognize my reflection in my apartment window.

If it hadn't been for that, I never would have discovered the seven words that changed everything.

Chapter 14

Puzzle Pieces

After Paul helped me uncover "It's my job to keep people happy," I brought the same exercise to my leadership team to help them discover their own limiting beliefs.

To most people, that might seem like crossing a line between personal life and work that shouldn't be crossed. But to me, it was a natural next step.

Since the earliest days of Student Maid, when something had helped me grow, I shared it with the team so that they could benefit, too. I hosted development workshops for our students for years until our leadership team took those over so that I could focus on developing *them*.

By the time I started working with Paul, I was already hosting a monthly workshop for the leadership team where we learned about ourselves and each other to help us strengthen our relationships.

With each new personality we'd added to the mix, tensions had grown. When one person chose to eat lunch alone in her office with the door closed, for example, the rest of the team took offense. It left them wondering why she didn't want to enjoy a meal with them in the kitchen, and she questioned why she was being judged for taking the solo time she needed to recharge.

Someone else on the team had a more straightforward, direct way of communicating. To her, it was efficient, but it came across to others as harsh and dismissive. Another person needed more time than others to complete certain tasks. While the rest of the team labeled their pace unnecessarily slow, this person saw it as being detail-oriented.

These misunderstandings disheartened me. I knew that no one was on a mission to frustrate their teammates; they each just moved through the world differently. Instead of taking someone's actions personally, I tried to get curious, meet them with empathy, and adjust my approach as needed.

Over time, that earned me the role of leadership team translator. I found myself decoding each person's behavior for the rest of the team to try to mitigate the tension between them, which was emotionally exhausting. But it also helped me see an opportunity: I could use our monthly workshops to make my leadership team more aware of their own behavior and how it affected others.

We started with self-assessments. We took all the classics—DISC, StrengthsFinder, Myers-Briggs—highlighting what felt true, laughing at what didn't, and exploring what our individual results meant for the team as a whole. With each revelation, the tension started to fall away. Once we had a clear understanding of who our introverts and extroverts were, for example, solo lunches were suddenly no longer a point of contention.

One month, we explored our communication "deposits" and "withdrawals"—the small actions that either built trust or eroded it for each of us. One person shared that not getting a reply to an email made her feel ignored, while another explained that having time to process feedback before responding helped her show up better in those conversations.

We also learned about the differences in our natural communication styles and began to see traits like "direct" and "sensitive" as instinctual rather than purposeful. We discovered our motivations, what we each needed to feel appreciated at work, and even our apology languages (yes, that's a thing). To make sure that the lessons stuck, I gave pop quizzes and asked everyone to list each other's assessment results from memory. The goal was to make understanding one another a shared responsibility.

Over time, these workshops helped the leadership team function as one. We didn't eliminate all the tension—there will always be some of that on any team—but we learned how to move through it in healthier ways.

Leading our workshops quickly became one of my most favorite parts of my job. No matter how stressful things were in the business, I knew I'd have two days every month where I could reconnect with my purpose as a leader and pour into my team.

All of that is why, when Paul taught me about limiting beliefs, I knew I wanted to bring the exercise to our next workshop.

By this point, the leadership team was smaller: A few people had naturally moved on, especially after we closed the second location of Student Maid and the software business. Now there were five of us—including me—and we mostly met virtually.

Everyone already knew that I'd hired Paul to help me become a better leader. I kicked off the workshop by telling the team how he led me to uncover "It's my job to keep people happy." I told them where I suspected it came from in my childhood and asked how they'd seen it show up in my leadership. I wanted to know how my belief affected them.

They didn't hold back one bit.

The team told me how frustrating it was when my fear of hurting people drove my decisions. They knew that when a choice might upset someone, I avoided it, even when it was the right one for the business. They brought up the times I hadn't let students go when I should have, especially when we'd given them many chances and they'd repeatedly failed to meet our expectations. They said the emotional energy I poured into those situations drained everyone involved.

As they spoke, I felt my shoulders relax a little—which probably seems like a weird reaction to tough feedback. But so much of what they shared matched what I'd already told Paul. Even though it felt vulnerable to open myself up to their perspectives, it also felt like a relief. Like I had permission to be *human*. To be seen for my imperfections and where they came from and to be able to sit there without needing to be anyone other than who I was. To be allowed to be a leader with flaws.

Then it was their turn.

I'd found a worksheet from Byron Katie's website that listed dozens of common beliefs and used it to guide my team the way Paul had guided me. I invited them to notice what they felt in their bodies as they read each statement. If a belief triggered an internal reaction, I told them to circle it. Then I asked them to think about where the belief might have come from and how they thought it was still affecting them today.

For the next 20 minutes, I watched their brows furrow in concentration as their eyes scanned the page. When the last person looked back up at the screen, I asked if anyone would be willing to share their discovery.

Before I could finish, Amanda unmuted herself. I could always count on her to go first.

Amanda was the only person on the leadership team who hadn't started at Student Maid as a cleaner. I'd always believed our leaders should "grow up" in our culture, but when we found ourselves without anyone internally who fit our front-desk role, we advertised for the position and chose Amanda. Her uncommon background made her stand out: From a young age, Amanda competed as an archer and qualified for the Junior US World Team. At one point, she was one of the six best archers in the country and trained for the Olympics.

Amanda applied at Student Maid because she was looking for something to supplement her work as an archery coach. I'd been dreaming about hiring someone with a coaching mindset who could reinforce our culture of learning with our students, and Amanda had all the strengths I was looking for. By the time we did the limiting beliefs exercise, her role had grown to overseeing the majority of Student Maid's culture and daily operations.

"I think my belief is 'I'm not good enough,'" she began. "And I know where it comes from."

She took a breath and looked at the screen. "When I was a kid, my grandma would tell me, 'Mandy, you're good at many things, but you aren't great at anything.'"

No one moved. It was devastating to hear.

"I know she meant well," Amanda went on. "She wanted me to have a better life than anyone in our family. I think it was her way of motivating me and pushing me to make something of myself. It's why I was so competitive as an archer. But now, when I mess up, it makes me feel like a failure. Like no matter how hard I try, it will never be enough. So I push myself harder."

My heart ached for little Amanda. I knew how much her grandma meant to her. I couldn't imagine hearing those words from the person you looked up to most.

I thought back to my feedback conversations with Amanda. Giving feedback was already uncomfortable for me because of my own limiting belief, but with Amanda, it felt even more challenging. She never got defensive, but she usually turned inward. Any time I gave her tough feedback, I'd watch her get upset with herself in real time, and it made me feel like I had to walk on eggshells around her. Now I understood why it happened.

Amanda's courage in sharing opened the door for others to follow suit. After she finished, Rachel asked to go next.

Rachel and I had worked together longer than anyone else on the team. She joined Student Maid in college as a cleaner, and the funny part is we hired her, trained her for one day, and then forgot to put her on the schedule. We only realized our mistake when she emailed the office weeks later and asked when she was supposed to work again.

After graduating with a degree in journalism, Rachel couldn't find a job in her field, so she stayed on the team and helped in the office. When we decided to open our second Student Maid location in her hometown, Rachel moved back to run it, but after a couple of years, she told me that her heart wasn't in it. We both knew her strengths weren't, either. She didn't want to leave the company, and I didn't want to lose her, so I had an idea: I had just signed my book deal for *Permission to Screw Up*, and I had no clue where to start. Rachel was a strong writer with a degree to match, so I asked her to be my editor. After we submitted the manuscript, she naturally moved into a content-centered role for both Student Maid and the speaking business, helping with everything from producing my weekly blog to writing internal policies for Student Maid.

"I'm pretty sure my limiting belief is 'People are judging me,'" she said with a nervous laugh.

"Tell us more," I said gently. I knew she'd need the invitation.

"Well, I overthink . . . a lot. I'll reread an email three or four times before I send it to make sure the tone is just right."

I had seen this in our writing work together—how carefully Rachel chose her words, how much intention she put behind every sentence. It was one of her greatest strengths.

"I think it's connected to me being an only child, but I can't point to a specific memory. I just know it's been a theme throughout my life."

She took a breath, as if putting the puzzle pieces together in real time.

"When I was a kid, it felt like all eyes were on me. And as I got older, I think I felt pressure to be worthy of that attention: If I got good grades, I had to keep getting them. If people said I was funny, I had to keep being funny. I've always cared so much about what others think, and it makes me second-guess myself. I'm always wondering how I come across and whether I'm saying or doing the right thing."

It helped me to hear that Rachel was aware of this in herself. She was one of the most thoughtful people I knew, but I could see where it held her back. She often got stuck in her head. Sometimes her worries transferred to others, and especially to me. Her fear activated mine. I would step in to try to reassure her and calm what she was feeling. Hearing her talk about her limiting belief helped me better understand that dynamic between us.

Cheyenne raised her hand next.

Cheyenne was newer to our leadership team meetings, but not new to our team. She had started as a student during one of our busy summers and quickly stood out, not just for her work ethic, but for the level of responsibility we could trust her with.

Within Student Maid, we had a hands-on leadership experience called the Ambassador Program, which we designed for students who wanted to learn the ins and outs of running a business. We gave them a sense of ownership by allowing them to assist with the operations of the company, and Cheyenne was one of our first. She partnered closely with Amanda to help keep the office running smoothly and did everything from booking clients to collecting invoices to managing our weekly schedule.

But what made her even more valuable was her perspective. As a student, Cheyenne noticed things about our company and culture that we didn't, and she always shared her ideas to help us make improvements. We assumed our time with her was short and that she would move on after graduation—still a couple of years away—to pursue a job in line with her degree in cybersecurity. We felt lucky for the chance to learn from her for the time being.

"Mine's the same as Amanda's," Cheyenne said. "I'm not good enough."

"I think it started when I was younger," she went on. "My brother was always getting into trouble, and my parents spent a lot of their time worrying about him. He was always the focus. And I felt . . ."

She stopped, searching for the word.

"Ignored." She gave a small shrug.

"I didn't always feel like I was good enough to earn their attention," she said.

A few of us nodded from our sides of the screen. "I didn't want to make things more difficult for my parents," she said, "so I stayed out of the way. And I think I still do that. I struggle to speak up for myself. Sometimes I don't feel like I'm . . . deserving, maybe, of things in my life."

Cheyenne was humble to a fault. When I recognized or praised her, it seemed like it was hard for her to accept it. She'd quickly deflect, passing the credit to someone else, and try to push away what was so clearly hers to receive. She could be hard on herself, especially when she made a mistake. And now, once again, I understood why.

Finally, it was Monique's turn. Up until now, she'd been doing what she always did: listening carefully, taking it all in, and letting everyone else speak first.

Monique joined our cleaning team during one of our busy summer seasons. That year, we held a friendly competition: Whoever cleaned the most efficiently—and with the highest quality—earned a spot on our year-round team. Monique was one of the winners.

I didn't think we'd have Monique on the team for long, and I dreaded the day she'd leave. Monique had always planned to pursue a career in interior design, and she had internships and job offers already lined up. But as graduation approached, Monique had a change of heart. When she interned with a major hospitality firm, she wasn't trusted to make any decisions—even small ones, like moving outlets on a drawing. She noticed that it was a stark contrast from the autonomy she felt at Student Maid and asked if she could build a future with us instead.

We didn't have an open role on the leadership team at the time, but I created one around Monique's strengths. In the years that followed, she helped wherever the business needed her. She trained new hires, led our student workshops, and eventually became my right hand in the speaking business, supporting the operations there. She had a way of bringing order to everything she touched.

"My limiting belief is 'I'm too much,'" she said.

I didn't expect that. Monique always seemed so sure of herself. She was one of the most confident people I knew—or so I thought.

"I remember waking up early one Christmas morning and seeing all the presents under the tree," she said. "I started shrieking with excitement. I was a typical kid, ready to rip into every present I saw. And I remember my mom telling me to be quiet and wait patiently."

She stayed with the memory for a second.

"I don't blame her," she said. "My stepdad was in the Navy, and I was with my dad every other weekend. Most days, it was just my mom at home with my sister and me, and she was overwhelmed. She also grew up in a house where she was expected to be seen and not heard. Her dad was like a drill sergeant. I don't think she knew how to let us be kids because she wasn't allowed to ever be one herself. Plus, that particular Christmas morning included both sets of my parents and all the stepkids. I'm sure there were dynamics at play that I didn't understand."

I wanted to jump through the screen and give Monique—and her mom—a hug.

"I think growing up like that is why I tend to hold back," she continued. "I don't always share my opinions, especially when they're strong or different from everyone else's because I'm afraid of how people might react. So that's why, sometimes, I just don't speak up."

I had seen this, and it always confused me. In meetings, Monique would appear to be in agreement with the group, but later, I'd learn that she had concerns all along. I never understood why she held back in the moments that mattered most, but now I got it.

Before we did this exercise, I thought I knew the four people on the screen in front of me inside and out. I had worked with them for *years*. I knew their assessment results by heart. We had logged countless hours of learning together. And yet what we learned in this one workshop surpassed all the others combined.

When I looked at their faces, I no longer saw my leadership team.

I saw Amanda, the little girl trying to make her grandma proud.

I saw Rachel, the only child hoping she was worthy of the attention she received.

I saw Cheyenne, the daughter trying to make things easier for her parents.

I saw Monique, the kid who just wanted to share her excitement and her voice.

This felt like the most important work a team could do. We had learned about one another's lives before, but not like this. I could feel our collective empathy expand even further.

And while that deeper understanding was powerful, I didn't want it to be the only outcome of our time together. I wanted it to challenge us to show up more courageously in our lives.

Now that we understood each person's limiting beliefs, we could call out the patterns that were holding us back when we saw them pop up. I took it seriously enough to pay for each person to have a one-on-one session with Paul so that he could help them further explore their own beliefs.

As for me? I felt a heightened responsibility to model what I had just asked of my team.

Now that they knew about my limiting belief, they needed to see me confront it.

Part II

Facing

Chapter 15

Baby Steps

In the weeks that followed our workshop, I tried to walk my talk.

In meetings, when someone disagreed or became frustrated, I fought the urge to smooth things over. Instead, I let them disagree and be upset. (And then I followed up with them after to make sure they were good. Baby steps, okay?)

When I let people sit with their uncomfortable emotions instead of rushing to fix them, I noticed the world didn't fall apart like I thought it would. The meeting went on, and usually that person came around by the end. Even if they didn't, they seemed to naturally get over it with time. Our meetings became more candid, and fewer people held back. Sometimes the tension led to better decisions. It was as if allowing people to feel their discomfort empowered them to do something with it.

Together, we made good on our promise from our workshop. Limiting beliefs became part of our shared language: When we thought a belief was getting in someone's way, we said so.

When Amanda started to shut down in a feedback conversation, we reminded her that receiving feedback didn't mean she wasn't good enough, and that awareness helped her remain open. When Rachel spiraled into overthinking, we reassured her that none of us were judging her, and she learned to give herself more grace. When Cheyenne deflected our compliments on her excellent work, we encouraged her to relish them instead, and it helped her see herself as a valuable part of the team. When Monique held back in a meeting, we invited her to share her perspective, and when we thanked her, it affirmed that she wasn't too much.

By this time it was January 2019, and I was nine months into my coaching journey with Paul.

I felt a little pep in my step again. Just a tad more energy. A bit more hope. A little less hitting snooze.

Working with Paul had shown me the difference that outside support could make, so I started looking for it in other areas of my life—even if it meant stretching an already tight budget. I hired a trainer and a nutrition coach to hold me accountable to getting healthy again.

I wish I could tell you that this decision came purely from a desire to take care of myself. But there was something on my left hand that was motivating me more.

I was engaged.

Spiros proposed shortly after the holidays. He had won a trip to the American Girl store near Washington, DC, at a charity auction, so we took his six-year-old daughter, Evie, for her Christmas present.

On our first night, we got dressed up to go to dinner at the Jefferson Hotel, a charming historic spot in the heart of DC. I should have known something was up when I tried to walk out wearing a loud, multicolored faux-fur coat: Spiros never comments on my clothes, but he looked concerned and asked if I had anything else to wear. (I realize now that he was imagining the engagement photos.)

At dinner, Evie asked if we could play a game of "I Spy," where you choose an object in the room, describe what color it is, and let everyone else guess until they figure it out. Spiros went first.

"I spy something pink," he said.

Evie had brought a toy with her—a small pink ball with a doll tucked inside. I assumed that's what it was, so I stayed quiet to let her win. But after a few minutes of her scanning the room with no luck, I decided to give her a hint.

"Is it somewhere over here?" I asked, pointing toward the table.

That's when Spiros reached for the pink ball and handed it to me.

"Open it," he said.

The ring was inside. They had planned it together.

It was one of the most beautiful moments of my life.

With a wedding now in my future, I wanted to feel better in my own skin. I was tired of waking up and not recognizing the version of myself staring back at me. I wanted to begin this next chapter with Spiros as my healthiest self—for me, for him, and for us.

Working out and eating better helped my clothes begin to fit again. But the more I focused on my health, the harder it became to ignore the one unhealthy habit of mine that was still going strong: Drinking wine.

I didn't do it every night. But after a long day filled with endless decisions, everyone needing something from me, and pressure that felt like too much for one person, sipping a glass of cabernet took the edge off. It was the one time of day I felt like I didn't have to be "on."

At the time, I called it "relaxing." But now I can see it for what it was: coping.

Though it was temporary, a glass of wine provided almost instant relief from my stress. It was the way I avoided having to think about the difficult emotions brewing inside of me and the truths I didn't want to acknowledge. It was the way I silenced the questions that haunted me when I was alone—questions like *If I don't want Student Maid in my future, what do I want? What am I really afraid of? How much longer am I willing to live like this?*

I'd tell myself I'd figure out the answers to those questions "tomorrow," but when tomorrow came, I was always too busy to spare them a thought.

When we're avoiding something, most of us have a go-to distraction: Some people watch shows. Some scroll, shop, or eat. Some immerse themselves in their work. Some stay busy so they never have to be still. No matter what they are, these distractions help us avoid the parts of ourselves we don't want to face. They aren't problematic on their own, but they become that way when we turn to them instead of processing how we feel—and doing something about it.

Wine had become a problematic distraction for me.

A few weeks after Spiros and I got engaged, I boarded a plane to Phoenix for my first speech of the year. I walked onto the jetbridge with a throbbing headache.

The night before, I'd had a few too many glasses of wine with friends. I'd wanted to celebrate my last bit of freedom before returning to work in the new year, and I felt anxious about the challenges in the business that I knew were waiting for me.

As I settled into my seat on the plane, I silently lectured myself:

> *Kristen, why did you drink so much last night? What if you don't feel better by your speech tomorrow? Is this really how you want to start a new year? Get it together.*

Two steps forward, one step back. That's how it was for me.

When I checked into my hotel later that day, I snapped a picture of the room-service menu and asked my nutrition coach what I should order to stay on track with my goals. She suggested that I get the chicken and grilled carrots and swap in olive oil in place of the butter. I called and placed the order, and just before I hung up, the person on the other end of the line asked, "Would you like a glass of wine with that?"

Absolutely not.

The thought alone made me want to throw up.

After I ate, I did my final preparations for my speech and turned in early. Right before I nodded off, I begged the universe to help me rock it on stage the next morning—and I promised myself I'd stop drinking.

One of those things came true.

Chapter 16

Right Now

I absolutely crushed my speech the next morning.

As soon as I stepped off the stage, I saw a man making a beeline for me.

I recognized him. He was the CEO of the company I was there to speak for. We'd exchanged a quick hello during my mic check, but now he was walking toward me with purpose.

He complimented my presentation, then asked, "Any chance you're free after this?"

It's not unusual for clients to want to grab a meal or do a quick debrief after an event, so I assumed that's what he had in mind. But after delivering a keynote and two workshops back-to-back—and recovering from a gnarly hangover—all I wanted was to be alone in my hotel room. My plans for the rest of the day included comfy clothes, a face mask, and answering emails from bed.

But, of course, there was no way I was going to say that to him. If the CEO was asking, I suddenly had all the time in the world.

"No plans!" I chirped, wishing I'd left the stage ten seconds sooner and missed him entirely.

"That's great news," he said, his eyes lighting up. "Would you be willing to facilitate a session for a leadership team here that is struggling?"

"Like . . . right *now*?" I asked, certain I'd misheard him. There was no way he meant right now. That would be crazy.

"Right now," he said.

He went on to explain that he had just stepped in as interim president of a global company, and the culture felt disjointed.

Several members of the US leadership team were there for the event, along with a few from Europe, and he wanted to take advantage of the rare opportunity of having them all in the same room.

He already had a vision for how to use the time: Onstage, I had shared what I'd learned from Paul about finding my own personal core values, along with the story of how we created Student Maid's values. He wanted me to guide this team through a similar process and help them discover a shared set of values for the company. He hoped it might unify the team and help the different regions feel more connected.

I did a quick mental inventory of what I had to work with . . . which was hardly anything. I didn't know this leadership team or have any context for the kind of work they did, aside from the few things the CEO had just told me. We also didn't discuss an additional fee for this, and we didn't really have time, considering the team was *already in the room waiting for me.*

But there was something about this guy's energy—combined with my love of helping teams work better together—that made me say yes before I had a chance to fully process what I was saying yes to.

Five minutes later, we were walking down the hall to a smaller conference room. As we stepped inside, 15 faces turned my way, all waiting for me to kick off a session I didn't yet know how I was going to lead.

The next two hours were what I was made for.

Voices rose. People pushed back. A few sat with their arms crossed and scowled. I listened to what they said (and what they didn't), and I made sure each person had a chance to share their perspective.

At first, the conversation centered on what wasn't working: The team acknowledged that there was a culture of finger-pointing and broken communication, and as a result their trust was fragile. Once we got it all out in the open, I shifted the conversation to the behaviors that might help remove those frustrations.

I captured notes on a large pad of paper propped up on an easel in the front of the room. I made sure it reflected the current state of our discussion, crossing things out and rewriting as we got clearer.

When I filled up a page, I'd tear it off and stick it to the wall. By the time we finished, paper covered the room, and all that was left on the easel was a sheet of paper with three words: Care. Ownership. Communication.

They decided that these were the values they wanted everyone in the organization to embody, including themselves—and the company still uses them today.

When we left that conference room together, it didn't feel like I was walking out with a group of frustrated individuals. I walked out with a *team*.

The CEO felt it, too.

"Would you like to join us for dinner tonight?" he asked.

I said yes—this time wholeheartedly. Something in my gut told me I wanted to be in this guy's orbit far more than I wanted to be in my hotel room alone doing a face mask.

His name was Jamil. And after Phoenix, we stayed in touch.

We debriefed the core values session over a call, and that's when he shared his next crazy idea.

"Will you join me in Amsterdam?"

Chapter 17

Heart of the Matter

Six months later, I boarded a plane to The Netherlands. This time, my "yes" came with a fee.

Jamil wanted me to attend his Quarterly Business Review (QBR). He asked me to bring the values work to the wider European team and help them explore how to live the values day to day.

At the Amsterdam office, we revisited the work we'd started. The European team thought the core values we had identified resonated with them for the most part, but they were adamant that two were missing: Curiosity and Fun.

The challenge was that those words didn't resonate with the US team at all. It was something we'd discussed in Phoenix. That group decided that while Curiosity and Fun reflected the spirit of the European office, they didn't represent the organization as a whole, so it didn't make sense to put them on the list of company-wide values.

Then, in what I had learned was typical Jamil fashion, he asked a question that changed the course of the entire discussion: Was there a way to approach the values so that the different regions felt connected to the company as a whole while still honoring what made them unique? What needed to be true everywhere, and what could be allowed to look different?

In the end, we empowered the European team to add Curiosity and Fun as their "identity values."

That's the kind of leader Jamil is. He noticed what energized people and directed that energy toward something productive. Over the next couple of days in Amsterdam, I got to see that up close.

After the core values session, the rest of the time we spent together was dedicated to the QBR. I watched Jamil lead his team through an honest look at the business. They examined their results, gave one another feedback about their performance that quarter, and spoke candidly about where the business was falling short and why.

I noticed that Jamil didn't rescue anyone from discomfort. Not once.

He asked questions that cut straight to the heart of the matter. He spoke last. When someone got upset, he didn't smooth it over, and he definitely didn't soften the truth. When someone operated below their potential, he said it plainly. When perception didn't match reality, he called out the gap. When someone said they'd "try," he followed up with "What's your plan? When is your deadline? How will you measure success?"

Hope wasn't a strategy to Jamil. Clarity was.

What struck me most was how candid he was without ever being unkind. He wasn't arrogant or unforgiving; he was authentic. When he spoke, it felt like an invitation for the person across from him to rise to the standard he knew they were capable of meeting. And rise they did.

It was obvious to everyone in that room that Jamil cared about them. He often described his company as a place where people could use their collective superpowers to do good in the world. In preparing for my keynote in Phoenix, I'd learned he was the real deal as far as leaders go: His company offered benefits I rarely saw in other businesses, like tuition reimbursement to explore interests outside of work and scholarship programs for his employees' children. He led with generosity.

But there were expectations. At Jamil's company, you were responsible for your results. I spotted a screen in the European office with little animated fish swimming across it. Each time a deal closed, the fish got bigger. At any moment, all anyone on the team had to do to see how the company was performing—and how they were performing within it—was glance up at the screen. There was nowhere to hide.

It felt completely different from how I led. I still believed it was my job to absorb the pressure so that no one else on my team had to feel it—and I still did so much of it behind closed doors.

In Jamil's company, the challenges belonged to everyone, not just him. Transparency fueled ownership. The team didn't resist hard conversations; they faced them together. And at the end of the QBR, after hours of intense work and difficult conversations, they celebrated. They boarded a boat and drifted through the canals of Amsterdam, cracking jokes and clinking glasses. I overheard more than one person tell Jamil how meaningful the last few days had been.

I sat there and watched in awe.

I'd never seen a leader hold such a high standard and still be so loved and respected by their team. Most leaders I knew were either results-driven or relationship-driven. Jamil showed me it was possible to be both—something I wanted so badly for myself.

When we spent time together outside of the sessions, over breakfast at the hotel and catching each other in the lobby after long days, I paid attention to how he carried himself when he wasn't "on." He seemed genuinely happy. He'd brought his kids along on the trip and spent time with them whenever he could. He spoke about his marriage with warmth. He drank his coffee slowly in the morning and kept a notebook nearby, jotting down reflections and setting intentions for the day. He was present.

Jamil was the person I had described in my eulogy exercise. On my flight home, I kept thinking, *That's who I want to become*.

A few days later, we debriefed our time in Amsterdam over the phone. I had a question for him, but I kept talking myself out of it. Right before we hung up, I forced myself to say it.

"Jamil, where did you learn to lead like that?"

I was prepared to go into even more debt to sign up for whatever coach or leadership program made him into the kind of leader he was.

He mentioned a couple things—a program at Harvard, an executive coach—but then he said something that shocked me. I'll never forget this moment, partly because I had a lice treatment soaking in my hair while I waited for his reply. (Spiros caught lice from Evie, and when I got home from Europe, I joined the club.)

As I stood there, breathing in the fumes escaping my shower cap, Jamil said, "How about I mentor you? As much or as little as you want. Free of charge. No strings attached."

He said he believed in me and my work and that he genuinely wanted to help. Looking back, I sometimes wonder if he saw something in me I couldn't yet see in myself.

By then, my time with Paul had come to a natural close. During his next trip to Houston to visit family, we met in person—something I never would have agreed to in the beginning. I got to thank him face-to-face. I had grown so much through our work together, and I was ready for my next step.

Paul had helped me confront my past.

And now, Jamil was the one I would trust to help me create my future.

Chapter 18

Crystal Ball

I was on the verge of a new beginning.

I kept trying to live differently. I experimented with taking breaks from drinking and downloaded an app to track my alcohol-free days.

The first time, I made it to 30 days. Another time, past 70.

When I went without wine, my mind felt clearer. I slept deeper. Instead of waking up with a headache after a night with my friends, I woke up before my alarm.

Removing my means of escape didn't make my difficult feelings go away; it forced me to notice them more. Fear, loneliness, resentment, uncertainty, unhappiness in my work, stress, shame—they were all still there and, if anything, they were louder.

I still didn't know what to do about these feelings, so I gave myself permission to just . . . feel them. I took them with me on walks and solo dinner dates, and I wrote them into the pages in my journal. Sometimes I'd cry. Even though it wasn't fun, it felt like progress. Like I was getting to know my heart.

I still had trouble resisting invitations to happy hour—even more so when they came on tough workdays. But I felt healthier than I had in years. I had my nutrition dialed in, I was working out regularly, and I'd picked up a newfound love for running.

It had started with just five minutes a day. There was a dirt track outside my apartment in Houston, and eventually I worked my way up to running lap after lap around it, sometimes logging six or seven miles.

People who hadn't seen me in a while started to notice: They asked me what I was doing differently because they wanted to do it, too. Even my parents did a double-take the next time they saw me and told me how strong and healthy I looked. It felt good to be seen in that way again. I hadn't heard that in a long time.

My new lifestyle also brought me closer to Spiros. On the days I felt overwhelmed, I took it out on the track instead of on him. I came home sweaty, more patient, and quicker to laugh.

Now I was eager to see more positive changes in my life and my business—and I really hoped Jamil's support would get me there.

Before our first session, he sent me a few thought-provoking questions to help him understand what I wanted to get out of his mentorship. He called it the "crystal ball exercise."

From the prompt at the top of the page, I could already tell this coaching relationship would be different than the one I had with Paul:

> "The year you envisioned has now come and gone. We are celebrating because we achieved the following specific and measurable outcomes."

It was so Jamil. He wasn't interested in vague goals; he wanted to know *exactly* what winning looked like.

Even though "specific" and "measurable" weren't words I used often (more like ever), I thought about what kind of achievements would make me want to celebrate. I didn't know how big to go or how realistic to be, but I pushed myself to dream. Having Jamil in my corner made me feel like anything might be possible.

When we started our work together, it was September. He asked me to complete the exercise for the remainder of the year and also for the one ahead—2020.

In my crystal ball for the last quarter of 2019, I wrote that I saw:

- Paying off an additional $89,000 in debt
- Making Student Maid profitable again
- Bringing in $140,000 in speaking revenue
- Taking three weeks off at the end of the year
- Hosting a retreat for other leaders

For 2020, I saw:

- Becoming debt-free (which would mean paying down $244,000)
- Doubling the profit margins of Student Maid
- Bringing in $375,000 in speaking revenue
- Being able to confidently communicate our growth plan
- Taking four weeks off at the end of the year
- Getting a contract to write a second book

Looking at the goals I wrote down gave me chills. I couldn't imagine how it would feel if I actually achieved them. It felt like all of my problems would vanish in an instant.

But then I felt a wave of panic.

It hit me that once I sent my goals to Jamil, he was going to see everything: the debt, my true aspirations for growing the speaking business, and the reality that Student Maid wasn't as financially successful as he might've assumed.

I wanted to go back and delete half the list. I felt exposed. And embarrassed. Jamil had started as a client of *mine*. What would he think of me now?

But I also knew that if I didn't own where I was and declare what I wanted, I'd be wasting his time and mine. Someone like Jamil wasn't giving up precious hours for surface-level conversations. He wanted to help me work through the real problems that kept me up at night and help me become who I was capable of being—and he couldn't do any of that if I didn't let him in.

I hit "send" before I could talk myself out of it.

Chapter 19

The "A" Word

Jamil and I met on video twice a month for 90 minutes. There was no hiding behind a phone call like I did with Paul.

He treated our time together as if it were his most important meeting.

Our sessions were scheduled months in advance and always protected on his calendar. Jamil was in a time zone two hours behind mine, but no matter what worked best for me, he was there.

I can still picture him on my screen: He always joined from the quiet of his home with the same yellow wall behind him. I usually showed up frazzled, thinking about the meeting I'd just left and anticipating the ones coming later, but Jamil was centered. Never in a hurry. From how serene he appeared, you'd never guess he ran companies that brought in hundreds of millions of dollars a year. Within minutes of being in his presence, even virtually, I could feel my nervous system relax.

That's what made him rare: As calming as he was, he was equally confronting. Just like Jamil had zero tolerance for avoidance with his team, he had zero tolerance for it with me.

He opened our first session by sharing the reason he chose to mentor me. "Kristen, I think you can become the Tony Robbins of the rising generation."

Sorry, what?

I just sat there, at a total loss for words. I didn't know how to take his compliment; I certainly didn't see myself that way. No one had ever dreamed so big on my behalf.

He went on to say that he thought I had a gift for speaking and facilitation, which he'd witnessed firsthand in Phoenix and Amsterdam.

"I want to see you grow your speaking brand and use your superpowers to their fullest," he said. "So that's where we'll start."

It was just like Jamil to get right down to business.

"Your first assignment is to work with your team to create a structure that will bring what you saw in your crystal ball to life."

He briefly explained that by "structure," he meant clear ownership of goals. He wanted the team to feel empowered to deliver results so that I could stay focused on speaking.

"Oh, we already have that," I said proudly. I walked him through the leadership team, who did what, and how we split our responsibilities across the two businesses.

He shook his head. "That's not a structure," he said. "That's a list of people and their jobs."

We were only five minutes in, and I was already feeling the heat.

"I want to know who owns what," he continued. "Not who *helps*. Not who is *involved*. Who is responsible for delivering the result?"

"We all kind of . . . share things." I said. I felt myself starting to tense up. "Our culture is pretty collaborative."

"I'm sure it is," he said. "But when everything is shared, that means nothing is owned."

He leaned in slightly toward the screen.

"If I asked each person on your team what they are accountable for, would they know how to answer? Would they be able to tell me the goals they're driving, what success looks like, and how they measure that success?"

Hmmm.

"They'd probably . . . have a sense." (Emphasis on probably.)

"A 'sense' isn't clarity," he said. "Before our next meeting, I'd like to see clear owners for all the major components of your businesses, the goals each person is responsible for, and how those goals tie to your vision."

He wasn't done. "And while we're at it, let's have everyone create a work map for the rest of the year, too."

"A work map?" I asked. It was like Jamil and I spoke different languages.

"A week-by-week plan," he explained, "for what each person will do to reach their goals."

A week-by-week plan. Oh, wow.

"Send it to me before we meet next," he added. "I'd like some time to review it."

I was suddenly missing Paul.

I thought Jamil's instructions had me looking like a deer in headlights, but it was nothing compared to the looks on my team's faces when I shared the assignment with them—especially when I got to the part about work maps.

It wasn't that we didn't have plans or goals; of course we did. I'd been a business owner for 12 years at that point. I knew how to rally people around a common goal and inspire them to believe in it.

The problem was the "A" word: accountability.

If you read my first book, you know I often thought of myself as more of a *cheer*leader than a leader. I wanted our culture to feel fun. We had a big bell on the wall in our front office, and when we hit a goal, we rang it like crazy.

And when we didn't hit a goal, I rang the bell like crazy to pump us up to try again.

No one on my team was lazy. They all worked hard. They all cared. They all could've had jobs that paid them far more than I could, and yet they chose to be here with me. If we missed a goal, why make them feel bad about it? I wanted them to be excited to keep going and try again, not crippled by feeling like they'd failed.

Whenever we fell short of a financial goal at Student Maid, I tried all kinds of ways to motivate people to turn things around. I even went through a phase where I rebranded revenue as "Difference Dollars," saying it was the money that helped us make a difference in the world. I thought if I could make it feel more fun and meaningful, my team would be inspired to book more cleanings.

But what Jamil was asking me to do—put a person's name next to each goal—was something we'd never done before. We had only ever had team goals that we all worked toward together. That way, when we succeeded, we all shared the win. And when we didn't, no one person was at fault.

And when we kept missing our goals? Well, I just booked more speeches.

Now I can see that so much of my approach was influenced by my limiting belief: I equated holding people accountable with making them unhappy. And when it came to my leadership team especially, I didn't want to take that risk.

I knew they weren't sticking around just for the paycheck, so I worried that if our culture felt too strict—or if my expectations were too high—it might push them over the edge and cause them to leave. Holding our students accountable for the quality of their cleaning work was one thing, but with my leadership team, I really struggled. I avoided those conversations like the plague because there was more at stake: These weren't just employees or peers—they were my friends. We had years of history and trust between us. We talked all the time. More than them not liking our culture, I was afraid of them not liking *me*.

But now that Jamil was holding me accountable, my fear of failing his homework assignment was enough to push me in a new direction.

Once they got over the shock of creating work maps, my leadership team and I started sketching out a new structure. I empowered them to choose the goals they wanted to own. It felt rocky and a little uncomfortable at first, but then things began to unfold more naturally than I expected. By the time we were done, every goal had a name next to it. No one loved creating their work map (actually, they loathed it), but I reminded them often it wasn't *me* making them do that; it was Jamil.

I realized I'd built up the homework to be a much bigger deal than it actually was. I'd expected my team to resist and be frustrated about what I was asking them to do, but it didn't go like that at all. The team embraced it, figured it out with me, and seemed energized once we got into it. It took all of two meetings to land on our new structure. I was beginning to notice that maybe things wouldn't play out the way I'd feared they would. Maybe I really could ask more of my team.

Jamil gave me a B on that assignment, which was better than I expected. He said a few of our goals were too vague, so I took them back to the team, and we tightened them up.

With that taken care of, Jamil switched his focus back to me. "What's the status of the leadership retreat?" he asked.

Jamil knew that was the goal I was most excited about from the crystal-ball exercise. For a long time, I'd been dreaming about growing the speaking business by hosting our own events. I'd met many leaders over the years and saw an opportunity to bring a group of them together to help them grow, build new relationships, and feel less alone in their journeys.

"We booked the venue," I said. "The date is in December."

Please don't ask me—

"How many people have you signed up so far?"

—dang it.

"No one . . . *yet.* But I'm working on it!" I assured him.

"It's already October," he reminded me. "You don't have much time to work on it."

Less than two months, to be exact, and I'd set a goal to register 20 people. No one even knew about the retreat yet aside from me, my team, and now Jamil.

"What's your holdup?" he asked.

"I'm not sure what to charge." It was partially true.

The real reason was that I was scared. It had been a long time since I put myself out there and tried something new, and I wasn't exactly overflowing in the confidence department.

"Just pick a number," he said, "and go for it. Your homework is to email your invitations by the end of today. Give me an update when you're done."

By the end of today? I checked the time on my laptop: 2 p.m. And it was Friday.

That was Jamil. He didn't wait for Mondays, especially when a goal was at stake. He pushed me right to my edges and made me face every inch of what I didn't want to.

That evening, I dragged myself and my laptop to a coffee shop. I stared at the screen, going back and forth on the price in my head for far longer than I should have. Finally, I picked a number somewhere in the middle and sent out all the invitations.

I was convinced I'd just embarrassed myself. But the next morning, I woke up to two yeses.

I couldn't believe it.

Over the next couple of weeks, I stuck to my end-of-day coffee shop routine, and I surpassed my goal: When all was said and done, I'd registered 30 people for the retreat.

Jamil was slowly teaching me how to face what I'd been avoiding.

I should've guessed that every push, every assignment, and every moment he didn't let me off the hook was just preparing me for what was coming next.

Chapter 20

Alarm Bells

"I think you're ready for your first QBR," he said.

Jamil and I were almost two months into working together, and he wanted to bring the same review process he used for his own team to mine.

But there was a catch.

"How about I facilitate it for you?" he offered. "It'd be a good way for me to meet the team and see how they work. I think it would help me coach you better."

Mayday! Mayday!

I was humbled by Jamil's generous offer—and also terrified. The mere thought of him joining one of our leadership team meetings made my heart race. We already had regular strategy meetings where we reviewed our goals and upcoming plans, but they were nothing like the one I watched Jamil lead in Amsterdam. I worried they might find his no-nonsense style jarring.

And yet that was kind of the whole point, wasn't it? Jamil's style couldn't have been more different from mine, which was exactly why I wanted to learn from him.

"I'm in," I said. "Let's pick a date."

We scheduled our QBR for the week after Thanksgiving. We decided to meet virtually and blocked off two full days.

Jamil gave me the heads up that he wanted everyone to complete some homework to prepare for our time together. The assignment hit my inbox the Monday of Thanksgiving week, and when I saw it, my stomach dropped:

- **2019 review:** What went right this past year? Wrong? What did you learn? What were your biggest challenges and opportunities?
- **2019 goals:** Where do you stand on your goals? Where were you on- or off-track? What specific activities will you focus on to finish the year strong?
- **2020 goals:** What are your goals for the upcoming quarter? What is the deadline for each goal and how will success be measured? Create a starting work map.
- **Starts, stops, and keeps:** What should we start, stop, and keep doing as a company as we head into 2020?
- **Winning moves:** What are two ideas that could double revenue or profit over the next three to five years?

You've got to be kidding me.

We were days away from a holiday, and our QBR was scheduled for shortly after we returned. I would never have assigned something like this to my team right before a break, especially because we didn't get many of them. But Jamil didn't operate that way.

The even bigger issue? We were behind on some of Student Maid's financial goals. And not just a little behind—*a lot* behind. What would happen when my team had to present that in front of Jamil?

Just imagining it made my limiting-belief alarm bells start blaring.

I thought about pushing back on Jamil's request and asking to reschedule the QBR to allow more time for the team to prepare. But it didn't feel fair to dictate the terms. He was giving his time to help us—and we sure needed it.

What ultimately kept me from backing out was an image I couldn't shake: Jamil's team laughing and clinking champagne glasses after their own QBR in Amsterdam. Although I suspected the journey to get there would be uncomfortable, I thought that maybe this was my chance to create a moment like that with my own team.

I can still picture their faces as I walked them through Jamil's homework for the QBR. It felt like they were all silently asking the same question: Why in the *world* are you asking us to do this right now?

Honestly, I was asking myself the same thing.

As we wrapped up our meeting, I wished the team a happy Thanksgiving and felt like the worst leader imaginable. How could anyone have a happy anything after all the work I had just asked them to do?

After I signed off, my body felt heavy. I couldn't shake the fact that *I* had gotten us here. If only I had led us better—if only I had made wiser financial decisions and faced the small issues before they had become bigger ones—maybe we wouldn't have needed someone from the outside to help us get back on track.

Despite all the progress I'd been making in recent months, I felt like a failure.

All holiday weekend, I was in my head. My mom, dad, sister, and I had rented rooms at a Florida resort to do something special as a family for Thanksgiving, but I was somewhere else entirely.

I remember playing checkers and other board games with them, nodding along and laughing at all the right times, but I was just going through the motions. My insides were crawling with the unease I felt about the QBR that was waiting for me on the other side of the weekend. We took a family photo together on the beach, and every time I see it now, I remember how far away I felt from them—and from myself. Several times that weekend, I reached for a glass of wine, hoping it would give me a break from the guilt and anxiety pumping through my veins.

It never did.

Friend, have you ever had a moment when you realized enough is enough? For me, that moment came on the last night of our trip.

I laid in my hotel bed looking up at the dark ceiling. I felt terrible about how little of the weekend I'd been present for, and I hated that this was the version of me my family continued to get. We never know how many holidays we'll get with our loved ones, and here I was, spending precious time with them like *this*.

Right there in that hotel bed that night, I made a decision. I decided that 2020 was going to be my year in a way that no year had ever been mine before.

It would be the year I finally faced Student Maid's problems head-on:

- The year I paid off all the debt
- The year I built the speaking business to its full potential
- The year I became the leader my team deserved
- The year I became the me that *I* deserved

I grabbed my phone off the nightstand, thinking I'd scroll Instagram before calling it a night. An ad for a "One Year No Beer" challenge caught my eye. That's when I made another decision: It was time to stop escaping.

I decided I didn't want to wait for 2020 to make any of that come true. I signed up for the challenge immediately: 365 days without alcohol, starting now. As I drifted off to sleep that night, I had never been more certain that this time, I would keep my promise.

The next morning, as my sister and I walked through the airport to our separate gates, I hugged her goodbye and started to cry. I felt fragile. No one knew what I had just decided about the year ahead or the fears I had about the QBR I was flying back to.

I just knew that once that plane took off, nothing in my life or my business would ever be the same.

Chapter 21

Half-Truths

I tossed and turned all night before the QBR.

When I realized my alarm would soon be going off anyway, I grabbed my sneakers and headed out for a run to burn off my nervous energy.

As I jogged around the track, my mind drifted to the last conversation I'd had with Jamil. We'd had a quick call right after Thanksgiving to review the agenda for the QBR, and before we hung up, he said, "Kristen, remember you have one challenge in this meeting. And that's to be the last person to speak."

This was my chance to become the leader I'd seen Jamil be in Amsterdam. When I got back from my run, I found my Post-it stack, peeled one off, and wrote "SPEAK LAST" on it in big, bold letters. I stuck it on the corner of my laptop where it could keep a close eye on me during the QBR just in case.

After a hot shower, a hearty breakfast, a few trips to the bathroom (thank you, anxious stomach), and some deep breaths, the moment of truth arrived.

I carried my laptop into the living room and set it on the coffee table, facing the same window where I caught my reflection on that lonely spring night the year before. I opened the virtual room a few minutes before our scheduled start time to see that Amanda was already there. She was always early, especially when she was nervous—just like me.

As the rest of the team trickled in, we exchanged our usual hellos and good mornings and took a minute to chat about how we'd spent our Thanksgivings. No one had to say it: My emotional spidey senses picked up on the butterflies stirring in their stomachs, too.

A notification appeared at the top of my screen, letting me know that Jamil was in the virtual waiting room.

No turning back now.

I clicked to let him in, and suddenly there he was: white polo shirt, yellow wall, camera angled slightly upward, just like always. Except this time, my team's anxious faces appeared right next to him.

As the team and Jamil introduced themselves to one another, my eyes flicked back and forth between the squares on my screen, each one of them a window into our separate worlds. It was starting to sink in: This was really happening.

Here we go.

Jamil kicked off the meeting by walking us through the day's agenda. As soon as he started to speak, I felt a calm wash over me. He was kind and disarming—because of course he was. Everyone seemed to warm up to him quickly.

Maybe this will be okay after all. Maybe it will even be great.

"Okay team, we're going to start with a check-in," he said.

That wasn't so unusual for us: We always began our meetings with a check-in where we each shared how we were doing in our lives, at work and outside of it. We used it as a chance to catch up personally before we talked about the business. I had a feeling that Jamil's check-in would be a little different.

"Okay, here's how this is going to work," he said. "I want you to rate these five areas: your trust as a team, your relationships, your teamwork, your communication, and your personal happiness at work. Give each one a score between 1 and 10, with 10 meaning things are the best they've ever been."

Yep, definitely different.

"Don't answer based on what you *wish* were true," he added. "Go with the score in your gut."

I watched a few pairs of eyebrows raise slightly.

"Alright," he said only a moment later, "Who wants to go first?"

Wait . . . what? We're sharing these scores . . . out loud?

We often evaluated our culture as a team, but we'd never done it like *this*. Usually, we focused on general reflections and feedback. We'd never done anything where we assigned scores and then owned up to those numbers out loud. And while I'd asked my team about their job fulfillment before, I'd never asked such a direct question about their personal happiness at work. I assumed that if something was off, they would tell me. We had that kind of trust. I braced myself for their answers and hoped that our strong culture would shine through.

One right after the other, the team listed off their scores for each category. Within minutes, everyone had shared, and I felt a smile tugging at the corners of my mouth: Their scores weren't just okay; they were *stellar*.

"And Kristen?" Jamil asked. "How about your scores?"

I started to rattle mine off.

"Let's see . . . for trust, I give it a 10. Relationships: 10. Teamwork: 10. Communication: 9. And personal happiness at work . . ."

For a split second, I debated with myself.

Do I say it?

Kristen, are you crazy? You can't say it. Everyone else's scores are so high!

"Nine!" I blurted it out before I could change my mind.

The truth? Five.

And that right there was my problem in a nutshell: I didn't know how to say what I actually felt, especially when it seemed to be so different from the way everyone else seemed to feel. I didn't know how to let the truth break through my facade, and I can't help but wonder what could have happened if I'd had the courage to say "five" out loud.

When I think back to that time now, I doubt I was the only one who shared an inflated score. It was our first time ever doing something like this as a team, and it was uncomfortable. It felt vulnerable. And once the unspoken standard of high scores had been set, no one—myself included—wanted to be the outlier. Jamil never said it outright, but we all suspected a lower score might require an explanation. He didn't seem like the kind of guy who would let anyone off the hook that easily.

I wasn't ready to go there. And I understand if my team wasn't, either. A higher number felt like a safer bet. But despite the half-truths, reporting these scores was still a turning point for our team. It was the first time we'd ever had a conversation like this out loud.

It was our start.

"Let's talk about the quarter," Jamil said, moving to the next item on our agenda. "What's worked well so far?"

And . . . *silence.*

My team looked to me, waiting for me to go first like I always did. With my finger hovering over the button to unmute myself, I felt my Post-it watching me.

Kristen, don't you dare.

Then, after the longest five seconds of my life, I heard:

"I can go."

It was Amanda. (Always.)

I let out a quiet breath and fixed my attention on her square of my screen.

"I think this was the first quarter I actually understood what we were working toward," she said.

That opened the floodgates. After that, each member of my team took turns describing how, before we implemented our new team structure, they'd never had a clear sense of our priorities. Many said they hadn't felt fully empowered in their roles until now. They liked having ownership over individual goals and the fact that they could now see their direct impact on the business.

They spoke with pride about accepting the challenge to get uncomfortable this quarter, *even* when it came to the dreaded work maps. While they said creating the work maps was time-consuming, they understood the value in having a plan instead of sticking to our usual style, which was to fly by the seat of our pants. Most of all, they liked knowing exactly who was responsible for what.

It was another small realization that maybe the things I feared weren't as bad as I made them out to be. I still had a long way to go before I could embrace the "A" word, but my limiting-belief alarm bells were a little quieter.

That is, until Jamil shifted to the next topic:

Numbers.

Chapter 22

Lurking Below the Surface

"Walk me through how Student Maid is performing," Jamil said.

All the air left the virtual room.

Amanda took her cue.

"Okay," she said, her voice wavering. She looked down at her notes and then back up at the screen.

"So far this quarter, here's where we're at." She read the revenue number—the same one we'd been reviewing in our team meetings for the last few weeks—and quickly added, "which isn't too far off from where we wanted to be."

I felt my stomach tense. It was *a lot* far off from where we wanted to be.

"And our labor costs are still high," she said. Her eyes strayed to the edges of her screen. I could tell she was trying to avoid making eye contact with Jamil.

For a moment, he didn't react. And then . . . "Why hasn't revenue gone up?" he asked.

Oh no. Oh no no no no.

A few people squirmed in their seats, including me.

"Well," she began, "we've been working on some ideas to get more clients on a regular cleaning schedule. We've tried—"

"That's not what I asked," Jamil interrupted.

I sucked in a sharp breath.

"How many of those plans have you actually executed?" he asked.

Amanda went quiet. My heart sank as I watched a familiar scene play out: She was shutting down. Retreating into herself. Telling herself she wasn't good enough.

This is all my fault. I knew I never should have let us do this QBR.

Jamil continued to push. "What's really going on here?"

By now, Amanda's face was blotchy. A few tears slipped down her cheeks. My finger was halfway to unmuting my mic before my Post-it stopped me.

I don't know how much longer I can take this, I thought.

I felt responsible for Amanda's predicament. Yes, she owned Student Maid's metrics: She had agreed to that when we created the new structure. But I didn't see our struggles as her fault. The cards she'd been dealt were tough, and she'd had an uphill battle from the start. Though it was slow, she was making progress. That was good enough for me.

I was torn between wanting to protect her and wanting to adhere to Jamil's advice. But I reminded myself that it wasn't my job to keep her happy, and it wasn't my job to save her. My job was to empower her. So I stayed silent, hoping she could somehow feel the encouragement I was trying to send her with my eyes.

Then, as quickly as they came, Amanda's tears vanished. I watched her regain her composure. More questions followed, and Jamil continued to challenge Amanda in the same way I saw him challenge his team at his QBR in Amsterdam.

And then I saw her rise.

"I think part of it is that I don't feel fully empowered to own Student Maid's numbers," she said after several minutes. "I'm not always sure where my ownership ends and Monique's begins."

I glanced at Monique, who I could tell was taking it all in.

"I don't always know what I can decide on my own and what needs to go through her. And that's been hard," Amanda said.

Monique nodded and unmuted herself.

"Yeah, I feel that too," she said. "I know we decided I'd own the overall profit goals of both companies, but I don't always know when to get involved in Student Maid's numbers. I don't know when to step in and push or when to back off and let Amanda take the lead. And honestly," she added, "I don't feel confident owning the numbers for the speaking business, either. Since you're so involved in speaking sales, Kristen," she said, looking at me, "that line feels blurry to me."

Monique exhaled. "I'm more energized by building new projects, like the retreat, and supporting the operations there. I'd rather be responsible for new business growth."

What in the QBR is going on here? How come none of this has come up before?

And then, I felt it—something that was true for me that I hadn't said out loud, either: "I think I should own the numbers for the speaking business," I said. It was one of the few times I spoke all meeting. "I thought handing them off was the right move to empower Monique, but I really miss that part of my role."

All of a sudden, I felt . . . lighter. It was *freeing* to say that out loud to my team.

And from the matching smiles on their faces, I could tell they felt the same way.

A lot shifted for us in those five minutes. In a single conversation, we uncovered issues that had been lurking below the surface for months. That was another small but mighty realization for me: The way things look on the outside don't always match what's going on behind closed doors. Not just for me, but for my team, too.

When I look back on it now, I can see how fragile that moment was in our QBR. If I'd unmuted myself to protect Amanda's feelings when I first felt the urge, she might've never opened up and shared all that she did. And if Amanda had let her doubt take over or decided that missing those goals meant she wasn't good enough, the conversation could have shut down completely. Instead, we both sat with our discomfort, and it opened a door to a conversation we didn't know we needed to have.

Thank goodness I didn't rescue her. And thank goodness Amanda found the courage to lead with vulnerability.

"Well," Jamil said, "it sounds like we've got a new plan."

We got clear on our goals for the year ahead and adjusted ownership based on our discussion. Then, just before our closing exercise, he gave us one more prompt.

"I want each of you to rate how confident you are that the team will achieve these goals. One to 10."

I didn't hesitate to break my rule and go first.

"Ten," I said. It was my true number.

Nines and tens followed.

This time, Monique went last. "Seven," she said.

Seven? Okay, where did that come from?

"Walk me through your reasoning, Monique," Jamil said, intrigued.

Yeah, I want to understand, too.

"I'm not as confident we'll hit our numbers," Monique said. "We've set big goals before, but we always end up making decisions that take us in the opposite direction. We keep spending when we should be cutting back."

I don't know if I like where this is going. . . .

"We've gotten into a bad habit of relying on speaking revenue to cover the gap when Student Maid falls short instead of actually fixing the issue."

Well, you're not entirely wrong there. Even if I'd say it differently.

"If Student Maid is going to work," Monique continued, "it has to stand on its own two feet. And that's going to take sacrifice and discipline. We're going to have to make tough decisions we haven't been willing to make so far."

Tough decisions? Definitely don't love the sound of that.

"We talk a lot about our culture. And that matters. But we need a better balance. We have to be willing to be uncomfortable in the short term so that we can get to where we want to be in the future."

When she says "we," is she talking about me?

I watched my team begin to nod as Monique finished. I nodded, too, but I felt unsettled.

"Thanks for sharing your perspective," Jamil said. He was his stoic self, as always.

I sat with Monique's words, unsure about what to do with them. She didn't share them with anger or frustration. She was calm as she spoke. Direct. Honest.

A part of me knew she was right, even if I didn't want to admit it: Our expenses had always been high, and the speaking business shouldn't keep carrying Student Maid. I could only give so many speeches. It wasn't a sustainable solution. But as much as I agreed with Monique and tried to stay open to her perspective, I also resisted it. Cutting back, discipline, hard choices—none of those sounded like things that would keep people happy.

I didn't have much time to dwell on it, though; we had already arrived at the closing exercise of our QBR.

It was a visioning exercise similar to the crystal ball one. Jamil asked us to write a postcard to ourselves from the future. He wanted us to describe the year ahead in vivid detail, as if the year had already happened. What did we accomplish? What were we proud of?

Here's what I read out loud that day (sorry in advance for all the exclamation points—I think you'll see how excited I was):

> It's December 31, 2020. I am sitting with my family on vacation after being off for a week, with 2 more weeks off ahead of me. This year was the best year yet—for me and my company.
>
> On the personal front, I got married. I kept my health strong, fulfilled my 365-day alcohol cleanse, and didn't burn out. I took regular time to spend with friends and family. I took more thinking time and read over 60 books. My parents are healthy. I continued my coaching with Jamil. As a team, we crushed our goals more than we ever have.
>
> The accomplishments I am most proud of are:
>
> - We are all still here, we love our jobs, and our trust in one another is more than we thought possible!!!!!
> - We are debt-free!!!!!
> - Our students are paid more!!!!
> - We are closer to everyone being at market value with their salaries!!!!!
> - Student Maid is profitable!!!!!
> - Speaking profit has tripled!!!!!!

- We hosted 9 more amazing and fulfilling retreats!!!!!
- Our blog community has grown to 10,000!!!!!

> Can't wait to ring in the New Year in the morning. Tomorrow I start writing my new book. This year will be hard to beat!

By the time we finished reading our postcards, we'd all declared that 2020 would be our best year yet—and it felt like every person meant it. It was our version of clinking champagne glasses on a boat.

I closed my laptop and exhaled so deeply, I'm sure my neighbors could hear it.

Jamil did it.

My Post-it and I did it.

But most of all, my *team* did it.

Just as I was about to sink into the couch and take the rest of the night off, Jamil called me.

I shouldn't have been surprised. We always debriefed after I worked with his team, so of course we'd do the same after he worked with mine.

He said two things. First, "Great job on being the last one to speak."

Then he paused.

"So, tell me about Monique."

Chapter 23

Traction

If you read *Permission to Screw Up*, you might remember Monique as the person I handed a giant ring of keys to.

It was in the early days of Student Maid, during one of our busy summer seasons. I was assigning units to cleaning teams at an apartment complex when I realized—to my horror—that every single apartment door was locked.

I had the keys, but they were all on one giant ring, and the property manager was adamant that I couldn't separate them. If I lost the ring, I'd have to replace dozens of keys at $50 a pop.

A long line of students was waiting on me for their cleaning assignments, and there was absolutely no way I could afford to pay them to stand around while I unlocked every door myself. I turned to the person closest to me and asked them to unlock the doors instead. It happened to be Monique.

It was one of her first days on the job and my first time ever meeting her. At the time, she was studying interior design at UF. She'd applied for a cleaning job when her boyfriend (now husband), Tim, told her we were hiring. He was one of our developers in the scheduling software business.

Without giving it a second thought, I explained the stakes and handed Monique the key ring.

She was just 19.

By the time I finished assigning all the units, she was back with the key ring fully intact—and what could have turned into an expensive, stressful day didn't.

Monique's work ethic that summer earned her a spot on our year-round team, and soon clients were requesting her by name.

She trained new team members how to clean the "Monique way," and on the days when she worked, there were fewer client complaints.

I always assumed Monique would move on after she graduated, so I was caught off-guard when she told me she wasn't sure she wanted to pursue interior design after all. The whole time I'd known her, that had been her dream, but her last internship left her feeling disillusioned. The culture of the company where she interned was nothing like Student Maid's, and it made her question what she wanted for her life. She wondered if there might be a future with us instead.

I didn't know how we'd afford another salary, but I was certain I didn't want to lose Monique, so I told her we'd figure it out. And we did.

Monique helped anywhere the business needed her. She brought consistency to our hiring and onboarding process; she learned how to facilitate leadership workshops for our students; and she even supported Tim in the software company, attending conferences and recruiting customers until we shut it down.

When my speaking engagements started to pick up, I reached a point where managing it all on my own became too much. Every event came with a flurry of emails, contracts to review, client calls, and all the moving pieces of travel logistics. It was a full-time job on its own. With the rest of the leadership team focused on Student Maid, I was the only one focused on the speaking business, and I was drowning.

I decided to pitch an idea to Monique one day while we were grocery shopping.

I had just flown in for a team-wide Student Maid event, and she'd picked me up from the airport. We made a quick run to the store to grab food and supplies. As we walked down the aisles, I tried to explain the kind of help I was looking for in the speaking business. I didn't love the word "assistant," but it was the closest thing I could find. I asked her if she wanted to be that person.

We were standing near the blackberries when she said yes.

I didn't know the first thing about how to structure her role, and I wanted to start this new stage of our working relationship the right way. I reached out to an assistant of someone well known in the speaking world and asked if she'd be willing to train us, and luckily she agreed.

On our training call, she told us to think of Monique as the quarterback and me as her coach. She explained that Monique's job was to understand my vision well enough to make decisions in real time: She needed to be able to call the plays, quickly adjust when things changed, and keep the game moving forward without having to stop to ask me what to do next.

I need to tell you that in high school, I was the captain of the cheerleading team, but I had to ask my fellow cheerleaders if we were on offense or defense to know which cheers to call. So, yeah—the football analogy didn't exactly work for me. But I understood enough to know that my job was to make sure I didn't slow Monique down. In my own words: I needed to hand her the key ring and let her run.

And run she did.

Almost as soon as Monique and I started working on it together, the speaking business took off. Our strategy was divide and conquer: I stayed focused on bringing in sales, nurturing client relationships, and delivering my best from the stage, and Monique worked her magic on the operational side. She implemented task-management systems, kept my calendar updated, and handled the chaos of booking travel like she'd been doing it for years. Every morning, we had a 15-minute phone call to set the tone for the day, and that was all it took to keep us in sync.

Even though I still felt weighed down by the debt and my fading passion for the cleaning business, working with Monique in this way was a bright spot for me. I was proud to watch her shine in what she was naturally exceptional at, and it was comforting to have someone else's focus on the work that made me feel the most alive.

The first test of our partnership came when Abby told me she was leaving Student Maid.

It's never great timing when you lose your right-hand person, but for me the timing was especially terrible. On top of everything else, I was also in the midst of my last writing sprint to finish *Permission to Screw Up*. The book was already overdue, and if I didn't meet the new deadline, I risked delaying its publication date even further—and maybe even losing my book contract.

Less than a week after Abby resigned, I was scheduled to fly to the Dominican Republic for a speech, and my dad was coming with me. Between his demanding work schedule and mine, one-on-one time was rare. We planned to stay for several days after the event to have quality time together. We'd been looking forward to the trip for months.

Abby's decision to leave wrecked me emotionally. Somehow, I still had to find a way to keep Student Maid running, finish a book, be strong for my team, and make memories with my dad.

I was falling apart. Monique became the glue that held the business together when I couldn't.

Abby had given us a month's notice, and up until her last day, Monique worked with her to redistribute her responsibilities across the team. She stepped into more of a coordinating role, becoming the go-to leader for the rest of the team and filtering out what truly needed my attention while I was writing. And she did it all in addition to her regular duties in the speaking business.

When I got the news about Abby, the last thing I thought I should do was go on vacation with my dad after my speech. But Monique knew how important this trip was to us both, and she wanted me to go. As I boarded the plane, she encouraged me to be present with my dad and promised she would help keep things moving in the business while I was gone.

She did.

I remember my dad and me sitting outside at a restaurant in the Dominican. I'd given my speech earlier that day, and he wanted to take me to a nice dinner to celebrate. I got dressed up and forced a smile, even though I felt heartbroken.

I can still picture his face across the table as I dabbed at the mascara running down my cheeks. He knew how much Abby meant to me and how much it hurt to lose her; she was a part of our extended family. I shared my worries about how I would be able to continue without her.

For the first time, I told my dad how much debt I had. He was aware that there was a lot, but he didn't know the exact number. After I said it out loud, I watched the worry settle into his eyes.

He stood up from his seat and wrapped me into a hug that I'll treasure for the rest of my life. While I was in his arms, it felt like everything would somehow be okay.

Monique gave me that moment with him.

I had wonderful relationships with everyone on my team, but the kind of support she offered me during that season was unique. While others were understandably processing their own emotions around Abby leaving and the uncertainty ahead of us, Monique kept her focus on me: not just Kristen the boss, but Kristen the daughter who needed time with her dad.

In the months that followed, Monique continued to help steady the ship. Even though I didn't think it would be possible after Abby left, Student Maid found its footing again. Through sheer force of will, I managed to finish writing *Permission to Screw Up* and submitted the manuscript. I took the leadership team with me to New York to celebrate its launch later that year. Monique was the one who arrived early to help me prepare for the big day and met me at a bookstore to see it on shelves for the first time.

As exciting as that season of life was, it was also when the misery I felt about Student Maid started to peak.

Monique's support certainly helped, but there was still a lot I shielded her from. At the time she wasn't heavily involved on the Student Maid side of things, in HR, or in the finances, and that's because I was careful not to pull her in. I didn't want the stress to bog her down or for her to carry the same kind of burden I regretted that Abby had to carry. At the end of the day, I was still Monique's leader. I didn't feel like I could share the reality of what I felt inside, no matter how much she'd earned my trust.

Just a few months later, in spring of 2018, I caught my reflection in my living room window—and then found Paul.

When he began coaching me, one of the first books he recommended I read was called *Traction* by Gino Wickman.

The book is about how to implement systems to scale a business. While its advice is invaluable, it wasn't the most thrilling read for me. More than once, I had to resist the urge to shut the book and take a nap—until I got to this one part.

I saw a page that described two roles every business needs: a Visionary and an Integrator.

The Visionary sets the direction for the organization. They stay big-picture, dream up big ideas, build key relationships, close deals, and drive the culture. The Integrator is the one who turns those ideas into reality. They manage the day-to-day operations, keep the team focused, remove roadblocks, and track progress on goals.

As I read it, I kept thinking, *That could be Monique and me.*

The relationship between a Visionary and an Integrator sure sounded a lot like what was already happening between us in the speaking business, and it showed me how we could be even more impactful together.

From the assessments we'd done in our monthly workshops, I knew that one of Monique's top strengths was "Significance." She was at her best when she knew she was making an impact and when she played an influential role. In the back of my mind, I worried I'd lose her one day. Monique was perhaps the most ambitious and driven person I'd ever worked with. Nothing rattled her; no challenge was too big. She was a go-getter who set a high standard for herself in every aspect of her life. I couldn't imagine she'd be content with being my assistant forever, and I feared that she might start to see my company as a place that kept her playing small.

But it wasn't just that.

I loved working with her. She just . . . *got me.* The way she could follow my thoughts, anticipate what I needed sometimes before I could, and bring order to what felt chaotic to me felt rare. I'd never clicked with anyone I worked with like that.

"Integrator" had a nice ring to it. It sounded like a title that matched her impact and hinted at what her role could become. I hoped it might help Monique see this as a place where she could build a future, so I asked her to read *Traction* and tell me if she could see herself as an Integrator, too.

She said yes. Again. (This time on the phone instead of near the blackberries.)

Calling her my Integrator didn't suddenly change our relationship. I didn't know exactly what to do differently, but I knew

I needed to let her into more of the business. I decided to start with our finances.

For most people, finances are probably the last thing they'd want to be transparent about, and it took me some time before I let her into *everything*. But I knew that Monique had a gift for managing money: She talked passionately about her goal of living debt-free in her personal life and operated with a level of financial discipline I'd never seen.

I invited her to sit in on meetings with me and my CPA so that she could begin to understand the financial picture of both businesses. I thought she'd enjoy it and that being included would matter to her, and I knew she'd bring valuable insight. Once she understood the reality of the debt, she helped me create an ambitious payoff plan so that we could get rid of it sooner.

That's when our relationship slowly began to change.

By this point, the rest of the team was aware of the state of our overall finances and the amount of debt we had, too. But they didn't have the same perspective Monique did. They didn't see how tough it was to manage our cash flow and how many impossible financial decisions I had to make to keep everything afloat. I could tell Monique was beginning to understand the pressure I was under in a way she hadn't before. Even though we never talked about it directly, I could feel her empathy in how she listened, the questions she asked, and even in the way she looked at me.

I could also feel her silently wondering how I'd allowed things to get this far out of hand.

So that's why, when it was Monique's turn in the QBR, she rated her confidence in hitting our financial goals a 7.

She was talking to me.

And she wanted Jamil to hear her, too.

Chapter 24

Idea Monkey

In our coaching session after the QBR, Jamil and I had a lot to talk about.

"I like Monique," he said. "She seems to see your challenges clearly. And she doesn't beat around the bush."

Just like you, I thought.

Jamil went on to say that he respected how Monique was the only one to share a different opinion when it came to her confidence in our future goals. (And considering that her limiting belief told her that her opinions were too much, I was incredibly proud of her for speaking up.) He pointed out that, more than anyone on the team, she focused on solutions and what we could do about our financial predicament, rather than blaming our circumstances.

I, on the other hand, wasn't so sure I liked what Monique had said about needing a better balance between our culture and numbers.

My mantra had always been "People first." I didn't want "numbers" or "finances" anywhere near my leadership philosophy.

I believed that if we took care of our people, the numbers would naturally take care of themselves. It had worked for us in the early days, and while we hadn't been able to pull off a profitable year at Student Maid since we'd taken on all the debt, I trusted that day wasn't far off. There had to be such a thing as good business karma, right? *Right?*

But I was starting to understand that Monique didn't see it the way I did. Underneath what she said in the QBR, I could sense her growing frustration with my leadership.

I had felt it before, like when I ordered lunch for the team as soon as she and I left a meeting with our CPA. Monique didn't say anything, but she gave me a look that clearly communicated, "Why are we spending money on this right now?"

Sometimes she'd suggest we pause or reduce an expense, and I'd list all the reasons why I thought we shouldn't. I'd say things like "I already promised this to the team," or "This is important for morale," or "We just need to give it a little more time," or my favorite one, "We'll make it up on the speaking side."

Monique didn't push back on me—probably because she could tell I didn't want to be pushed—but I'm sure she found my choices confusing. Here I was, clearly under massive financial pressure, and I kept spending money. I'd say that the numbers mattered to me and that I wanted to get them back on track, but then I didn't act like it. And that was the disconnect: I knew I needed to change my approach, but I was so afraid that getting strict about money would jeopardize the most important part of our business. To me, cost-cutting was culture-cutting.

From Jamil's perspective, the contrast between me and Monique wasn't a problem. In fact, he thought it could be the key to a more successful future.

"You need someone like her to keep you grounded in reality," he said.

Grounded in reality? What's that supposed to mean?

"You have someone in your business who sees where you want to go," he said, "and she also sees what's standing in your way. The more you can be open to her way of thinking, the better."

I wasn't convinced. I loved working with Monique, of course, but I didn't know if I *wanted* to see things the way she did. I struggled to imagine how our two ways of thinking could coexist while keeping our strong culture intact.

That is, until Jamil shared something that sparked another shift in the way Monique and I worked together.

"I have a different way that you can think about your relationship with her," he said. "You, Kristen, are an Idea Monkey."

I cocked an eyebrow at him. *I'm a what?*

He told me it was a concept from one of his favorite books, *Free the Idea Monkey to Focus on What Matters Most* by G. Michael Maddock and Raphael Louis Vitón.

"You're creative," he continued. "You constantly generate ideas. You make connections that other people don't see. You inspire people with what's possible, and you challenge the way things have always been done."

Oh, I like this. Please go on!

"But . . ."

Uh oh. Here it comes.

". . . Idea Monkeys lack focus, discipline, and follow-through."

I winced.

"They ignore the practical side of their ideas," he continued. "They don't always think about things like profitability or budgets."

You got that right.

"They can be inconsistent," he added, "even a little chaotic, jumping from one shiny object to the next. They like to chase what's new and exciting."

Kristen Confetti: That's what my team affectionately called it when I'd go into a meeting and suddenly change the plan.

"Idea Monkeys need someone who can rein them in," he said. "Someone who grounds them. And that person is called a Ringleader."

A Ringleader, he explained, doesn't get overwhelmed by an Idea Monkey's chaos. They can take it in, make sense of it all, and turn it into something that people can actually work with. They ask the questions that ensure ideas are practical and have a real chance of being successful.

"The Ringleader sets the Idea Monkey free," he said. "Someone in the business has to think about the budgets and the follow-through, but it doesn't have to be you. You get to dream."

He smiled. "I know how liberating it can feel because I'm an Idea Monkey, too."

Wait, what?

Jamil was the most numbers-focused leader I knew. And his demeanor was the opposite of chaotic.

He laughed at the look of confusion on my face.

"Most founders and CEOs are Idea Monkeys," he said. "I have a Ringleader who does the same thing for me in my own company, and I'd be lost without them. They've rubbed off on me a little."

Well, now you have my attention.

Maybe it wasn't that Jamil was naturally better at all of this than I was. Maybe he just had someone who balanced him out, and *that* was what made him so effective. Maybe Monique could be the one who balanced *me* out.

If you think the Idea Monkey and the Ringleader sound similar to the Visionary and the Integrator, you're right. But hearing Jamil describe the relationship this way made it click for me in a way it hadn't before. My homework after that session was to start sharing my ideas with Monique. It didn't matter if they were big, small, or half-formed; Jamil wanted me to share them *all* with her and remain open to what she had to say. He urged me to run everything by her before acting on it and encourage her to challenge me.

"She'll know what to do," he promised.

So I tried it. After that session I started sending her my ideas anytime inspiration struck.

Without me even having to ask, she started a running list where she captured all the ideas I sent her so I didn't have to keep them in my head. Almost immediately, I felt lighter; I hadn't realized how many thoughts I'd been storing up there—and how much real estate they took up in my mind—until I started handing them over to Monique.

But more than relief, I felt seen for the dreamer I was.

It used to be that when I tried to brainstorm with the team, they couldn't quite go there with me. Instead of voicing excitement and building on the ideas I shared, people seemed to get overwhelmed by them, sometimes not even responding at all. And when I shifted directions or came back with a better idea, they became visibly frustrated, saying that it felt like starting over and like the work they'd already done would go to waste.

I walked away from those moments feeling utterly deflated, often believing that something was wrong with me. I would think that maybe my energy was too much, or my ideas too big, or my passion too intense. So I started to tone down that part of me.

When I shared ideas with Monique, it was different. She could listen to me ramble for 20 minutes—thinking out loud, jumping from one disjointed thought to another, barely making sense even to myself—and then, somehow, she'd pull out the most critical parts and say, "So, what I think you're saying is . . ."

And she was spot-on. Every time.

She gave me permission to be messy. To let my imagination flow wild and free. Where I once felt like my thoughts were too much, with her I felt empowered to think even bigger. Knowing she was holding the other end of my tether let me dream and drift without worrying I'd float too far. Even when she challenged me, she did it with such compassion and understanding that it still felt like love.

One day I came to her with an idea that I was *convinced* would be our next big break.

"Okay, hear me out," I said. "We create a planner. A beautiful one. It'll have bright colors, inspirational quotes, and tons of space to write. It could be a whole new revenue stream! We could sell it online . . . maybe even in stores."

She nodded, patiently letting me finish.

"Okay," she said. "Have you thought about . . ."

For the next couple minutes, she walked me through all of the steps involved in what I was proposing: the cost of design, production, and inventory. What it would take to mass-produce something like that. The reality that we still had six figures of debt, which meant it probably wasn't the right time to take on the risk of a new venture. And then, of course, there was the fact that we weren't in the planner business to begin with.

Hmmm. Hadn't thought about any of that.

I felt myself slowly floating back down to earth.

"How about this," she said. "It really does sound like an amazing planner that could help keep you organized, so why don't I make one for *you* to use?"

I laughed. "Okay, fair."

A few weeks later, it was waiting on my desk when I got back to Gainesville.

To this day, it's the most perfect planner I've ever used. Each page was so detailed that she had to split it into multiple volumes to cover a whole year. It was exactly how I imagined it but better: There were daily inspirational quotes and she even added little water glasses at the bottom of every page so I could track my water intake.

That was us.

She didn't shut down my ideas. She got curious. She clarified them. Grounded them. Made them better. And sometimes she saved us from them.

And the most special part of it all? She let me be me.

Monique promised to keep every idea on her running list so that even if we chose not to implement one right away, we could come back to it in the future. (Selling a planner is still on there to this day. You never know.)

This way of working together started to help in many parts of the business—even the ones where I was most hesitant to bring her in.

Once, I came to her and said I wanted to take our leadership team on a retreat to Mexico. In my head, I saw chartered yachts, ten-course meals, and massages on the beach. Nothing less than extravagant. I wanted to forget about the debt for a minute and do something really nice to reward my team for working so hard. We went on a retreat every year, and this time I wanted to go bigger than usual.

Monique was all for an international team getaway—just not with the price tag I had in mind. So she reworked the itinerary. Instead of a five-star resort, she found a beautiful Airbnb. Instead of chartering a private yacht, we joined a group catamaran for a day trip to a secluded beach. Instead of fine dining every night, we chose to make one meal extra special.

In the end, we spent a fraction of what I would have spent and probably had even more fun. We still talk about that trip.

Our partnership also influenced the way we led team meetings. Instead of presenting ideas to the team on my own, Monique and I started doing it together. I would lead with the vision—the what and the why—and Monique would follow with the plan—the how. I got to inspire and motivate people while Monique helped them understand what this new idea would mean for their day-to-day work and responsibilities. She'd lay out a clear plan with defined roles and timelines and then hold the team accountable to their deliverables.

For the first time, the team didn't feel overwhelmed by my ideas; they were eager to get started.

We couldn't have been more different.

I'd ask, "What could this become?" She'd ask, "What will this cost?"

I'd say, "Let's go!" She'd say, "Let's think."

I'd ask, "How do we take care of them?" She'd ask, "How do we make sure we can keep taking care of them?"

Jamil was right: Monique had never been against me or our culture.

I would soon learn she was protecting us both.

Chapter 25

Blue Sky

With Monique and me in our new groove, I felt it was possible to do something I never thought I'd be able to: I took three weeks off.

I'd "seen" it in my crystal ball, but I didn't really believe it would happen. And yet here it was: three whole, empty weeks on my calendar at the end of 2019. No meetings. No calls. No speeches. It was a dream.

I hadn't taken off more than a week at a time since I started my company, and even that had been rare.

I always thought that if I ever took that long a break, I'd want to go on vacation. But instead, I spent three glorious weeks at home where I didn't set an alarm, I wore pajamas at every opportunity, and I only returned an email if I *really* wanted to. I spent my time doing the things I rarely had time for that filled my cup: reading, cooking, watching movies, soaking up time with my family. I couldn't remember the last time I had so much control over how I spent my days. I felt so free.

On Christmas morning, Spiros and I chose our wedding venue as our gift to each other. We searched online and fell in love with a resort in Mexico. After taking a virtual tour, we decided that it was perfect for us, and we set a date to get married there at the end of 2020.

We rang in the New Year with a celebratory toast—still only water in my glass—and for the first time in a long time, I didn't feel dread about the year ahead of me. I felt ready. Excited, even.

Things on the business front were looking up. Student Maid's numbers were steadily improving. We were making a dent in the debt. Speaking was keeping me as busy as ever, and the leadership retreat I hosted had gone so well that I had another 30 people signed up for my next one, which would take place in a couple of months.

All signs pointed to 2020 being our best year yet.

Ha.

When COVID-19 hit the United States, I was in Seattle.

I gave a keynote and signed books within miles of "ground zero," unsure of what that actually meant but cautious enough to awkwardly bump elbows instead of shaking people's hands.

On my way back to the airport, one of my speaking agents called. "Clients are starting to get nervous about the virus," she said. "Some are considering rescheduling their events."

A jolt of panic shot through me. It felt like everything around me was moving in slow motion.

"I'll give speeches in a bunny suit if I have to," I told her.

It sounded like I was kidding, but I wasn't. I didn't know enough at the time to be afraid of the virus; I was more afraid of what would happen if our revenue dried up. If my speaking events got canceled, we wouldn't be able to make payroll, let alone our debt payments.

At that time, it was early March, before large parts of the country began to shut down, and I was on my way to Gainesville for the next leadership retreat. I told myself to focus on that and try to forget about the conversation I'd just had with my agent.

Knowing what I know now, I would have canceled the retreat in a heartbeat. Thankfully, none of our attendees got sick. But after we wrapped up our closing exercise, we all stood in the hotel lobby, staring dumbfounded at the TV screens announcing that we were officially in a pandemic.

After learning the news, most people probably didn't keep their dinner reservations. But nothing in Gainesville had shut down yet, so Monique and I went ahead and enjoyed a sushi dinner at our favorite place as planned, after which I suggested we go back to her house and watch *Contagion*. (Part dark humor. Part attempt to wrap my head around what was happening.)

We all know how quickly things escalated after that. With just the one suitcase I'd packed for the retreat, I ended up staying in Gainesville for the next four months.

It was my choice to hunker down there. Spiros worked at one of the busiest hospitals in Houston, so we knew there was a high risk of exposure if I went back home. But beyond that, I felt a responsibility to be physically near my team. Luckily, my parents still owned a house in Gainesville, so I had a place to stay.

Within days, all of my hopes and plans for 2020 went up in a cloud of disinfectant, just like everyone else's. This time, my empty calendar left me feeling petrified. There wasn't a single speech on it, and on top of that, client after client had started canceling their cleanings at Student Maid. Spiros and I also decided to push back our wedding, just in case.

And then Student Maid started getting requests to clean spaces for COVID-19 prevention. I found myself at a moral crossroads.

We needed revenue to make payroll and cover our debt payments, and it seemed like cleaning would be our only option for the foreseeable future. I wanted to keep everyone safe, of course, but I also knew my team needed their paychecks, and I didn't want to undo all of the financial progress we'd been making. With no money coming in, it was only a matter of time until the business would be no more.

For a few days, I tried to do both: I made cleaning voluntary, provided protective gear, and only accepted jobs where there was no known exposure. But that plan didn't sit right with me. I could feel it in my gut.

It was a phone call from a team member's father that made me slow down and pay attention to the feeling I'd been dismissing. He was a mentor of mine back when I started Student Maid, and he told me he thought I was making the wrong choice by keeping the business open for cleaning services.

That conversation brought me back to the values I'd discovered with Paul. He'd told me my values could be my compass in impossible moments, and for the first time, I understood what he meant.

None of the options in front of me were good. If I continued to offer cleaning services, I could risk my team's safety. But if I closed the business, I might ruin us financially and cost everyone their jobs. I went for a long walk and listened to what my values had to say.

Courage told me to close Student Maid until it was safe to reopen, no matter what it did to our numbers. It told me that I'd figure it out like I always had and that nothing was worth jeopardizing my team's safety. Compassion told me to keep our team paid throughout our closure, which, at the time, I thought would be just two weeks. It told me that my number-one goal was to take care of my team no matter what it did to Student Maid's balance sheet.

After my walk, I ran the numbers and found a flat amount we could afford to pay our students for a short time while still covering our minimum debt payments. I decided I wouldn't take a paycheck unless I absolutely had to, and even then, I would only take the bare minimum. I brought my plan to the leadership team, and something remarkable happened: They all told me they were willing to defer their own paychecks in the short-term if push came to shove so that we could prioritize paying our students.

Together, we shared the plan in our first company-wide virtual meeting of the pandemic—and something even more remarkable happened.

"I don't need a paycheck," one student said. "I'd rather it go to someone who does."

"Same here," another said. "I can make do with half of mine and give the rest to anyone on the team who needs it."

"I could really use more," someone else said, quietly. "I'm not sure how I'm going to pay my rent."

I watched as our team took care of each other. Students, some still in high school, making sure everyone had what they needed. And by the end of that call, every person did.

That meeting remains one of my favorite moments in Student Maid history. When things were at their hardest, our culture was always at its strongest.

Student Maid was one of the first businesses in our community to close and to commit to keeping our team paid. We inspired other companies to follow in our footsteps. And even though those first two weeks turned into many more, we kept the paychecks coming. It's a choice I would make again in every lifetime.

After that meeting, I dove headfirst into emergency mode.

I moved fast. I reached out to every client who had canceled their speaking events and offered virtual keynotes at a pay-what-you-can rate. Almost immediately, I was back to work, speaking about change, resilience, and how to lead through uncertainty. I had never done a virtual speaking event before, but now I had dozens on my calendar and enough revenue to keep everyone paid for another few weeks.

It was a short-term fix. Luckily, we'd scheduled our next QBR long before we knew about the pandemic, and Jamil offered to join us for it. With decades in business, he'd learned a thing or two about how to navigate a crisis.

I expected we'd go straight into creating emergency plans, but instead, Jamil started with "Let's dream."

I blinked.

Sorry, what?

"We're going to have what I call a Blue Sky conversation," he said.

Jamil really is a man of mystery.

"In a crisis, anything goes," he continued. "This is your chance to toss out wild ideas for the business. The sky's the limit. Nothing is too big."

Normally, a conversation about dreaming and big ideas would be my jam, but I felt stuck. The Idea Monkey in me was nowhere to be found—and neither was anyone else's.

Jamil could tell by our silence that we were struggling, so he switched tactics.

"Okay, let's try something else," he said. "I want everyone to answer two questions. On a scale of 1 to 10, how passionate are you about cleaning? And how passionate are you about leadership development?"

Where is he going with this?

"We'll start with cleaning," he said. He didn't give us much time to think. "Monique, what's your score?"

"Zero." She answered with no hesitation.

Wait, what is happening right now? And did she just say zero? That wasn't even an option.

"Two," another said. As we continued around the virtual room, everyone else also said two.

Then Jamil looked at me.

"Kristen? What will it be?"

I knew my answer. I just didn't know if I was ready to say it. I couldn't believe we were having this conversation.

I glanced at Monique.

"Zero," I said. It rolled off my tongue faster than I expected.

That felt . . . good.

Wait, what is happening right now?

"Interesting," Jamil said. "Okay. How about everyone's scores for leadership development?"

"Ten," Monique said. Again, no hesitation. This time she looked at me and smiled.

"Nine," from another voice. More nines followed.

"Kristen?" he asked.

I looked at Monique again. "Ten." I smiled at her.

That felt even better.

But what is actually happening right now?

"Well, we just learned a lot," Jamil said.

We sure did. But what on earth does it mean?

We sat there looking at each other, stunned.

We all knew we hadn't stuck around because we were passionate about cleaning. Cleaning was just the vehicle for building the kind of culture we wanted to have. But we had never admitted our shared lack of passion for it out loud. No matter how much we loved our students and believed in the mission of our company, the day-to-day reality of running a cleaning company took a toll on all of us. No one could deny it.

It was liberating for me to hear us say aloud what had weighed on my heart for so long. The thing that had caused me so much secret pain was now out in the open. Something I'd built up in my head for years had come out in a one-minute conversation. And now I knew I wasn't the only one who felt that way.

But my relief lasted only a few minutes.

Even though I wasn't in love with Student Maid anymore, it was still the company I'd built. It was where all of our stories began. It was the place our students depended on, their home away from home, the place they felt like they belonged. The place I felt *I* belonged.

For everyone else, Jamil's question was about cleaning. For me, it was about everything: My life. My purpose. My responsibility as a leader.

Suddenly, I was terrified.

What did I just do?

Chapter 26

The Perfect Plan

"Let's take a pulse," Jamil said. "Reopen Student Maid once it's safe to do so. Close it for good. Or undecided."

Speaking of pulses—mine was off the charts.

Close it for good?

I don't remember who said what next. I don't remember the final vote tally, though I think most of us landed in the "undecided" camp. I didn't take a single note in our meeting. I couldn't. My jaw was on the floor.

All I remember after that is having one conversation out loud with the team and Jamil and an entirely different conversation with myself.

Stay calm, Kristen, I thought. *Your team just rated their passion for cleaning at zeros and twos, and so did you. You have to do something about that.*

"We can't just abandon our students," I said to the team.

Of course you can't. You aren't the kind of leader who abandons people you love.

"No matter what we do, we have to take care of them," I continued, seeing nods of agreement in each square on my screen.

'No matter what we do'? What are you saying? What are you going to do? You can't really be considering—

"What if we sell the business?" I heard myself say. "That way, our students can keep their jobs."

Sell Student Maid? Are you out of your mind? This is your company. Your everything. Your baby. What do you mean sell it?!

"We could reopen the business when it's safe," I said, caught up in the excitement beginning to spread across my team's faces. "We could get it profitable, and then sell it to someone else."

Stop. Don't rush this. Student Maid is your whole life. No matter how miserable it's made you, you can't walk away from it after one meeting. You don't really want it to end. You're just going through a rough patch. You'll get back to how you felt in the old days. Can you even imagine not having it in your life? Try for just a second to picture it. How sad would that be? Who are you without Student Maid?

"I could start looking for a buyer," I suggested. More nods from the team.

Find a buyer? For the company you built from nothing?! For the thing that gives your life meaning? What are you talking about?

"That would be the best of both worlds," I added, "and free us up to focus on growing the speaking business."

Closing your pride and joy will 'free you up'? How can you say that! Sure, Student Maid is stressful sometimes, but it can go back to feeling the way it used to. Just give it more time. You and the team are making progress. Things are improving. And besides, what would happen to your speaking without Student Maid? That's what people know you for.

Out loud I was calm, measured, logical. I was acting like the leader I thought I needed to be, especially with her calm, measured, logical coach watching. I could see him nodding out of the corner of my eye.

But inside, everything in me was still pushing back.

Slow down. You don't have to decide this right now. Once you make a choice like this, you can't take it back. You love Student Maid. You want it to be part of your life forever. Maybe there's another way. Maybe you don't have to say goodbye for good.

"I have an idea," I said. "What if we transitioned ownership of Student Maid to one of our alumni instead?"

Yes, that's it! Find someone who understands the culture, who grew up in it, who could keep it all going with no interruption . . .

"It's what we're all about: Student Maid develops leaders. What could be better than having one of our own take it over?" I grinned at my team. They grinned back.

Yes. This is who you are. This is a much better decision than selling Student Maid to a stranger.

"We could get the business to a strong place first—make it something someone would actually want to take on. And that way, we could still be involved. We could support that person, mentor them. Help protect the culture. They could take over the operations and the parts we're ready to move on from, and then we can put our energy into growing the speaking business and go fully into leadership development and what we're most passionate about."

This is perfect. No one gets hurt. Nothing has to end. You'll never have to say goodbye to Student Maid. You know, sometimes you really are a genius.

"That person could be the new owner, and I could stay the founder."

Even better. You'll get to keep your identity.

"We won't pass on the debt. The speaking business will keep paying it down. And instead of selling Student Maid outright, we'll structure it so we get a small percentage every month."

Exactly. It's not about the money. You're keeping what matters.

I remember looking around the virtual room, pleased to see some smiles and even more enthusiasm—but not so much from Jamil and Monique. They seemed . . . less enthused. But they didn't speak up to oppose my plan, so I took that as permission.

"I have just the person in mind," I said. "Katie!"

It really did seem like the perfect plan.

Chapter 27

Thought Partner

Katie couldn't have been a better fit.

She had literally grown up in the company: She'd started working with us at just 17, but you would never have guessed she was years younger than most of our other students at the time. On top of being a meticulous cleaner who earned rave reviews from clients, she was also kind, teachable, and someone everyone loved to work with—a leader's dream.

Even after Katie left Student Maid for grad school, she often came back to work with us during our busy summer seasons. She would single-handedly manage hundreds of team members at several apartment complexes with zero complaints, and she hit every goal I gave her. All I ever had to do was tell Katie what needed to be done, and she did that—and then some.

Katie and I had stayed in touch over the years, and I knew she would soon be finishing her PhD in youth development and family sciences (another reason she was a perfect fit for leading students). She and her husband—whom she met while working at Student Maid—had moved to a city close to Gainesville, so she wouldn't even need to relocate.

The more I imagined handing over the reins to Katie, the more the idea lit me up. Within days of our QBR, I met with her and her husband on a video call.

We talked through everything, including Student Maid's financial history, the profitable years before the debt, and the progress we'd made leading up to the pandemic. They saw what I saw: a business that had worked before and could work again. More than that, they saw how it could fit with the life they were building for their growing family.

Shortly after that meeting, it was official: Katie would become the new owner of Student Maid in the spring of 2021. We decided to keep the news to a small circle who needed to know. The plan until then was to continue to grow the speaking business so that it could support the leadership team's salaries after the transition, and once it was safe, we'd reopen Student Maid and work to stabilize it, all while preparing Katie to take over.

I had my work cut out for me.

In addition to making sure our future plans stayed afloat, I was determined to keep our promise of paying our team throughout our closure. So I did what entrepreneurs do best: I hustled.

I turned my dining room into a speaking studio. I sat in the same chair for 12 hours a day, surrounded by a miles-long ethernet cable, lights I didn't know how to use, and a camera that had suddenly become our lifeline. I gave two, three, sometimes four speeches a day. In between speeches, I led team meetings to help us continue navigating the crisis, and at night I applied for every pandemic relief grant I could find. I was lucky if I slept five hours.

It paid off. We secured relief funds, and by the time they ran out, speaking revenue was rolling in to make up the gap. Soon I began facilitating monthly virtual mastermind groups for leaders to help them feel less alone while navigating the pandemic, and I started getting asked to do one-on-one sessions for those who needed extra support. Our revenue was multiplying by the week.

I was operating on pure adrenaline. The growth was exciting, but it also felt like being in a pressure cooker. I kept a photo of my team on my desk to remind myself who I was doing it all for. On the days when it felt like too much—and with wine no longer an option—I went for a run and pounded my stress into the pavement. I went on like that for *months*.

Before I knew it, it was time for our third QBR.

This time, Jamil thought I was ready to lead it alone, and I agreed. On paper, we were doing well. Speaking revenue was the highest it had ever been, and we were paying down debt at record speed. Student Maid was back open, and while its revenue was still far from pre-pandemic levels, we were starting to find our footing again.

But something wasn't right with the team. I could just feel it.

"Let's start with Jamil's check-in question," I said, kicking off the QBR. I hoped I could get to the bottom of whatever it was.

Nothing immediately stood out. We all rated our trust, relationships, teamwork, and communication at eights and above.

But then we got to their scores for personal happiness at work.

"Mine's a 5," Amanda said.

Yikes.

"I'm a 6.5," Cheyenne added.

Double yikes.

"Mine is an 8," Rachel said.

That's actually low for her. Triple yikes.

That left Monique.

"I'm a 3.5," she said.

I felt sick.

"Okay," I said slowly. "I appreciate everyone being honest with their scores."

Wow. This is not good.

"I'll put myself at a 6," I said.

This time, that was my honest answer. Now that we had a plan to transition Student Maid—one I felt good about—that wasn't what was dragging down my score. It was the frantic pace I'd maintained for months, and my stress wasn't a secret to my team.

But their scores were a mystery to me.

"Tell me more," I said, my eyes flicking between their faces on my screen. "What's behind your numbers?"

"I mean," Amanda started, "everything just feels different."

"Yeah," Cheyenne agreed. "We're all doing things we didn't sign up for."

Rachel chimed in. "That's true," she said. "And of course the pandemic is part of it, but I tried not to let that influence how I answered."

The conversation went on like that for a few minutes, with no one pointing to a specific reason for their lower scores.

Then—

"It's not just the pandemic," Monique said.

She looked at me. "Kristen, you've been really intense this quarter." That caught me off-guard.

"Okay," I said. "Tell me more."

"It feels like everything we worked so hard to build this last year just disappeared," she said. "You have your hands back in everything. And it's been hard for us to work with you."

I pictured my "SPEAK LAST" Post-it as I fought to keep quiet.

"This quarter has felt like whiplash," Rachel added.

"It definitely has," Cheyenne said.

Whiplash? Ugh, Kristen. Not again.

I could feel it. I knew I'd been all over the place.

As they continued to share, I forced myself to stay present instead of mentally spiraling.

"When you step into everything," Monique said, "it pulls me out of my role, and it makes things chaotic for the team. It's been whiplash times a million."

"It's felt like you and Monique are out of sync," Amanda added. The rest of the team nodded.

"I used to hear your ideas first," Monique said. "We'd talk them through and get aligned before bringing them to the team. But now I'm hearing about them for the first time in our team meetings, and I don't agree with how we're going about things."

Ouch.

"It's stressful," she said. "There's no clear plan. Every week, the priorities shift. And all the pressure is on you. You're stressed and overwhelmed, and we can all feel it."

She looked at me again. "It doesn't have to be this way."

I fought back tears.

"I want to help you," Monique said. "*We* want to help you. But we can't. You're moving too fast. It feels like you're in your own world. I want to lead our team meetings again. I want to work with you on the vision for the future. I want to bring more structure to the team. I miss those parts of my role."

More nods from the team. They seemed to want her back in that role, too.

"My score is 3.5," Monique said, "because this is the first time in almost 10 years that I haven't loved my job."

My heart dropped into my stomach. *Oh no. I can't lose her.*

"Yeah," Amanda added softly, "when Monique said she might look for other options, that really scared me."

What? Monique looking for other options? This can't be happening.

"Not because I wanted to leave," Monique said quickly, "which is why I didn't say anything to you. But I was really frustrated, and I didn't know if this was how my role was going to be from now on. And if it was, I couldn't keep doing that."

"Thank you for telling me," I said, trying my best to keep a tremble out of my voice. Inside, I was being eaten alive by shock, guilt, and fear.

The feedback was a gut punch, but I was grateful for every word of it. I'd rather know how my team really felt than not know. As we wrapped up the QBR, I promised everyone—and especially Monique—that I would return to the systems we'd created before the pandemic and partner with Monique the way we used to.

But even as I said those words, all I could think about was how dangerously close I'd come to losing her—and how I hadn't even seen it coming. I couldn't shake how much it bothered me, so I brought it to my next coaching session with Jamil.

"You're not letting her in," he said after I walked him through everything. "And I'm not talking about letting her into your ideas. I'm talking about letting her into your heart."

My heart?

For the rest of our session, Jamil and I walked through the events that led to the tough feedback from Monique and the team:

When the pandemic hit, I snapped into emergency mode. I became so focused on keeping the business—and everyone in it—afloat because that's what caring leaders do. I knew from all the books I'd read that you don't learn who your leader is when things are going well; you learn who they are in a crisis. I made it my mission to be the kind of leader I'd want to follow in a pandemic: someone who would protect, reassure, bear the brunt of it all, and keep the weight off my team's shoulders.

I didn't realize that the very same care had pushed me to bulldoze my way back into every project, process, and piece of the business we'd worked so hard to pull me out of. While it was never my intention, it turned my team upside down. More than anything, it turned me and Monique upside down.

When the pressure built up, I shut Monique out. When I felt unsure about how to lead through a crisis, I retreated into myself. When I could feel that I was running myself into the ground, I didn't stop to ask for her help.

I thought I was protecting her, but I was actually pushing her away. I didn't let her lead with me. I didn't let her carry anything for me. And while I was keeping everything moving on the outside, on the inside I felt completely alone—and I had done it all to myself.

"Monique isn't just your partner in strategy," Jamil went on. "She's your partner in all of it: the good, the bad, and the ugly. And in order for her to be that, she needs to know how you're feeling, especially when things are challenging."

Then he said something that would radically change how Monique and I worked together from that day forward.

"I want you to think of Monique as your thought partner," he said.

He explained it as the deepest kind of relationship two people on a team can have. No issue is too big. It's the place where you can bring the toughest challenges that keep you up at night. You can talk about your fears, your worries, and the things that feel vulnerable to say out loud.

"But it requires trust," he continued. "And a shared understanding of confidentiality. What's said in a thought partnership stays there. You have to feel safe enough to tell the truth about what's really weighing on you as a leader. And your team has to understand that, too—that there will be things you and Monique discuss that they won't be a part of. But it's in everyone's best interest.

"There's a saying in leadership," he continued. "It's lonely at the top. But it doesn't have to be. And I think that's what Monique has been trying to tell you."

I took a deep breath and let it out slowly. I had a feeling that this would be an inflection point for us.

I've called Monique a lot of things in this book—my assistant, my Integrator, my Ringleader, and now, my thought partner. I debated simplifying our relationship and skipping straight to this part of our journey, but doing so would've made it look too easy.

Letting someone in doesn't happen in a single conversation. It would take many years, many attempts, and many failures on my part before I learned to open up in the way Jamil described. I didn't know how to let people into my thoughts or my heart like that. I didn't know that difficult emotions were meant to be shared out loud or that it was possible to feel safe while doing so. Rarely is anyone taught how to be vulnerable, especially when you're leading a team and everyone is looking to you.

But I was willing to try.

Not long after my conversation with Jamil, Monique accepted her new role as my thought partner. We shared the news with the team and told them about our social contract—that there would be discussions kept between Monique and me—and they gave us their full support. They wanted us to do whatever we needed to find our groove again.

This time, it wasn't that Monique's role felt different. It was that *we* felt different.

This time, it felt like neither of us was going to hold anything back.

Chapter 28

Intervention

"It's time to walk away from Student Maid. For good."

The walls of my favorite sushi restaurant started closing in around me as I tried to make sense of what Monique had just said. I stared at her, waiting for her to take it back. This was supposed to be a celebratory dinner—not whatever kind of dinner *this* was about to become.

It was December 2020. After spending the last few months in Houston, I'd flown back to Gainesville to close out the year with the team and honor some big milestones. So much of what I'd seen in my crystal ball had come true.

My speaking gigs had brought in almost $700,000 in revenue, and I'd done nearly all of them from behind a computer. The six-figure debt that used to keep me up at night? *Completely gone.* We'd paid it off more than *five years* ahead of schedule. We were still on track with our plan to transition ownership of Student Maid to Katie, and the leadership team and I were just a few months away from being able to put all of our focus on growing the speaking business. The team's happiness scores had climbed back up in our last QBR, and my thought partnership with Monique was thriving. I'd even hit my biggest personal goal: 365 days without alcohol. And now I was about to take off another three full weeks from work, which I'd encouraged the leadership team to do, too.

It was hard to believe it was real. I'd finally achieved what I'd spent years working toward, and it felt like I was becoming the person and leader I'd been trying to be. Now, when my head hit my pillow at night, sleep came peacefully.

I had pictured a night of celebration with Monique: laughing, sharing our favorite foods, taking in all of our accomplishments, and dreaming about the new possibilities ahead.

But to Monique, this was no celebration. It was an intervention.

"Kristen." She looked me straight in the eye. "We can't give Student Maid to Katie. We can't keep doing this."

"What do you mean?" I shot back. "The debt is paid off! We're finally in the place we've been working so hard to get!"

People seated near us started turning toward our table as I passionately gave Monique an excuse for every word that came out of her mouth.

She reached into her bag and pulled out her laptop. She'd come prepared.

"Look," she said, turning the screen and Student Maid's P&L toward me. "Even if we give Student Maid to Katie, it will still weigh us down. The debt might be gone, but Student Maid isn't stable yet. We're still using speaking profits to keep it afloat."

If people weren't watching us before, they definitely were now. We had invited Monique's husband and my cousin to join us for what was supposed to be a laid-back dinner with light work talk, but when words started flying and the laptop came out, they moved to another table to allow us to continue our heated debate.

"We can't do all these things you say you want to do—because of *this*," she said, pointing to the spreadsheet.

I didn't like the numbers in front of me. And I liked the conclusions Monique was making even less.

"Kristen," she said, softer now, "I know how big your dreams are. I want you to go after all of them. But Student Maid is going to be the reason they can't happen."

She tapped her screen furiously, pointing to one cell in particular.

"Look at this. Cleaning revenue is still down *50%* from where we were before the pandemic."

She looked back at me. "A lot of the profit we make from your speeches will continue to go toward covering that gap. And that also means it will be harder to give the raises you promised."

Now that we'd finally paid off all the debt, I'd promised everyone on the leadership team that big raises were coming—including one for myself.

I knew we'd still need to support Student Maid. I just hadn't realized how much.

"We need a clean break," she said. "And giving it to Katie isn't that. I know you don't want to be involved in Student Maid anymore, but when you give the business to her, you will be. It won't be less than you are now; it will be *more*. You'll want to mentor her and help her because you care. And at the very least, you'll be tied to Student Maid until the numbers are where they need to be."

She let her words sink in.

"And I'm not sure if the numbers will *ever* get there."

I stared at the screen, clinging tighter to my plans with Katie than the piece of salmon sashimi pinched between my chopsticks.

"But I can't do that," I said. "I've already committed to Katie. She's built her entire future around taking over Student Maid. And not just her, but her family, too." Tears began welling in my eyes.

Monique didn't flinch. "So you're going to give her a business that's struggling financially?"

I looked away. "Of course not," I said. "We'll help her."

"That's my point," Monique said. "We'll *always* be helping her. I can't imagine a time when we won't be."

She locked eyes with me. "That's why I'm saying we can't do this anymore."

By now, the server had come by twice to try to offer a dessert menu, each time hesitating to interrupt.

"We can't just walk away from Student Maid," I said, my voice unsteady. I grasped for a reason that would change her mind. "The speaking business won't exist without it. We need Student Maid for credibility. Why would anyone book me for a speech if I'm no longer connected to the business I speak about?"

"That's not true," she said. "Nothing erases what you've built. You don't need Student Maid to prove anything. You've already proven it. Look at your speaking calendar—we can barely keep up as it is."

I shook my head, refusing to hear her.

She continued: "I'd rather we just close the business completely. But if you aren't willing to do that, we can sell it. We just can't give it to Katie. That's not a solution."

"But what about our students?" I practically shouted. "What happens to them?"

If there was anything that might make her reconsider, I was sure it'd be this.

"We've always taken care of our people, and that will never change. But this might be one of those moments where we have to make hard choices. I don't have all of the answers, but we'll figure it out. Together."

I tried to stay open and let Monique challenge me in the way Jamil had always encouraged.

But this? This felt impossible.

I couldn't fully process what she was saying. All I could think about was our students and Katie. In that moment, all I wanted was to wake up from this bad dream.

And yet . . . I could feel the truth of Monique's words in every bone in my body.

Here it was again: The same decision to make. The same chance being handed to me. The same door I could walk through. I could almost taste the freedom Monique was offering me. I could see it all: the life and future that was waiting for me on the other side of the decision to walk away.

How was it possible to want something in my heart so badly while feeling the need to fight it with equal force?

Because that's what happens when you love something.

Just like all the times before, when the chance to walk away was right in front of me, all I could think about was how much Student Maid meant to me.

All I could remember was ringing the doorbell for my first cleaning job. And the night I cut tiny ornaments out of sponges. And when the 45 people who'd quit on me gave me another chance and I realized, for the first time, that I wanted to be a leader.

All I could see were the students who were imprinted on my heart—the ones who had come through our doors feeling unsure of themselves who were now out in the world, confident and chasing their dreams. How it had always been me and Student Maid against the odds. And how, no matter how big the challenges were, we found a way through them. Every time.

All I knew was that Student Maid was the one thing I could always count on. I'd had different friends over the years. Different relationships. But Student Maid was the constant throughout it all. The part of my life that was always there, no matter what.

And so, once again, I wondered: How do you just walk away from all of that?

But the numbers didn't lie.

We'd paid off more than $200,000 of debt that year—and still, Student Maid needed more money. Still, it swallowed up resources. Still, it demanded *everything*.

By this point, it had been hours since Monique and I first sat down. The restaurant staff was hovering near our table, hinting that they were trying to close. Monique's poor husband and my cousin had left to go on a walk long ago, when it became clear we weren't going to be done anytime soon.

Just before I paid the bill, Monique leaned across the table and looked me right in the eyes.

"Your decision to transition the business to Katie isn't really moving on from Student Maid," she began. "It's another way to avoid doing it. I know you're afraid to hurt people. That's what I love about you. But you don't have to keep sacrificing yourself, Kristen. You don't have to come last."

"All the money from your speeches could be going to you and our new chapter," Monique continued. "But instead, with this plan, a significant amount will need to keep going back to Student Maid. Eventually, you're going to resent that. You'll resent being on the road away from Spiros and not seeing financial growth that makes it feel worth the sacrifice."

She kept going, barely taking a breath. "I know you love the idea of mentoring Katie and continuing to support Student Maid, but what happens when you want to grow your family? I know that's something you want one day. What happens if you can't slow down on your speaking because you're still trying to keep Student Maid afloat? I want you to have the flexibility to take on less work and prioritize your marriage and a future family. I want you to be free."

She looked at me and the tears slipping down my cheeks, and finally, she said, "Kristen, it's not your job to keep everyone else happy. Isn't it time you made yourself happy for once?"

That's what did it for me.

There it was—my limiting belief, sitting between me and Monique at the table.

I could finally see it all. By holding onto one company, I was holding back the one I was most excited about. By giving my time to Katie, I was taking it away from my family and what I felt most called to do. By continuing to make Student Maid a place where students could grow, I was stunting my own growth. By protecting everyone else's hearts, I wasn't listening to what my own had been whispering to me for so many years.

And if I kept choosing everyone else, I would never be able to choose me.

For so long, I had been trying to write a version of my story where I didn't have to let go, where I didn't have to say goodbye, where no one had to feel any pain.

As I sat across the table from Monique, I accepted for the first time that a version like that wasn't possible.

I finally admitted to myself what I truly wanted: to go all-in on speaking. I wanted to help leaders on a larger scale. I wanted to have the courage to build a life on my terms.

The only thing standing between me and that life was fear.

Monique and I were the last ones in the restaurant that night. As we walked out of the same doors I'd walked through to spend my first business loan on sushi and sake, the irony hit me: I'd just decided to end Student Maid in the same place I'd celebrated its start. In the same room where we hosted our launch party for *Permission to Screw Up*, just steps from the table where I signed hundreds of books for our students and the community that night.

And the person I once trusted with a ring of keys was now the one giving me the courage to unlock our next chapter.

A full, heartbreaking circle.

Chapter 29

Closer to Me

It's four weeks after my dinner with Monique. I'm sitting in the living room of a new apartment, where Spiros and I have lived for only a few months.

I'm still high above Houston. Light pours in through the windows, and when I turn toward them, I catch a glimpse of her in the glass.

It's a different window, a different time, a different version, but still her.

I pause to study the face looking back at me.

The first thing I notice is the stress-induced cold sore on her lip. Proof, I think, of how much she cares.

As I continue to take her in, I'm struck by the differences I see.

In her posture, there is more certainty and steadiness. She doesn't have it all figured out just yet, but she's more willing to make hard decisions.

Behind her eyes, she is calmer. Grounded in who she is and what she believes, even though I know she's also terrified of what lies ahead.

Instead of feeling far away, she's closer to me now.

I nod, wanting her to know that I'm with her.

That I love her.

That I'm proud of her.

I tell her: *It's time.*

I open my laptop and click the link.

Soon, dozens of faces fill the screen. In front of me are students I've hired. Coached. Watched grow. The ones who stayed with me through the uncertainty of the pandemic.

They are looking at me, their leader, waiting for me to begin.

"This is going to be a difficult conversation," I say.

I take a steadying breath. "I've made the decision to close Student Maid."

The words feel inconceivable as they leave my mouth. On a few faces, I see looks of surprise and concern—and if I didn't have everyone's attention before, I certainly had it now.

"When I cleaned my first house, I never thought it would lead to starting a company. It was supposed to be a way to make money in college. But it grew into all of this—something I'm so grateful for and that I'll carry with me the rest of my life."

I look at the faces looking back at mine.

"Along the way, I learned a lot about myself. I discovered that my true passion isn't cleaning—and you know that. We're all here because we care about growing as leaders. That's what Student Maid has always been about."

I swallow.

"I've realized I'm ready for my next chapter. I have a new dream, and I need to follow it. I need to follow my heart and focus on speaking and leadership development full-time."

With every word, I feel both lighter and heavier. Happy and sad. Never one without the other.

"We're going to look for other cleaning companies to take over our clients," I continue. "And on May 9—Student Maid's anniversary—we'll officially close. The goal is for each of you to have the option to keep your job with the new companies. I'm going to do everything I can to make that happen. And if it doesn't . . ."

I pause, letting my eyes move across the faces on the screen, hoping each one can feel the love in my words.

"We will take care of you. We will help you find your next step."

I look at them again.

"We will take care of you *no matter what.*"

I stop.

I let myself breathe.

I let them breathe.

"What questions do you have? What are you afraid of? I want to talk about all of it. Anything that's on your mind."

Seconds pass, and then the first student raises her hand. She doesn't have a question.

"Student Maid is a place you built for us to follow our dreams," she says. "It's okay for you to follow yours, too."

After all these years, the memory still takes my breath away.

Chapter 30

The Other Side

On May 9, 2021, I walked out of Student Maid's doors for the last time.

Just before that, surrounded by our students, alumni (including Katie), our leadership team, and my family, I signed the same wall that every team member signed when they graduated from the company.

Even years later, I struggle to describe how it felt to face the end of the business I'd built from nothing. I can only say it was difficult, beautiful, intense, and everything in between—emotions I felt all over again as I wrote about it.

After pouring my heart and soul into Student Maid for more than a decade, I walked away for less than $5,000. But what I took with me could never be measured. Student Maid taught me how to lead. It helped me discover my purpose and introduced me to some of the most incredible people I've ever known.

I wish I could tell you that in the end, no one got hurt. But that's not what happened.

I did hurt people.

Katie was devastated. When we reconnected years later, she told me how confusing she found my decision at the time, especially after all we'd talked about and planned for. I wish I'd had the courage to tell her from the beginning that my unhappiness was the real reason I wanted to hand over the business. And actually, I wish I'd never offered her the opportunity at all, and that I'd found the courage to close Student Maid the moment the leadership team admitted our zeros and twos. Still, it worked out for the best: Katie went on to land a role as an assistant professor at a university and is now working toward a dream she's had her whole life.

Katie wasn't the only one I crushed with false hope. After the meeting where I announced the news, I *still* couldn't let go. I kept trying to find ways to bring our students with us into the next chapter—even attempting to find places for them in the speaking business at one point—but of course, none of that worked. And having to take it all back only made things harder. In the end, the two companies that took over Student Maid's clients offered jobs to all of our students, but not one person took them up on it. Turns out they weren't passionate about cleaning, either.

The longer I tried to protect others from pain, the more pain I caused. The more I worked to appease everyone, the more I confused them. The more I avoided hard conversations, the harder they became to have. By hanging on, by fighting, by trying one more time, I thought I was doing the right thing. But in the end, I only caused others more harm—and hurt myself, too.

As sad as it makes me to think back on it all, I know I never meant to hurt anyone. I understand why I made the choices I did, and I don't fault myself for them. That version of me did the best she could with what she was capable of at the time.

And I can only love her for that. Because no matter how messy and painful it was or how long it took to get there, she did it. She found the courage to face herself and finally choose what she wanted most.

I wish it didn't take me as long as it did to make that choice. If I could go back and talk to the version of myself who wrestled with the decision to walk away, I know exactly what I'd tell her. And maybe, friend, this message is meant for you, too:

> *There is no path that gets you where you most want to be that also guarantees no one will get hurt. It doesn't exist. But you can't let that stop you from choosing yourself.*
>
> *I promise: It won't be as scary as you think.*
>
> *I know you're afraid that if you close this chapter, it will change everything. I know you're afraid that people will see*

you differently, judge you, and label you an uncaring leader. I know you fear that letting go means erasing yourself and all you built.

But when you actually say it out loud? When you actually speak the words you've been terrified of but longing to say for years?

Most people will go on with their days as if you told them what you had for breakfast. You'll realize that all the fears that kept you stuck will never unfold the way you convinced yourself they would.

You will hurt people. You can't avoid that. But with time, they'll understand. They'll see you as human, just like them. And they'll be okay.

And you?

One day, you'll look back and say that even though it was one of the toughest things you ever did, it was right.

Growth is a part of life. If we deny ourselves the permission to evolve, we'll never know what we're truly capable of. When I was in the thick of our transition, I found a book that really helped me. It's called *Necessary Endings* by Dr. Henry Cloud. In it, he uses a rose bush as a metaphor for making hard choices, saying that roses are the areas of your life that you most want to nurture and give your energy to. Speaking was one of my roses. But in order for your roses to bloom, he says, you need to have the courage to prune the bush. You can't start a new chapter unless you are also willing to close one.

Student Maid will always be a part of me.

There are still moments—when I stumble upon an old photo, or I hear a vacuum humming in a hotel lobby, or I get a text out of the blue from a former student—that take me right back.

I'll always miss it. I'll always love it. And I'll always love myself more for choosing to say goodbye.

I thought that ending Student Maid was the only thing I'd have to do to give myself the life I had been dreaming of. That it was the hardest thing I'd ever have to face.

But it wasn't. It was just the beginning.

Part III

Courage

Chapter 31

Brace Yourself

I was giddy as I opened my laptop.

The moment is finally here!

My hands hovered over the keyboard as I grinned to myself.

All of your hard work is about to pay off—literally!

Now that the debt was gone, I was able to do things I'd dreamed about but could never afford. Amanda, Rachel, Monique, and Cheyenne (who stayed with us after she graduated college) had all chosen to step with me into the next chapter to focus on the speaking business and our shared passion of leadership development full-time. Speaking revenue continued to soar, so I'd just paid them a significant bonus. I had tears in my eyes as I confirmed the amounts that would soon hit their bank accounts. I'd always hoped to give them a deposit with that many zeros; I knew it would make a huge difference in their lives.

And now it was time for a bonus of my own. After all the years of being the guarantor of the debt, enduring the stress of keeping Student Maid afloat, and delivering close to 250 virtual speeches to ensure we survived the first year of the pandemic, it was time to cut myself a check that matched my hard work and sacrifice.

I pulled up our financial spreadsheet and closed my eyes, savoring the moment just a second longer.

Pinch me! This is it!

My fingers flew over the keys as I plugged numbers into formulas.

I leaned back with a grin stretched across my face.

Brace yourself. It's going to be BIG.

I hit enter. And . . .

Wait.

I stared at the number on the screen.

That can't be right. Maybe I'm looking at the wrong . . .

I blinked and leaned in closer.

. . . no, that's definitely the right one.

I reran the formula, certain I'd made a mistake.

And then I ran it again.

And again.

And once more manually, just to be sure.

Same number.

I swallowed hard.

This is . . . my bonus?

I felt a sting somewhere in my chest but smothered it before it could grow.

Don't be ridiculous, Kristen. How can you be upset? That's still the biggest bonus you've ever taken. You should be grateful.

I ignored the feeling trying to fight its way out and snapped my laptop shut, trying not to dwell on my disappointment. But later that night when Spiros got home, he asked about my bonus. When I told him the amount, he looked at me for a second before he said, "You deserve a lot more than that."

His words sent a spike of heat up my neck and into my face. The stinging feeling I'd been trying to push down all afternoon came back with a vengeance.

Spiros was right. I *did* deserve more.

My inner monologue went off the deep end:

After all the hours I worked, THIS is what I get?

I've given EVERYTHING to my company.

Why am I ALWAYS the one who has to sacrifice?

The more I thought about it, the angrier I felt.

But then, in the middle of my rage spiral, Jamil's face appeared in my mind. He had encouraged me to let Monique into my heart and to share the good, bad, and ugly with her—and what was brewing inside of me certainly felt bad and ugly.

I took some time to simmer down before I grabbed my phone to text her.

"I'm sad and mad about my bonus," I wrote.

My fingers couldn't type out my feelings fast enough. I told Monique that my bonus just didn't feel fair, especially after all the time and energy I'd poured into the business that year in particular. I felt like the company just kept taking from me.

Monique's response quickly crashed the pity party I was throwing myself:

"I love you, so I'm going to be honest with you," she began.

I watched impatiently as three dots appeared and disappeared over and over again. I could tell she was choosing her words carefully.

Finally, she wrote: "The business doesn't take from you. You take from you."

Whoa.

After I read her text a third time, the uncomfortable truth of it finally started to sink in.

She was right, of course.

I'd thought that making the decision to walk away from Student Maid meant leaving my problems behind with it. But Monique was shining a spotlight on what I'd refused to see:

You can take the leader out of the business. But it's a lot harder to take the patterns out of the leader, especially when those patterns began long ago.

Chapter 32

Over the Top

Let's go back to a sunny day in December 2015.

I walked into Student Maid's office with a smile that stretched from one ear to the other. In my hands were more gift bags than I could comfortably hold, the thin handles digging into my fingers as I made my way to the conference room.

I moved slowly around the long table in the center of the room, placing a bag topped with a big red bow at each seat. When I was done, I stepped back to take it all in.

They're going to love this, I thought.

That morning, on my drive to the office, a row of small, brightly colored Bluetooth speakers caught my eye in a store window while I was at a stoplight. Before I could think twice, I was making a U-turn into the parking lot.

I walked in and asked the sales associate how much they cost. I remember feeling a pang of sticker shock at the price, but my mind was made up. I swiped my credit card and bought 10 of them, one for each member of my leadership team. I carried the boxes out to my car and stuffed them into the backseat, trying to ignore the anxious voice telling me, *Kristen, what are you doing? Go back in and return them.* But by the time I'd set down the last bag on the conference room table, my anxiety had evaporated. All I could think about was how excited my team would be when they opened their holiday gifts.

The speakers weren't the only surprise waiting for them that day. I'd also gotten each person a gift card to a store I knew they loved, and I'd hand-selected five books based on their interests and where they wanted to grow in their lives and leadership.

I leaned against the wall, arms crossed, trying to act casual as people started to trickle in. Just as I imagined they would, each person stopped in the doorway, their eyes wide and jaws hanging open.

"What is *this*?"

"Kristen, are you *serious*?!"

Soon, tissue paper was flying everywhere, and when they saw the speakers in their bags, the room erupted in shrieks.

"This is *insane*!"

"Are you *kidding* me, Kristen? You're the best boss *ever*!"

"You're like Oprah! *You* get a speaker! And *you* get a speaker!"

It was everything I'd hoped it would be. Maybe even more. I took a mental snapshot so my heart wouldn't forget it. *This is what it looks like to take care of people*, I thought, already planning my next surprise.

Back then, when it came to treating my leadership team, very little was out of the question. I frequently went over the top to make sure they knew how much I appreciated them.

Once, I took them to a spa for facials and let them each pick a product to take home. Another time, I sent them on a scavenger hunt across Gainesville—every stop came with a gift—before asking them to meet me at my favorite sushi restaurant (you know the one). I picked up the four-digit tab like it was nothing.

Holiday parties meant open bars and an invitation to bring their friends. At the end of Student Maid's busy summer cleaning season, I'd rent a limo to take them bar-hopping to celebrate. (I loved a good limo.) I didn't just spoil them on special occasions; I took them out to dinner often, ordered lunch to the office, and bought them all coffees whenever I got one for myself. My team worked hard, and I never wanted them to question how much they meant to me.

But before my Oprah moment with the speakers, I had a very different surprise waiting for my leadership team in that same conference room.

Months earlier, I'd gathered them in our newly remodeled office and stood at the whiteboard. With my back turned to the faces watching from around the table, I gripped a marker in my sweaty hand and wrote a number on the board as big and bold as I could. I can't remember exactly what it was, but I know it was more than $300,000.

"So," I said, turning around, "this is our current debt balance."

The reaction was worse than I expected. One person gasped and put her hand over her mouth. Another stared at the floor. Most simply looked at me without saying a thing.

"That's . . . a lot of debt," someone eventually piped up. (Pretty sure it was Monique.) "I wish you'd told us sooner."

My team wasn't just shocked; they were upset. And rightfully so.

They knew I had taken on six figures of debt to open our software business and our second Student Maid location—and that the amount had continued to grow ever since—but I'd never shared specific numbers with them.

I'd rationalized my choice to be vague about the total by telling myself I was protecting my team. It was bad enough that I was so stressed out by it; I didn't want them to carry the same burden. But now I can see that underneath the guise of protection was shame. Even though I'd had good reason to believe that our two new ventures would take off, neither had gained the traction I'd hoped for, and it left me with regret. We now had more debt than we could handle, and I felt like I'd failed my company and team. I didn't *want* to let them in on the reality of the situation, but I'd reached a point where I had no choice: I needed their help to improve our numbers—and I also needed their understanding. In order to pay off the debt and get us to a better future, I explained, big salary raises would have to wait.

As I walked everyone through the repayment terms, I could hardly believe the words I was saying: If we made only the minimum payments, it would take more than *10 years* to pay off the balance. The best way to change that—and allow for big raises sooner—was to start bringing in significantly more revenue so that we could pay down the debt faster.

In those days, Student Maid's growth was holding steady, but the business wasn't performing well enough to support future raises *and* repay our creditors. And while the speaking business was starting to take off, it wasn't bringing in enough to cover it all, either. We needed everyone committed to increasing the cleaning revenue, booking more speeches, and finding ways to make our two new ventures financially successful.

I'd hoped that revealing the amount of debt we were in would light a fire under everyone, and after the shock wore off, it did. The team not only rallied around the challenge of bringing in more revenue, but they also supported the plan of delaying big raises in favor of making extra principal payments. I promised to make it worth the wait: I told them that when the debt was gone, in addition to a salary raise, everyone would get a "debt bonus," which would be a five-figure sum based on their tenure with the company. It was important to me to honor their years of sacrifice.

You'd think that in a season of financial strain, I'd also cut back on unnecessary business expenses. And in some places, I did. But there was one area where that was out of the question: celebrating my team.

Debt or not, I was committed to making them feel valued. I wanted everyone in my company to know they weren't just "employees" to me but people I truly cared about. I knew the paycheck certainly wasn't keeping them there.

For our students, that looked like continuing to pay them to attend leadership workshops and investing in an office remodel that wasn't typical for a cleaning company. Our team members had 24/7 access to the building so they could always have a quiet place to study and a home away from home.

As for my leadership team, I kept giving small raises and handed out bonuses when I could. And I kept finding new ways to surprise them, like the day I gave them the speakers. The lunches and dinners out never stopped, and neither did the epic parties and elaborate leadership team retreats.

One year, I took the leadership team and their significant others to a luxury resort a couple of hours away from Gainesville. When they checked into their rooms, I had matching pajamas, slippers, and a personal gift I knew they'd love waiting for them on their beds. (Monique's was a Tory Burch purse, which was *the* item of that season.)

But I didn't stop there: I invited each of their parents to join us, too, and I paid for hotel rooms and meals for those who could come. I wanted my team's families to feel just as special and included in our culture. Before we arrived, I asked the leadership team to write letters to each other's parents highlighting their child's strengths and why they appreciated working with them at Student Maid. I wrote letters, too. When the parents met us in the lobby for dinner that first night, you could tell they'd all been crying from reading the letters in their rooms. That moment is still one of my most treasured memories.

At this point, you may be wondering how in the world all of this spending kept happening even after the team knew about the debt. Why didn't anyone try to rein me in?

Well, because from the team's perspective, the problem was under control. We were paying down debt each month, the speaking revenue kept growing, and they had a leader who had always made the numbers work before, so why would any of that change now? Besides, they're only human. Who *wouldn't* want their boss to buy them lunch, surprise them with gifts, and take them on trips?

But, of course, there *was* a problem. A big one. I just kept it hidden from them.

No one knew how much pressure I was under to make it all work. The money for treating my team had to come from somewhere—and it often came from me. In order to keep up with our debt payments and maintain the culture that everyone had come to expect, I paid myself less than what I could have. Some months, I didn't pay myself anything at all.

For part of that time, I lived in the home my parents had bought in Gainesville when I started college. Because my compensation was unpredictable and I couldn't consistently pay them rent or utilities, they kept a running tally of what I owed them instead. I watched that number grow along with my guilt. I felt self-conscious that I was in my mid-20s and still relying on my parents to float some of my living expenses. Later, when I moved to Houston, Spiros helped me a lot, too.

No matter where I was or what I was doing, an unsettled feeling came with me. I felt like a financial failure. I had personal credit card debt, almost nothing in savings, and a bank account that didn't match the image I was projecting to the world. In social settings, if the topic of money came up, my heart would start racing. I felt pressure to look and act successful even when I didn't feel financially secure, and because I wasn't great with managing money in the first place, it only made my situation worse.

That external pressure began in the earliest years of Student Maid, when I started attending networking events with other local business owners. I was often the youngest person in the room, and I wanted to prove I belonged. When people would ask what I did, I'd tell them I owned a cleaning company, and some would respond by changing the subject. That reaction told me that they didn't see my work as important or impressive, and I was determined to do everything I could to try to change that. I bought nicer clothes and leased a Mercedes I couldn't afford, hoping they would earn me credibility as a successful entrepreneur. I told myself that if I could present something different on the outside, people would see me and Student Maid differently. And they did.

But I began to feel trapped. Not just because I felt like I had to maintain my outward appearance, but also because of the standard I'd set in my company. I felt tremendous pressure to keep spending and maintaining the culture everyone had come to know—but now I can see that almost all of that pressure was coming from me.

Anytime I did something for my team, I told myself it had to be better than the last thing I did. I had to throw a nicer party, plan a bigger surprise, buy more expensive gifts, and pick up the tab, just like I had every time before. What started as something I *wanted* to do now felt like something I *had* to do because of the precedent I'd set. But no one was forcing me to swipe my credit card. I was the one consistently raising the bar, and I was also the one who refused to lower it.

Doing less for my team didn't align with the generous and fun leader I wanted to be. I feared it would make them feel like I was taking away one of the biggest reasons they'd chosen to keep working with me. I can't deny that it also felt good to be seen that way. It was validating to hear, "You're the best boss ever!" and to watch parents beam with pride that their children worked for a leader and company that treated them well.

As time went on, the money got tighter, and the more difficult it all became. The software company and second location didn't work out, as you know, and by then Student Maid had started to struggle, too. We'd maxed out our lines of credit, and when I added up the total debt we'd accrued over the years, it now amounted to nearly half a million dollars. But none of that stopped me from treating my team. I kept stretching to meet the standard I'd set, which kept me stuck in a never-ending cycle of spending, stressing, and making up the difference by giving more speeches or taking less of a paycheck for myself.

The financial pressure consumed my thoughts, and the strain I felt sometimes manifested as frustration with my team. Even though I tried so hard to keep my feelings tucked away, they came out at the most inopportune times.

One afternoon, I took the leadership team on another spa getaway. It was during a stressful season at Student Maid, and I wanted to surprise everyone with a few hours of relaxation in the middle of the workday. But I could feel it in me when we got there. Something was bubbling right beneath the surface.

And then it boiled over.

"We're behind on cleaning revenue," I said to my team between our spa services. (It's only now that I can see the irony of discussing lagging revenue while simultaneously treating everyone to an expensive spa day. *Yikes.*) "We've had this conversation so many times, and our numbers are not improving. We *need* to figure it out." It came out more direct and intense than anything I'd ever said to them before.

Now that I can see it clearly, my reaction wasn't really about revenue. It was about how much I was sacrificing behind the scenes and how much pressure I was under just to make a spa day like that possible. But my team didn't know that, and at the time, neither did I. All I felt was anger, and all they heard was my disappointment, and it blindsided them. One even started to cry.

That day was supposed to be relaxing. Instead, I walked out of my facial to find them huddled around a laptop, scrambling to make a plan to fix something they didn't fully understand.

Fortunately, times like those were rare. I tried to keep a lid on my growing resentment, but it was becoming harder to do. Every dollar I gave to my team started to remind me of what I wasn't giving myself.

Another surprise for them or picking up the dinner tab meant more pressure on me to make the numbers work. A luxury retreat meant more speeches and more time away from my family to cover the cost. And while my team usually thanked me when I treated them to these things, sometimes they didn't, and that hurt. I shouldn't have been giving to them and *expecting* any thanks in return—that's not truly giving—but as my therapist once said, "Sacrifice breeds entitlement." I've learned how true that can feel when you're resentful.

All of that is why, years later, I felt mad and sad when I looked at my bonus check. Even though the debt was finally paid off, I still felt like I was sacrificing more than I should have been.

Monique's text helped me see the situation for what it was. It wasn't the business that took from me. It was *me* who chose to take from me, over and over again. The bonus was just the latest example.

I knew how it had happened: I'd created a bonus structure to motivate my leadership team during the pandemic and reward them for growth in the business. The higher the revenue level we hit, the bigger the bonus I'd pay them. Because the speaking business had skyrocketed, they hit the highest tier, which meant I paid them the largest bonuses they had ever received. And that was *on top* of the even larger debt bonuses I'd committed to that day in the conference room that were still to come.

None of that was the problem. I was more than happy to reward them for their hard work and our growth. The problem was that I hadn't factored myself into that bonus structure at all. My bonus was an afterthought instead of part of the plan. I decided I would take it from the remaining profit, but then I realized there wasn't as much left as I thought there would be. Even though it was the largest bonus I'd ever taken, it was less than I felt I deserved.

My heart pulled me in two different directions.

I was proud that I had done exactly what I'd promised my team all those years ago when I first told them about the debt. The moment our financial picture changed, I made sure they saw a significant difference in their paychecks, and it meant everything to me that I could do that. I couldn't wait to also give the salary raises I'd said were on the horizon.

At the same time, I knew that I had sacrificed more than anyone. As a business owner, sacrifice is what you sign up for. But after more than a decade of taking care of everyone else, carrying immense financial weight, and working more hours than ever, I wanted a check that reflected it all. The anger I felt that day about my bonus amount was misguided: I wasn't mad at my company. I was mad at myself and my repeated decision to put my financial needs last.

I knew deep down that this way of giving wasn't sustainable.

And yet I didn't know how to stop.

Chapter 33

No Matter the Cost

This time, instead of pouring a glass of wine or searching for a life coach, I'd dealt with my misery by reaching out to the person who had become my confidant and voice of reason: my thought partner.

In answer to Monique's truth bomb of a text about my bonus, I acknowledged that she was right. I chalked it up as a hard lesson learned and told her that I wanted to figure out how to prevent myself from feeling this way again.

As our conversation over text continued that night, I shared a fear about the future: I couldn't see a path for my own financial growth because of the salary raises I'd said were coming to the team. And I didn't know how to fix it.

Instead of summarizing what Monique wrote back to me, I want to share her exact words. I know it might seem strange that she and I talked about such a serious topic over text, especially considering that these days I often give speeches where I actively *discourage* people from having meaningful conversations that way.

There were times—like the infamous confrontation over sushi—when we had no problem saying hard things out loud. But there were also moments when we connected like this. Early on in our thought partnership, texting was one of the ways we built trust. Writing gave us space to process our thoughts and choose our words intentionally, which often led us to be more honest than we might have been otherwise. I'm proud of our willingness to speak candidly, even over text, and I want to show you the reality of how we built our relationship.

Here's what Monique wrote back to me that night:

I completely understand where you are coming from. I understand why you feel like the company keeps taking from you. But it's not the company—it's you who keeps taking from yourself.

It's a lot of small things you don't notice until it's too late, and then you're bitter.

I personally feel like you overpromise to the team. The only reason they think they are getting a salary increase soon is because you mentioned it.

With the structure you created, you started everyone's bonuses at a ridiculously high amount. I know you did it so the team would feel valued, but it's super hard to sustain.

I prefer not to talk about something financially as a team until it's actually happening. Doing that leaves us no room to pivot or adjust, and no runway of cash.

I know you trust me, and I know the way I think about money is very different from you. I can say with absolute certainty that we can get you to a better place, but I'm struggling with how to make that happen because of the expectations you've set with the team.

I think it's connected to your limiting belief: You worry the team feels undervalued. Or you feel you have to make the things people want happen overnight, so you promise it and then don't want to go back on your word.

You didn't have to promise the bonuses you did, and I want to help you never do that again. Because once you promise something, you always make it happen. It's a huge strength of yours, but also a weakness. You make that promise happen no matter the cost to you. You run yourself ragged to keep all the promises you didn't need to make in the first place.

> The big question is what now? It's hard to fix it overnight because we're still fulfilling past promises.
>
> I hope it goes without saying but I'll say it anyway. I'm thankful for you—with my current pay, and no bonuses or end-of-the-year surprises.

Once again, she didn't hold anything back.

She could see right through me. It's not easy to be seen so clearly, especially when your weaknesses and the parts of yourself you aren't proud of are on full display. But as it always was with Monique, her kindness and understanding shone through every word.

I knew she was spot-on.

But thinking about what it would take to get to the better place Monique was describing paralyzed me with dread. Creating a different financial future for myself could only mean one thing: I'd have to lower the standard my team had come to expect.

My worst leadership nightmare.

Chapter 34

Taboo

"Kristen. You can't be serious."

Monique stared up at me from the center of my laptop screen, her eyebrows practically reaching her hairline.

I'd just told her my annual salary. It was the first time I'd ever shared it with anyone on my team.

"Everyone else needs to know, too," she said, her tone softening. "If they did, they would feel the same way I do: Your raise should come first, even if ours have to wait. You deserve so much more."

At the time, my annual salary was $46,000. But that number wasn't the whole story. As a business owner, my compensation is made up of a few components: my salary, plus any bonuses and distributions I take throughout the year (including my disappointing bonus check). That particular year was one of the rare times when those payments collectively brought my compensation to six figures. It was the highest-earning year of my career up to that point.

But the $46,000 salary number bothered me more than I wanted to admit. It wasn't guaranteed: My salary fluctuated based on what the business could swing and was anywhere from the low- to mid-five figures over the years—even $0 during some pay periods. No matter what the number was, it never matched the level of responsibility I carried. When I was lucky enough to be able to take bonuses and distributions on top of my salary, those were inconsistent as well. There was little predictability in what I could count on for myself.

This conversation with Monique had started because of a bonus, but I quickly realized the issue was so much bigger. It wasn't really that I wanted a larger bonus. I wanted a level of financial stability and security that I didn't have. I wanted to be able to count on my pay and build my life around it, and I wanted the amount to reflect the fact that I was the owner of what was on track to become a million-dollar business.

But that desire was complicated. When I took into account all of my compensation, I was already the highest-paid person on my team. I felt guilty for wanting more when they were earning less. Especially because these were people who had been with me for years, and they had sacrificed so much, too. I tried to convince myself many times that what I made was more than enough. But the reality was that I couldn't see a clear path for my financial growth in the company I had created. The only way to get where I wanted to go, I thought, was to go back on the promises I'd already made to my team, and that wasn't something I was willing to do.

I was stuck between what I wanted and needed for myself, what I wanted to give to my team, and my identity as a servant leader.

I told Monique about all of it. And sharing it with her opened the door to some of the most vulnerable conversations about money of my leadership journey and my life. We'd moved quickly from our text exchange to long video calls where we both tried to get to the bottom of such a complicated and sensitive topic. Before then, Monique had a bird's-eye view of our numbers and helped me with budgets here and there. She had sat in on meetings with my CPA and knew where things stood overall, but she didn't see the most sensitive numbers. She didn't know anyone's compensation aside from her own. She also didn't know how inconsistent my pay was or about the times I'd had to lean on Spiros and my parents to float my living expenses.

It felt awkward and embarrassing to share these things with her. But each time I opened up, Monique met me with empathy and grace, which made it easier to keep letting her in. She never once made me feel judged for my poor financial choices. She recognized that managing money wasn't my strength and that many of my decisions had been driven by generosity. We both agreed that I needed to grow in these areas, but she made me feel seen rather than ashamed.

Together, we reached a new level of candor in our relationship that made me wish I had told her about all of it sooner. But I know why I didn't: It felt taboo to talk about money in this way.

We were a small team. We didn't have a CFO; I had always believed financial decisions were mine to make as the owner. Even though Monique was my thought partner, letting another person into the numbers at this depth felt like crossing a line. I wasn't sure how to involve her in decisions that would directly affect her. I also couldn't think of a single small-business owner I knew who operated with that level of transparency, likely for the same reasons I didn't. Money is something that many of us are taught to keep quiet about. To me, it felt like the touchiest subject of all.

There was another reason I kept it to myself: I liked having control. I knew Monique thought differently than I did when it came to finances, so before these conversations, I'd only let her into the parts of the business that felt "safe" to share. I worried that if I let her see everything, she might question my decisions or expect me to make different ones. And if that meant cutting back on things that made our culture special, I wasn't willing to do it.

But the more Monique and I talked about money, the more I realized how isolating it had felt to make all of these decisions alone. I hadn't fully recognized the emotional toll it had taken on me, and seeing her disbelief and concern over how much I'd been managing behind closed doors opened my eyes.

Monique was adamant that our next step should be figuring out a new financial structure before I increased the team's salaries. She wanted to help me create something that rewarded me more fairly and that would prevent me from future resentment. She also wanted to build emergency savings into the business so that I wouldn't have to operate under the financial pressure I'd become accustomed to.

We both knew that to do that, we needed to talk it all over with the team. There was no way to increase my compensation without having it affect everyone else's. But we realized that there was an even bigger issue than raises, which was that I didn't have any kind of system for determining how much we each should be paid. Up until then, I had only relied on my own judgment to make decisions about team compensation. I'd decided what felt fair and what I thought people deserved, but that subjectivity was stressful.

The way to fix that, Monique and I decided, was to create a clear hierarchy that matched compensation with each person's role in and impact on the business. It felt like the right time to tackle it because we had just entered our new chapter. It made sense to have a conversation with the team to define each person's position more clearly and ask them how much responsibility they actually wanted moving forward.

To help prepare for our discussion, Monique sent each person a series of questions to get a better understanding of their goals. Instead of making assumptions as we built a new structure, she wanted facts: Where did they hope to be compensation-wise over the next few years? What numbers did they see in their wildest dreams?

I was surprised by how different the team's answers were from what I had imagined. Their financial goals didn't come close to the expectations I'd been putting on myself. I still wanted to give my team beyond what they asked for, but it became obvious that the pressure I felt to do more was largely self-imposed.

I was ready to dive into next steps, but before I could get very far, Monique interrupted me.

"Hang on," she said. "There's one person on the team I still haven't interviewed."

She smiled at me. "What's *your* dream? How much do you want to make a year?"

Her question caught me off-guard. No one had ever asked me that before.

"I want the *real* number," she continued. "Nothing is too high. What do you see in your wildest imagination?"

I laughed, remembering how she'd told me she had to practically drag dream numbers out of the team. And now here I was, needing the same encouragement.

I took a minute to factor it all in: Everything I'd built. All the risks I'd taken to be an entrepreneur. The energy I'd poured in for well over a decade. The fact that our revenue came from speeches that I personally prepared and delivered.

"I can't say it," I told her, rolling my eyes at myself to cover how vulnerable it felt to share a dream so big. "It's *ridiculous*."

Monique didn't let me off the hook. "We're dreaming here," she said. "There's no such thing as too big. Tell me!"

I took a breath.

"One . . ."

I stopped myself.

I can't say it. I don't want her to think I'm greedy.

Another raised eyebrow from Monique got it out of me.

"One million dollars." It sounded even more ridiculous out loud.

I can't believe I actually said that.

It's so much money.

Too much.

Way too much.

She's going to think I'm so selfi—

"I was hoping you'd go that big." Monique interrupted my swirling thoughts with a grin.

Wait, what?

"You deserve to make a million dollars a year," she continued. "I know how much you sacrifice and how hard you work. There's no reason we can't build a plan to get you there one day."

I sat there, dumbfounded.

Both Monique and I knew that me making a million dollars wasn't anywhere close to reality—not back then, and not for the foreseeable future. It wasn't something I expected or even needed. It was just a dream.

But when I said it, Monique didn't flinch. Or laugh. Or act like I'd gone too far. She dreamed right along with me. She made me believe that I deserved to reach that high, and I have no doubt that's how she made every person on the team feel when she asked them that same question.

"The sky's the limit," Monique said. "We can build a better way forward, and we'll do it together." No matter the conversation, she made me believe that anything and everything could be possible.

This was now about so much more than my compensation. It was about building a company that could take us where we each wanted to go. Now that we knew everyone's financial dreams, we could work backwards and create a path to get us there—and we could do it in a way that was sustainable, fair, and benefited everyone.

As excited as I was, I couldn't help but worry about how the team would react to a more formal structure. I didn't want them to feel like I was becoming a different kind of leader, and I felt guilty knowing that anything I gained financially would reduce what was available to them. But I also knew that the way we'd been doing things wasn't working for me or for the business, and that if I didn't make a change, it was only a matter of time before my messy feelings resurfaced.

It was time to talk to the team.

Chapter 35

Everyone Wins

"This might be a little uncomfortable," I said to the three faces next to Monique's on my screen. "We've never talked about money like this before, but we need to. It's time to create a new kind of pay structure based on our roles and responsibilities."

I braced myself for the team's reaction. But to my surprise, they simply nodded. No one looked upset or concerned. If anything, they seemed curious about where this was going.

"The conversation we're having today isn't about who works harder or who matters more," I continued. "We all work hard. We all matter."

I paused, unsure of how to say what needed to be said next.

Monique jumped in. "If we're serious about growing the business," she began, "we need to talk openly about the kind of responsibility each of us wants to take on in this next chapter. We need to make sure our pay matches that, even if it creates differences in what we each earn."

She's so good at this, I thought gratefully.

"We need a team hierarchy that aligns our compensation with the level of responsibility we each have," she continued. "The bigger the impact of those responsibilities on the business, the higher in the hierarchy you'll be. And instead of Kristen and me determining a new structure without you, we want your input."

I took that as my cue. "So," I said. "Tell us. What do you think our team hierarchy should look like?"

Please let this conversation go well. Please, please, please.

"Well, Kristen should be at the top and make *way* more than the rest of us," Cheyenne piped up immediately. "That's a no-brainer."

And then:

"Yeah, for sure."

"Obviously."

Whoa. What is happening?

Monique caught my eye and gave me a small wink.

"Speaking for myself," Rachel said, "I don't want the kind of responsibility that Kristen and Monique have. I love how much flexibility I have with my role, and I like staying focused on content. I'd genuinely be happier lower in the hierarchy."

That surprised me: Rachel had worked with me the longest out of anyone, so I'd assumed she would want to be further up.

"Same," Amanda said. "As we're figuring out my new role on the speaking side and I'm adjusting to being a new mom, I want to stay focused on doing that well instead of taking on more responsibility. I'm comfortable being lower in the hierarchy and having my pay reflect that."

Amanda and I had talked about her role often, and she had shared similar thoughts with me before. But I had no idea she was fine with being lower in the hierarchy, too. Another surprise.

"I'm a little different," Cheyenne said. "I'm excited about taking on more responsibility. Now that I'm leading the speaking operations, I see a lot of potential there. I don't want to be at Kristen or Monique's level, but I see my role as having more influence on the business as a whole."

Another revelation. Though Cheyenne had seemed eager to take on more, it was nice to hear her confirm she enjoyed the additional responsibility.

"I love how easily this is coming together," Monique said. "For me, I really like being involved in the bigger picture of the business and in decisions that impact our future, and I'm okay with the pressure that comes with that."

She glanced at me and then back at the team. "I also think it makes sense that a larger portion of my pay is tied to how the business performs. I'm comfortable with more ups and downs in my compensation because of that."

"I'd prefer more of my pay to be predictable," Rachel spoke up. "I like knowing what I'm going to make each month."

"Same," Amanda added. "That stability is really important to me."

"I'm somewhere in the middle," Cheyenne said. "I like having a solid base salary, but I don't mind a little fluctuation in my bonuses."

Assumption after assumption fell away as the conversation continued. It was no longer up to me to guess what each person on my team wanted and needed; I'd asked, and they'd told me. (Imagine that.)

"Kristen," Monique said as we were wrapping up, "Would you be willing to share your current salary? I think it's important for everyone to know."

My heart jumped. We hadn't shared any actual numbers with the team yet. Monique and I had told them we would take what we'd learned from this meeting, create the new hierarchy along with the compensation the business could sustain, and then present it to them.

Oh . . . we're really doing this, huh?

I could feel everyone's eyes on me. I hesitated for a second before ripping off the Band-Aid.

"$46,000."

Silence.

"But that's before bonuses and distributions!" I quickly added. I explained that my total compensation fluctuated year to year and gave some examples of how much I'd made in higher-earning years and low ones.

More silence. Then—

"Kristen."

"What?" I asked, only half-chuckling.

"You've got to be joking."

"That's not okay."

"You need a raise."

"*Immediately*."

Monique was right. (Of course she was.)

In a single meeting, my team had completely changed my perception of what they actually needed from me financially and what they expected me to take for myself. They *wanted* me to make more money. They *wanted* my paycheck to reflect the effort I was putting in. And they *still* wanted that for me, even though it meant there would be less money available for them. I could hardly believe it.

I know that as the owner, I could have just given myself a raise. But there was something about hearing my team come to that conclusion on their own that shattered a story I had been telling myself. My team didn't see my gain as coming at their expense, and it showed me that the guilt I felt about paying myself more was unnecessary.

After that meeting, Monique helped me crunch the numbers. By the time I got my next paycheck, my salary had doubled, and there were more raises for me to come. The team decided on their own to delay their salary raises a few more months so that mine could come first. (It still blows me away.) We also found a way to work me into the bonus structure so that I could earn more reliable bonuses as well. I made sure to honor what I'd committed to: Soon after our conversation, I paid out the debt bonuses I'd promised that day in the conference room.

Now that we knew what everyone truly wanted, Monique and I could build a structure that supported everyone's needs and dreams. It felt like our partnership was working the way Jamil had always envisioned for us: We each brought our strengths to the table, challenged each other to see things differently, and worked together to create a better future for us all.

We both wanted to have a business that could take care of its people and allow them to grow financially; we just had very different ways of going about it. Where I operated with emotion, Monique brought a system. I thought in feelings; she thought in percentages. I wanted to give, give, give; she wanted to make sure we could sustain that generosity over time. In so many ways, we complemented each other, and the company thrived because of it.

A lot has changed since we had those conversations—and it's only gotten better.

Today, our financial structure is built on a simple philosophy: When the business wins, everyone wins. We still have a compensation hierarchy based on roles and responsibilities, and each position shares in the company's revenue growth. As the business grows, our compensation grows with it. And when growth slows or declines, our compensation reflects that reality, too.

We've built in discipline. Every quarter, we set aside money for taxes, savings, and investments in the business before we fund anything culture-related. At any time, the team can pull up our master financial spreadsheet and see how much money the company has, what each person on the team is making (me included), and how much we have saved for each budget category. They're even empowered to spend within certain categories without needing permission. Not a single number is hidden.

Within the first year of implementing our new structure, nearly everyone surpassed the financial goal they'd set for that timeframe. Since then, I've watched my team buy homes, pay off debt, purchase new cars, take incredible vacations, and give generously to their loved ones.

As for me, my own compensation finally reflects the business I've built. I may not ever make a million dollars a year, and that's okay, but now there are moments when I look at the check I'm writing myself and feel overwhelmed with gratitude. I think about how far I've come, what it took to get here, and the role my team played in encouraging me to take care of myself financially.

Our structure isn't perfect; it's human. We want it to grow with us as our needs change. At least once a year, I conduct "stay interviews" with my team where I ask them to tell me what they hope will stay the same in our company and what they hope will change in order for them to remain fulfilled. Our financial structure is a part of that conversation, and I ask for their feedback to ensure it's still serving us. Nothing is set in stone, and when something needs to evolve, we choose how to do it together. When there are tough financial decisions to make because of slower seasons in the business, we make those calls as a team. I'm no longer on an island alone.

I've learned that talking about money can be so freeing—but only if you have the courage to face yourself financially. When I was unwilling to make hard decisions, set better boundaries, or spend less, I put the stability of my entire company at risk. And by not prioritizing my own needs, not only was I hurting myself, but I was also hurting my team. I eventually reached a place where I couldn't give to others without also feeling resentful about what I wasn't getting in return.

Now that I feel taken care of, I don't keep score. I know what it means to give from a truly generous place. I still love surprising my team and going over the top for them, and while I could use company funds to do it (and often do), there are times I choose to pay for things out of my own pocket simply because it makes me happy.

I now know that a better gift than limo rides, bluetooth speakers, and luxury retreats is a financially secure company. *That's* what it really looks like to take care of people. And with that comes a responsibility to be a good steward of what I've built and to model what it looks like to prioritize myself financially so that my team feels permission to do the same.

It's amazing what can happen when you break a taboo.

Chapter 36

Unrecognizable

The Houston sun warmed my shoulders as I sat in the pool, a book in my hand, and marveled: *How is this my life?*

It had been a year since I'd walked out of Student Maid's doors for the last time. I'd taken myself to my favorite local day spa to celebrate, relax, and reflect on how far I'd come.

I still had many days when I missed our students, but my life felt unrecognizable—in the best way.

The speaking business had continued to grow along with everyone's paychecks. We'd blown past revenue benchmarks we thought were years away. My calendar stayed packed with virtual speeches, and in-person bookings were ramping back up as the world reopened in the wake of the pandemic. I still felt pressure to keep it all going, but it was *good* pressure. It kept me reaching higher and wanting more for myself and my team.

One of the things I enjoyed most about having only one company to focus on was that I had more space in my mind to dream.

One night, while lying on my couch and looking out at the city lights, I had an idea to create a virtual leadership development program and open it to the public. Up until that point, the only way my message could reach people was if their organizations brought me in to speak. I envisioned creating a new space where leaders from all over the world could come together to connect with, learn from, and grow alongside each other.

The pandemic had made the already lonely job of leadership feel even lonelier. I talked to so many who felt disconnected, not just from other people, but from their purpose: They'd spent so long in survival mode that they'd lost sight of why it was all worth it. I saw an opportunity to bring these leaders together and build a community. I imagined a two-day experience filled with music, energy, real conversations, and a fresh take on how to lead with humanity in a changing world.

Rarely has an idea come to me as fully formed as this one did that night. The next day, I pitched it to Monique, and shortly after that, to the team.

That's how the Human Leadership Program was born.

By the time I was sitting in that spa pool, we had already run the program five times. More than a thousand people from around the globe had been through it so far, and now it was growing by word of mouth. On top of that, I was still facilitating the monthly mastermind groups I'd started during the pandemic and advising leaders one-on-one.

My days were full to the brim, and my heart was even fuller. I smiled when I remembered the quote I'd scribbled down on a Post-it years before: I was getting my music out. It felt like my career was on track to make the kind of impact I'd written about in my eulogy.

My work was thriving, and my personal life was flourishing right along with it.

Spiros and I finally had our wedding in Mexico, in the same place we had planned to tie the knot before the pandemic forced us to postpone. We were surrounded by our closest friends and family, including some of my team. Jamil also made the trip, which meant so much to me.

Just before that day at the spa, Spiros and I had put an offer on a hundred-year-old house in our dream neighborhood in Houston—and got it. It needed a complete renovation, but we had a vision for what it could become. For the first time, I had a salary that made me feel like I could meaningfully contribute to the life we were building together, and I was proud of that.

And now, here I was, sitting in a pool, reading a book and actually feeling relaxed. I couldn't help but think about how a moment like this wouldn't have been possible in the Student Maid days. No matter how calm I looked on the outside, I was always waiting for something to go wrong, my phone never far from reach.

I couldn't remember the last time I'd felt such . . . *peace.*

"Excuse me?" I heard someone say. I looked up to see one of the spa attendants standing near me at the edge of the pool.

"There's someone here to see you."

I looked around for a second. "Me?"

She nodded. "They're waiting in the lobby."

What in the . . .

I set down my book, hopped out of the pool, and wrapped a towel around my sopping wet body.

I made my way inside, and when I turned the corner, I saw them.

My *team.*

Somehow, improbably, amazingly, they were all standing right in front of me: Rachel, Cheyenne, Amanda, and Monique—with her seven-month-old baby in her arms.

I stood there in my towel, mouth open as water puddled at my feet.

"You didn't think we'd let you celebrate alone, did you?" Amanda said.

Between hugs, they told me they'd been planning this for months. They had all flown to Houston and rented an Airbnb for the week to surprise me. I later learned how much effort it had taken to keep it under wraps. They put the expenses on their personal credit cards and met with our CPA so they could be reimbursed with the funds we'd set aside for a team retreat without tipping me off. That's the funny thing about running a financially transparent company: Surprises are harder to pull off, but when they happen, they're that much sweeter.

I laughed, and then I cried, and together we created quite a spectacle in the quiet spa lobby.

I'll never forget the week we spent together. We soaked up every minute and made some of my favorite memories. In between my virtual speeches, we enjoyed each other's company with as little work talk as possible. We lingered over meals, played card games, and reflected on how much we'd each grown over the last year, both in and outside of work. I took them on a tour of the house Spiros and I had just bought. They were the first people in my life to see it in person (aside from Spiros, of course).

This was our reality now. And it felt as close to perfect as I could imagine.

But even though things couldn't have been better, I didn't take any of it for granted. I continued to meet regularly with Jamil so he could keep an eye on my blind spots and hold me accountable to my growth as a leader. Only now it wasn't just me; Monique was part of our sessions, too.

With Student Maid's challenges in the rearview, we got to focus on growing the speaking business and exploring ideas like scaling the Human Leadership Program. It was valuable to talk things out with Monique in front of Jamil so that he could witness our dynamic and help us learn how to make better decisions together. Each session strengthened our thought partnership and pushed us to think bigger. We left feeling more connected and capable than when we started.

Jamil always opened our sessions with the same four questions: What gave you energy since we last met? What took your energy? How happy are you at work, on a scale of 1 to 10? How focused were you on what mattered most, on a scale of 1 to 10?

They were simple questions, but they had a way of immediately revealing the issues that needed the most attention.

Before long, there was one topic that kept rising to the top of the list.

"What took your energy?" Jamil asked us, as usual.

Monique didn't hesitate. "Figuring out Amanda's role."

Here we were again.

"Yes, we've been spending a lot of time on that," I said. (That was putting it lightly.)

Jamil leaned back and was silent for a moment. Then he looked at the screen and said, "Kristen, do you realize how often Amanda and her role have come up in our conversations recently?"

I knew exactly where this was going.

And just like that, things didn't feel so perfect anymore.

Chapter 37

Sweet Spot

I met Amanda the day she interviewed at Student Maid in 2015.

She was walking out of the office as I was walking in, and I stopped to introduce myself. Her energy was bright and warm, and somehow, even in our brief interaction, she made me feel like she cared about me.

I wasn't surprised one bit when the team chose to hire her over the other candidates they had interviewed for the front-desk position. It didn't take long for Amanda to show us her potential as a leader beyond answering the phones. She had a natural ability to connect with people—particularly our team members—and she quickly earned the title of Chief of Culture at Student Maid.

If you read *Permission to Screw Up*, you may remember Amanda as the one who fought to revamp some of the stricter policies in our Guidebook, which was our version of an employee handbook.

The Guidebook was born out of necessity: When we created it, Abby was still with the company, and she and I had opposite approaches for handling HR issues. Abby wanted hard-and-fast rules that applied across the board, while I preferred handling issues on a case-by-case basis. She and I usually made decisions together, but when my speaking-related travel ramped up and Abby became more focused on Student Maid's operations, Amanda and other leaders took over accountability conversations. I realized we needed to bring consistency to the process, so Abby and I—along with the rest of the leadership team—came up with a set of policies that blended both of our approaches, and that became our Guidebook.

I had thought we'd done a pretty good job of striking a balance between having empathy for our students and holding them accountable, but Amanda made me think twice.

Once, one of our most reliable student team members texted Amanda before his shift and said he was sick. According to our Guidebook, any absence from work could only be excused with a doctor's note, and too many unexcused absences would cost someone their job. This student said he couldn't afford to go to a doctor, and he didn't think he needed to. He just needed rest. Still, he told Amanda he was going to come to work anyway because he was afraid of losing his job.

Amanda thought the policy was unfair, especially because we would never enforce the same rule for our leadership team, so she brought the issue to me. It broke my heart to think we'd made someone who was sick want to come to work out of fear. That was the last thing I wanted.

Thanks to Amanda, we reworked the Guidebook to be more human, and we replaced strict policies with ones that had a greater emphasis on trust and care for our team.

That was the kind of leadership Amanda embodied, and her impact on our people couldn't be measured.

She also oversaw our Ambassador Program, a paid internship where students learned firsthand what it took to run a business, which became a launchpad for many of our leaders, including Cheyenne. Amanda led coaching conversations with our students, challenging them to reach the personal and professional goals they set for themselves. She met with them one-on-one often, checking in on how they were doing in their lives outside of work and making sure they felt supported.

And then there was her office.

The door was always open and a candle was always burning under the dim glow of her desk lamp. In one corner was a comfy papasan chair with a blanket draped over it and snacks within reach. She wanted people to feel safe coming to her, and they did. The whole space felt like a hug.

After a couple of years, Amanda came to me with a dream: She wanted to move back to the Pacific Northwest, but she didn't want to lose her job. We came up with a plan for her to work remotely and keep our culture alive from afar. She set up cameras in our office so she could see when team members came back from their shifts and chat with them, and she continued the one-on-one conversations she'd become known for over video calls. She even left her office intact so that team members could be cozy while they talked to her.

When I first decided to hand over Student Maid to Katie, I saw Amanda staying on as Chief of Culture. I felt confident that if she stayed with Student Maid, she could keep the culture strong. Both Amanda and Katie loved that idea, too. But if it turned out that Student Maid couldn't sustain her salary, the backup option was to change Amanda's role completely and find a place for her in the speaking business. Once it became clear that staying with Student Maid was no longer an option, I got to work figuring out Amanda's new role.

It was tricky. Everyone else's positions translated easily into our next chapter: Monique was still my thought partner who would help me grow the business. Rachel was already editing my blog and helping me create content for speaking events. Cheyenne had run operations at Student Maid and would now handle contracts and be the go-to for our speaking clients.

And then there was Amanda.

Amanda's gift was culture, but our small team didn't have the same needs that Student Maid did. Our culture was already strong, and the responsibility to maintain it sat with me. But I couldn't fathom leaving Amanda behind. I wouldn't even consider it. She meant too much to me and our team, and I was determined to find a way to keep her with us, even if it meant I had to get creative.

Around then, I needed help in my personal life. Speaking and traveling took up most of my waking hours, and it had gotten to the point where basic things like booking appointments had become challenging. By the time I was done with my day, the places I needed to call were already closed.

I couldn't justify bringing on Amanda full-time only to help me with personal tasks, but I needed plenty of help at work, too. Every speaking event came with dozens of details: booking flights and hotels, arranging for ground transportation, even figuring out where

I could eat when I had only short breaks between sessions. Monique had helped me with these things in the past, but she had limited capacity now that she was focused on new business opportunities. Having Amanda's support, I thought, could be a game-changer.

I presented Amanda with the idea of taking on some of my personal tasks and also managing my calendar and travel logistics for speaking. Because I knew she was most passionate about culture, I told her she could help me find ways to surprise and delight the leadership team, too.

She was all for it.

We both acknowledged that we were in new territory and that there wasn't a blueprint for a role like this one. We didn't know if it would work, so we agreed it would be an experiment and committed to giving it our best shot. Not long after, Amanda came up with a name for her new role, which is still the best title we've ever had in our company: Chief of Compassion. She saw her role as taking care of me and our team so that we could make a bigger impact on others.

Almost immediately, her support really did change the game for me.

For the first time, I got to experience the level of care our students had always felt from her. Amanda was always looking out for anything and everything she could do to make my life easier and more manageable.

Before I knew it, she'd blocked off time on my calendar not just for work tasks, but for *me*. She made sure I had time for the things that helped me feel my best: hair and nail appointments, massages, doctor's visits, and date nights with Spiros. When I came home after several days on the road, she made sure the kitchen was stocked with groceries. She tracked important dates in my relationships, reminding me of birthdays, anniversaries, and significant life moments I wanted to reach out about and recognize.

It got to the point where Amanda knew pretty much everything about me. She had my Social Security number memorized, had access to all of my passwords and personal credit card numbers, and handled sensitive appointments. She was listed as my emergency contact in more than a few places. I trusted her completely. She made me feel safe.

She also helped me create some of my favorite memories.

When we celebrated team anniversaries, she made my ideas larger than life. For one of Monique's anniversaries, I flew to Gainesville to take her to the spa and out to dinner. Amanda made it unforgettable: She and Cheyenne rented a luxury car, dressed up as chauffeurs, and drove us around Gainesville. The car was filled with decorations and charcuterie boards. Amanda's heart was in every detail.

She also arranged for me and Spiros to get married on the rooftop of our apartment building right before we flew to Mexico to celebrate with friends and family. She found our officiant, arranged for a bouquet and photographer, and coordinated the time of the ceremony so that the sky would be the perfect shade of blue in our pictures. After we said our vows, she had our favorite sushi delivered to our apartment.

Over time, Amanda took on more of the heavy lifting when it came to my travel logistics for work. In between texts about flights and car-service pickups, she encouraged me. She sent me pep talks when I had nightmare travel delays, surprised me with handmade cards or flower deliveries when she knew I'd had an especially demanding week, and showed up every day as my biggest supporter.

There was just one problem: Amanda struggled with keeping track of details.

At first, I couldn't blame her. My schedule changed so often that even I had trouble staying on top of it all. But after a while, I couldn't deny that it had become a glaring issue.

There were times when she scheduled my ground transportation on the wrong day. I'd get a call from a driver saying they were downstairs waiting for me in a totally different city than wherever I was. It frustrated them, and it cost us money to make it right. Another time, she forgot to reserve a hotel, and I didn't realize it until I landed late at night and had nowhere to go. Appointments, too, would get booked at the wrong times, and I'd only discover the mistake after I'd shown up.

I found myself frequently double-checking Amanda's work. I felt like I couldn't stay hands-off: Not only was there a cost to my time when things didn't go as planned, but I couldn't risk a travel mishap affecting a speaking engagement. I spent hours working with Amanda to build systems that would help her better manage the details, but inevitably the same issues would pop up again.

For most people, this would have been a sign that Amanda wasn't the right fit for the role, but I wouldn't allow myself to go there. Amanda was extraordinary. She *was* our culture. She lived our values and took ownership *every single time* something went wrong. She apologized, never got defensive, and worked to fix every mistake. She was always more frustrated with herself than I was, and she didn't shy away from responsibility. I'd only met a few people in my journey with her level of commitment to her job.

I gave her feedback using the same methods I taught in my speeches: the FBI (how I felt, the behavior that made me feel that way, the impact of that behavior) and Keeps and Considers (what I wanted her to keep doing and what I wanted her to consider doing differently). During our regular one-on-ones and in our quarterly 360 reviews with the team, we talked about the areas where she needed to improve.

But nothing worked. The issues kept happening.

I didn't know what else to try, so I asked Monique for help. Her strengths were different from Amanda's, and she was excellent at managing details when she was in charge of travel logistics. I thought maybe she could coach Amanda in a way that would make things click. But after extensive meetings with Monique and another round of new systems and accountability plans, Amanda continued to miss details. Involving Monique only seemed to make things harder for Amanda. It was confusing and frustrating for her to hear the same feedback from both me and Monique when nothing she tried seemed to make a difference.

With nowhere else to turn, I often brought up Amanda and her role in our sessions with Jamil.

In one of our earlier conversations, Jamil had introduced the idea of a "sweet spot." He described it as the place where people come alive in their work and where they have the biggest impact. For someone to be working in their sweet spot, he said, two things have to be true: The work has to align with the person's strengths, and they have to feel motivated to do it.

For months, Jamil had been trying to help me see that this role likely wasn't in Amanda's sweet spot. She might have been motivated and excited to do it, he pointed out, but it didn't seem like she was naturally suited for it.

I refused to listen.

I felt responsible for Amanda being in this situation to begin with. I was the one who had created the role, and I was also the reason that her previous one—her dream job at Student Maid—no longer existed. Despite the fact that we had called this an experiment and openly acknowledged that it might not work out, I knew how much Amanda loved our company. She often said she wanted to stay with us forever. She was also the primary breadwinner in her family, and she and her husband at the time had a young son. How could I possibly tell her this wasn't working out and deliver news that would change everything for her and her family?

I couldn't.

So, even though I knew that we spent far too much time on this topic with Jamil, and that it was taking up Monique's energy and mine, and that we had tried *everything*, I wasn't willing to face it. Instead, I told myself that Amanda lived our culture and values, and that was enough. That if I kept managing and helping her, eventually the issue would resolve itself. That even a year and a half into our experiment, there was still hope we could turn things around.

But in this meeting with Jamil and Monique, I couldn't avoid it anymore.

That morning, I'd learned that Amanda had booked my car service at the wrong time to take me to the airport. The driver was upset because this same situation had happened not long before, and I had to spend time fixing the reservation and calming him down.

I showed up to the session with Jamil thinking for the hundredth time that there had to be a way to help Amanda better manage the details.

But this time, I had to admit it:

There wasn't.

Chapter 38

Painful No Matter What

I could feel where the conversation with Jamil was heading, and I wanted it to go anywhere other than that.

"Kristen, it's your responsibility to make sure Amanda is working in her sweet spot," he reminded me for the umpteenth time. "If you take your emotions out of it for a minute, do you think she is?"

I knew the answer in my gut, but instead of saying it, I made excuses.

"What about the surprise trip to Houston?" I said. "She planned that. It was incredible. That was definitely her sweet spot."

"She came up with the idea," Monique said gently, "but I had to manage a lot of the details."

I got quiet. "Oh. I didn't realize that."

Jamil pressed a little further. "Monique, you shared that this has been taking a lot of your energy. Could you elaborate?"

She didn't hold back. "I'm spending more time supporting Amanda than I am on my own work. I can't focus on my projects. It's been frustrating."

I could feel Monique's patience wearing thin. We'd come up with all these ideas for growing the business, but I'd asked her to put them aside and focus on helping me get Amanda's role on track. I knew I was pulling her away from work she was excited about doing.

"It's not Amanda's fault," Monique added. "I know that she is trying everything she can and she cares so much. It's just that the role isn't in her strengths. And at some point, we have to call it what it is. It's not working."

"I know it's not working," I said. By admitting it out loud I think I surprised everyone, including myself.

I went on to share that Amanda was the only person on the team I had to support in this way. It's not that others on the team didn't make mistakes—we all did—but they didn't keep repeating the same ones. Deep down, I knew this wasn't the right role for Amanda. I had seen what it looked like for Amanda's work to match her strengths. I had watched her thrive as Chief of Culture, and I knew her at her best. This wasn't it. Even worse, I didn't have another position to offer her.

"I don't want to give up on her," I said passionately. "She always tries to learn from her mistakes and do better the next time. I can't imagine letting her go when she's working so hard to improve. It just doesn't feel like our culture. Or like me."

"I know you care about Amanda," Jamil said. "That's why she's still here. But if you don't have another role that will allow her to be in her sweet spot, she deserves to be somewhere she can use her strengths every day. Wouldn't you agree?"

I searched for something to say, but I couldn't find it. I was frozen in my heartbreak.

"Kristen," he continued, "the longer you hold on, the more you're hurting Amanda. And yourself."

After that, Monique and Jamil kept talking, but I wasn't really hearing them anymore. I was stuck on one word: hurting.

This whole time, I'd been telling myself I was helping Amanda by keeping her on the team. But what if that wasn't true?

I couldn't imagine that the last few months had felt *good* for Amanda. It had to be defeating to hear the same feedback again and again and to show up every day wanting to do your best but feeling like you were falling short. If I'd realized the role was out of her strengths, I suspected she'd figured it out, too. I knew what it was like to work on things that didn't come naturally to me. It drained me and left me feeling exhausted. What if that's how she felt every day?

I was also hurting myself: Trying to stay on top of the details for Amanda meant stretching beyond my own sweet spot. On days when I was heavily involved in her work, I felt zapped because the details weren't in my strengths, either. Plus, I knew that the majority of my time went to helping her instead of supporting others on the team, which wasn't fair to them.

Worse than any of that was the awful feeling brewing inside me: I'd started to resent the fact that I was paying Amanda to own a role I was so involved in. With our financial transparency, I worried that the team might start to feel an imbalance there, too. We had discussed Amanda's struggles together in our 360 reviews. Every quarter, we each shared two things we felt we could improve on and two things we thought we were doing well, and then we invited additional feedback from the rest of the group. Amanda often brought up her challenges herself in these conversations, so the team was aware of them. They had even offered their own ideas to help her better manage details, but none of them worked.

I could feel my frustration growing with every mishap. I noticed at times that I was shorter with Amanda in our meetings and less patient than I wanted to be. When something went wrong, I had a harder time summoning my empathy. I didn't want to feel this way because I knew she wasn't doing any of it on purpose, but I couldn't help it. And now I could see that it was affecting Monique, too. I could feel a wedge forming between us.

I could no longer deny it: Keeping Amanda on the team was hurting her, me, and Monique, and it would eventually ripple to the entire team, if it hadn't already.

But letting Amanda go would hurt, too. Losing her job would wreck her. And it would wreck me and the team.

Which hurt was worse? Which one do you choose?

Once again, with no good options in front of me, I turned to my values. Compassion told me that Amanda deserved to be in a role where she thrived, and that even though it would be devastating to let her go, in the end, it was the kindest thing for her—and for everyone. Courage told me that I needed to have an honest conversation with her and tell her what I'd just decided.

"I know what I need to do," I said to Jamil and Monique. "I know it's time to let her go."

The words were painful to say out loud.

"When will you do it?" Jamil asked.

I hesitated. "Next week."

"Next week?" he repeated.

I recognized it as soon as I said it: That was my limiting belief, looking for any way to delay hurting someone.

I knew I owed it to Amanda to talk to her soon. This conversation was going to be painful no matter what, but if she found out I'd been sitting on it for any length of time, it would hurt even more.

"I'm going to do it as soon as I get to the airport today," I said. I could tell that both Monique and Jamil were proud of me for not putting it off any longer.

I shut my laptop and zipped up my suitcase. As I headed downstairs to catch my ride, the only things pushing me forward were my values. They helped me take step after step, each one bringing me closer to a moment I'd been avoiding at all costs.

As soon as I got in the car, I texted Amanda and asked if we could FaceTime once I got to the airport.

I knew she could sense that something was off. I never asked for a call like that, especially on a travel day. After her mistake that morning with the car service coming at the wrong time, I imagined she was already worried. She told me she was free, and I said I'd call her once I got through security.

To ease my nerves for the rest of the ride, I called Monique.

"Do you think I'm making the right choice?" I asked her.

"I do," she said. "And I know it's going to be really hard."

I could feel the sadness in her voice. She loved Amanda, too. But she also recognized that this was one of those decisions that breaks your heart, even when it's right.

When we pulled up to the airport, I turned to my driver, who had overheard enough of the conversation with Monique to understand the situation.

"Do *you* think I'm making the right choice?" I asked him, desperate for validation.

"Why don't you give her one more chance?" he offered.

It was tempting.

I wanted to take the pass he was giving me and tell Monique and Jamil that I'd changed my mind. But I knew I was fooling myself.

One more chance would lead us right back to the same place, and it would only make things harder.

I walked through security and made my way to the gate, my pulse climbing with each passing minute. I tried to think of what I would say to her, but every version of the conversation I played out in my head felt wrong.

How do you tell someone you care about so much that they no longer have a future with your company?

How do you tell the girl whose grandmother told her she was good at many things but not great at anything that she's losing her job?

I found a spot near my gate as far away from other people as I could manage. As I looked at everyone around me going about their days, it didn't feel fair. I didn't want to be a leader. I didn't want to have to make a decision like this. I wished I had chosen a different path in life.

Why does leadership have to be this hard?

I sat down against the wall and pulled out my phone.

With trembling fingers, I unlocked the screen. For a moment, I couldn't move.

Then, shaking, I pressed the green FaceTime button.

Chapter 39

Two Things Can Be True

I could see it in Amanda's eyes before I said a word. She knew this call was serious.

For once in my life, I didn't beat around the bush. "This is going to be a difficult conversation," I said. "I've made the decision to let you go."

Tears filled her eyes as she nodded.

"When we started this, we called it an experiment," I continued. "And I know in my heart that we both gave it everything we had. But it isn't working. If it were, we wouldn't keep having the same challenges."

It took everything in me not to break down.

"You are one of the most incredible and dedicated people I've ever met and worked with," I told her. "It's just that this role isn't fully in your strengths. If I had another position to offer you in your sweet spot, it would be yours in a heartbeat, but I don't."

More tears ran down her cheeks as she kept nodding. I wanted to cry with her, and almost did.

On the outside, I tried to stay calm and grounded. But inside, I wanted to shake my own shoulders and ask, *Kristen, what are you doing? How can you do this to her? Why can't you just keep trying?*

I felt like a terrible leader. I never thought I would make this choice, and neither did she. She was gutted. Amanda had told me countless times that my company was the only place she ever wanted to work. How was it possible that I was here, having this conversation with *her* of all people?

But I was. And though it wrecked me to do it, I knew it was right.

"You've given so much to me and this company," I said with as much love as I could possibly hold in my voice as I watched her tears fall. "And I'm going to take care of you. Once you've had time to process this news, we'll build a plan together for your next steps. I want to support you financially so that money isn't an added stress, and I want to help you find a job that's in your sweet spot."

As gently as I could, I encouraged Amanda to think about what the best version of this transition would look like for her. How much money would help her feel safe? When should her role end so it didn't feel so abrupt? How did she want to say goodbye to our clients and people she'd grown to love? I promised that the following week we'd reconnect and make the most compassionate plan we possibly could for our Chief of Compassion.

Just before we hung up, Amanda and I decided we'd break the news in our virtual team meeting the next day. I'd let them know about my decision, and Amanda could share anything she wanted. We would take time, as a team, to absorb what this loss would mean for all of us.

"Now boarding all passengers to Dallas," a voice came over the intercom.

We looked at each other, neither of us knowing what to say next.

"I'm so sorry," I said. "I love you."

"I love you, too," she said. "Good luck on your speech. And I want you to have fun on your trip this weekend."

She knew that Spiros and I were going on a vacation to celebrate our one-year wedding anniversary because she had planned it for us. Even in the midst of her heartbreak, she was thinking about someone else.

After we hung up, I boarded the plane feeling utterly destroyed. *How do other leaders do this?* I thought mournfully. How could anyone work beside a person for years, getting to know and care about them, and then end it all in a 15-minute phone call?

When I landed, Cheyenne was there to greet me. She had flown to Dallas to support me at my speech. It felt wrong hiding something so enormous from her, but I wanted to honor what Amanda and I had agreed to.

That night, I was restless in my hotel bed, anxious about telling Cheyenne and Rachel the following morning. I knew they would be crushed. They loved Amanda as much as I did. All night, I worried about Amanda and how she might be feeling. I imagined that she was lying awake in her own bed, just like me.

First thing the next morning, I texted Amanda to make sure she was still okay with the plan to tell the team during our meeting. She was. Cheyenne came to my room for the virtual call, and when it began, I shared the news.

Rachel and Cheyenne looked shell-shocked. Beside me, I could feel Cheyenne's deep sadness radiating through the hotel room. Monique looked as upset as I felt, though we'd both known it was coming.

As for Amanda, she exuded nothing but love and strength on that call. Less than a day after being let go, she was comforting her teammates when we should have been comforting her.

I left that meeting and went straight to a stage to speak about leadership, with Cheyenne in the audience. It was one of those days when my job seemed impossible. I felt like I had no business teaching others how to lead. It was even harder knowing that there was someone from my team sitting in the crowd who I'd also hurt with my decision.

Somehow, I pulled myself together and ended up on a stage with a microphone in my hand. I didn't pretend that everything was okay, though. I opened my speech by admitting that I was having one of those days when I was questioning whether I was cut out to be a leader. I didn't share exactly what had happened, but the audience could tell it was something serious from the sadness in my voice. I caught Cheyenne's eyes from across the room, and I felt the ache of the morning all over again.

It was an emotionally tough day for all of us.

On the way back to the airport, I was surprised to see a voice note from Rachel. She reached out because she wanted to make sure I felt good about her performance in her role. Her message showed me how much my decision had shaken everyone.

While Amanda's struggles were no secret, what shocked the team was that I had acted on them in this way. I think they expected, just as I did, that as long as someone remained a good fit for our culture, I would keep them around no matter what. Making the decision to let Amanda go marked the start of a new chapter of my leadership, one where I made tough decisions like these when it was necessary.

I still went on my anniversary trip with Spiros and tried my best to be present with him, but Amanda was never far from my mind. I could see her fingerprints in every detail of the trip she'd planned for us. It went off without a single hiccup, which made me question my decision and contemplate taking it all back.

But by the time I got home, I felt more at peace with my choice. I knew Amanda deserved to use her strengths to the fullest each day, and preventing her from doing that was the opposite of caring for her. Just because it didn't feel good to part ways with her didn't mean it was wrong. The hardest decisions can also be the right ones. That's how it felt when I closed Student Maid, and it was how this felt, too.

As promised, Amanda and I met the following week to plan her exit. We agreed she'd stay on for two months to wrap up her work, which would allow her to say goodbye to our clients and spend a little more time with the team. Monique helped me make a plan to give Amanda six months of severance pay at her full salary. I shared her résumé far and wide, calling clients who led companies where I thought she could use her gifts.

Those final months of working together were some of the best through my eyes, which made everything more painful. I got to see Amanda's character shine even more brightly. She continued to give her best right through the end, and I had to remind myself that letting her go was better and more caring for her than keeping her on the team. Just before she left, we collaborated on a blog post where we wrote about how excruciating it felt to part ways, and yet it somehow felt beautiful, too. We hoped our story might inspire others in similar positions to handle departures with care, no matter which side of the equation they were on. Things only ended well because we chose to act with compassion for each other.

Amanda's last day with our company was in December 2022. Within a year, she started working one-on-one as a job coach for people with disabilities as they entered the workforce—a role that matched her strengths perfectly. I didn't help her get that job, and at first I felt guilty about it. But now I'm proud that she found it on her own. *She* did that. It's no surprise to me that she quickly worked her way up and that her career has only continued to blossom.

I've often thought back to the days with Amanda and what I could have done differently. I recognize now that while I gave her feedback, it often took me a while to share it with her, and when I did, I sugarcoated it. I wasn't clear about how much the issues were affecting me and the business or that the future of her job was at stake because of it.

My lessons from that time changed the way I lead. Today, I'm more direct about expectations, and I commit to the "24-hour guideline," which means bringing up feedback within 24 hours of an issue arising. These practices have made me more consistent and caring in how I communicate, and they've helped build trust because my team knows where they stand with me.

I don't always get it right. There are still times when my instinct is to delay a difficult performance conversation because I don't want to hurt someone. Sometimes I let that instinct win. But in the moments I feel tempted to cushion my feedback or avoid it altogether, remembering my experience with Amanda helps me choose differently. I only wish I could have been that leader for her.

I also know what to look out for now: If I'm doing parts of someone else's role, something has to change. Help them out? Sure. Support them? Absolutely. But if I'm too involved, then that dynamic needs attention.

Years later, while writing this book, Amanda and I reconnected.

I wanted to know how she felt about the way things had ended now that so much time had passed. I was curious about how my leadership in that season affected her, and if she was open to it, I wanted to share my own reflections, too. I also made sure she felt comfortable with me telling our story.

Soon enough, we were FaceTiming again—under entirely different circumstances.

Without knowing it, we had both met with our therapists beforehand to prepare for the conversation. Both of them asked us the same question: What do you hope to get out of this? We knew it wasn't about closure because that might not be possible. Instead, our goal was to share openly and be interested in each other's experiences.

When Amanda appeared on the screen, she looked *happy*. She was beaming and full of joy, and seeing her glow brought me so much peace.

I asked her to share first. She had notes.

Amanda told me that what happened between us left her confused and hurt. She knew that parts of the role weren't working, but she hadn't realized how close she was to losing her job. She could feel distance growing between us, but she hadn't understood why. What made it more painful was that, at that time, we all talked as if we would work together forever. We often said we were "lifers."

Now that I'm writing those words, I can't believe I ever promoted that idea in our culture, but I know where it came from. After years of hiring people, I felt like I'd found my dream team. I didn't want them to go anywhere, and the feeling was mutual: The team would often talk about wanting to stay in it with me for the long haul because they loved our culture and mission. I didn't think there was any harm in encouraging that mindset, but now I understand that as the owner, I need to have the freedom to make the best decisions for the business. And it's important that the people who work with me feel free to grow, change, and choose whatever is best for them, even if that path leads them elsewhere.

Amanda told me that when I called her from the airport that day, she had wanted to resist and ask me to make a different choice. The reason she didn't, she said, was that she loved me. She knew it was already hard for me to decide to let her go, and she didn't want to make things any harder. Once again, I was in awe of her compassion.

When it was my turn, I told her everything I've shared with you: the reasoning behind my decision, how I wish I'd been clearer sooner, the conversations with Monique and Jamil about her role, and the events that led to me calling her that day. She listened to all of it with an open heart.

Near the end of our call, we talked about grief. She said losing her job brought her through its many stages. I told her that I had grieved, too. I *still* miss working with her. I miss her presence, her friendship, and her support. Talking to her again brought all of it rushing back.

Before we hung up, we talked about how two things can be true at once:

You can love someone and still feel hurt by their choices.

A decision can be painful and still be right.

You can be grateful for the life you have now and still grieve the one you used to have.

Amanda and I are both happy. We are both thriving. And we both wish parts of our story had gone differently.

That, to me, is what it means to be human. Sometimes growth isn't closure. Sometimes it's having the courage to sit together in your complex feelings, stay open, and choose compassion even when there is pain.

I will always miss Amanda. I will always be rooting for her. And I will always be humbled by her tremendous courage in allowing me to share our story with you.

Chapter 40

Heart Monitor

I think I'm having a heart attack.

It was a Monday afternoon in June 2023, right before a full week of speeches and travel. I'd scheduled a massage in an attempt to squeeze in some self-care, but shortly before I was due to leave for my appointment, I suddenly felt my chest tighten. Sweat prickled across my skin, and I couldn't catch my breath.

What is happening to me?

Freaked out, I called the spa to cancel my massage, my heart pounding so loudly I could barely hear the person on the other end of the line. The world around me seemed to slow, and I felt dizzy.

This wasn't the first time I'd experienced concerning symptoms like these. Over the previous several weeks, my heart had started racing at strange times, but it had always settled down quickly, so I hadn't thought much of it. This felt scarier—and it wasn't going away.

I headed for the stairs to my bedroom, thinking I should lie down. I gripped the handrail and pulled myself up one stair at a time, stopping halfway because I thought I might pass out. When I finally reached my room, I went straight past the bed and into the bathroom where I stood over the toilet and gagged, certain I was about to throw up.

Something was very wrong.

I called Spiros, who was in another state at the time.

"I think you should go to the ER," he said, his always-calm voice noticeably less calm.

A few minutes later, I was in an Uber, convinced I was dying. The five-minute ride felt like hours. I watched traffic crawl by and thought about how the people in the cars next to me had no idea that someone's life was ending mere feet from them.

As I walked up to the reception desk, my pulse continued to hammer in my neck. I pulled out my license and insurance card with shaky hands, and someone took my vitals. My blood pressure was higher than it had ever been.

I waited to be called back and kept my eyes on the clock on the wall. Aside from my terrifying symptoms, there was just one thing on my mind: work.

The next day, I was scheduled to give three virtual speeches, the first of which started at 3 a.m. for a team overseas. The day after that, I was delivering an in-person workshop a few hours away from home. Cheyenne would be flying in soon from Gainesville to meet me; she was planning to go with me to the event and then stay with me for the week. It was her six-year work anniversary, and we thought it would be fun to take a road trip, eat great meals, and make memories together between my speaking events.

So, while I sat in the waiting room wondering if I was dying, I was also hoping I'd be discharged in time to keep my schedule.

After a while, they called me back to triage and brought me to a room where they ran EKGs and did chest X-rays. Nurses moved in and out, and I lay there staring at the fluorescent lights, trying my best to breathe normally.

I'd texted Cheyenne to fill her in, and she met me at the ER as soon as she landed, just in time for the doctor to tell me I could go home. Things looked okay for the most part, he said, except for a slight abnormality on the EKG. He recommended I follow up with a cardiologist within the next few days.

I felt overwhelming relief. For the fact that it seemed like I wasn't dying after all, yes. But also because I didn't have to cancel anything work-related.

That night, I didn't sleep a wink. My symptoms came in waves. Anytime I started to drift off, my racing heart would jolt me awake again. Still, I got up to give my 3 a.m. speech, powered through it, and somehow managed to deliver two other virtual keynotes that day. Before each one, I sent my clients a text and warned them that I was having some breathing issues. To ease their worries—and mine—I told them it was probably just my asthma flaring up. (It was the only thing I could think of, even though I hadn't had any trouble with it in years.)

Cheyenne and I were supposed to leave on our road trip for my in-person workshop the following day, but I worried I might not be able to pull it off. My heart was still beating out of my chest, and I didn't feel like myself. Having breathing issues while giving a speech from my home office was one thing, but standing in front of strangers while feeling like I might collapse was another.

I wrestled with canceling for hours.

I had never canceled an event because I was sick. Not *once* in all my years of speaking. There had been times I probably should have, like when I had a stomach virus and had to run offstage to throw up the second I finished my keynote. The only time I'd ever missed a speech was because of circumstances completely beyond my control: A snowstorm had grounded every flight, and there was no other way for me to get to the venue. But even canceled flights didn't usually stop me. More than a few times, I'd found car services willing to drive me through the night, sometimes arriving 30 minutes before I was supposed to walk onstage.

Canceling felt unthinkable. My clients spent months planning every detail of these events, and I couldn't fathom being the person who threw a wrench in their plans. What would they do if their speaker didn't show up?

With my symptoms showing no signs of improvement, though, Cheyenne encouraged me to do what was best for my health. Together, we decided that I would call the client, explain the situation, and explore our options.

"I can definitely still come," I assured my client. "I don't want to leave you hanging. If you can put a stool at the front of the room, I can sit down when I need to and facilitate the workshop from there."

At first, there was silence on the other end of the line. Then my client said, with concern and care in his voice, "Why don't we just reschedule? We can find another time to do the event. Your health is the most important thing."

I took the first deep breath I'd taken in days.

I can't believe that *my client* had more compassion for my well-being than I did that day. (Or that Cheyenne had to witness him caring more for me than I was willing to care for myself.) But that's how it went down.

Instead of going to the event, Cheyenne went with me to see a cardiologist. (An anniversary celebration she'll never forget, that's for sure.) By this time, Spiros was there, too, and he and Cheyenne stayed by my side as the doctor ran several tests and did an ultrasound of my heart. In the end, the doctor couldn't find a cause for my symptoms, so he asked me to wear a heart monitor for two weeks. Every time I had an episode, I was supposed to tap the button stuck to my chest and make note of what I was doing.

Within those two weeks, I tapped it more than a *hundred* times.

It was always the same: My heart would race, and I'd feel sweaty, dizzy, panicked, and short of breath. There seemed to be no connection between what I was doing when the symptoms came on. I could be walking, sitting still, inside, outside, in a car, on a plane. I could never predict when an episode would strike.

They followed me into my speeches, too.

I had a couple of in-person events during that stretch that I did anyway. One was my biggest event of the year with close to a thousand people in the audience. I knew my heart monitor might be visible through my shirt, and saying nothing about it felt inauthentic. So when I got onstage, I talked openly about the fear and uncertainty of the situation and tied it into my message that day. Oddly enough, telling the truth calmed me down, and the speech went great.

During this time, I even spoke at my cardiologist's own hospital on the topic of well-being (I couldn't make this up if I tried). I joked to the audience of women physicians that just a few days before, I'd been sent home with a heart monitor from that same hospital.

When I finally got my results back from the heart monitor, they indicated that everything was normal, which was just as comforting as it was maddening. I started to think that this might be my new reality, and I couldn't imagine dealing with these symptoms for the rest of my life. Every attack left me feeling scared and helpless. I was trapped inside a body I could no longer control.

My primary doctor prescribed anti-anxiety medication for me to have on hand in case things got really bad. I appreciated having that as an option, especially because I was about to go on a two-week vacation with my family to Greece. I'd never been before and had been looking forward to it for months. Spiros had lived there for a few years growing up and still has family in the area, so it was extra meaningful for me to go there with him. But instead of enjoying it, I spent a lot of the trip feeling miserable in hotel rooms, recovering from episode after episode.

Everyone was worried about me: my family, my friends, my team. Spiros even called my parents to express his concern. I remember breaking down one night in his arms. We'd gone out to dinner, and my symptoms had popped up while we were sitting at the table, so we abruptly left. On the way home, in between sobs, I dramatically gave him permission to marry someone else if this was how things were going to be from now on.

The doctors scheduled another follow-up, and in the meantime, I became desperate for answers. I Googled late into the night, trying to diagnose myself. I got acupuncture and massages. I visited energy healers. I replayed every episode and tried to find the common thread. No matter what I did, I couldn't figure it out.

Until one night, I made a connection I hadn't before.

The racing heart.

The sweat.

The terror.

It all felt familiar.

It felt like that one time, in Mexico. . .

Chapter 41

Enlightenment

Three months before my ER visit, I'd flown to Mexico for a week of relaxing and healing.

I'd been traveling constantly, living out of two 70-pound suitcases, juggling dozens of speaking events a month, leading a team, sitting in nonstop meetings, and serving as the primary driver of revenue for my business. I felt grateful for the success and exhausted by the pace.

I was making time for self-care: Peppered in between meetings and events on my calendar were plenty of spa appointments and massages. But what I craved now was something even more rejuvenating. I needed a true getaway. I wanted to spend time in a place where no one needed anything from me. I wanted to disconnect from the world, spend time in nature, and talk to no one but myself.

I had just the place in mind.

I'd heard about a retreat in a remote part of coastal Mexico from a few author friends of mine, and when I looked into it, I saw salvation. It promised a private casita by the ocean, no alarm clocks, and fresh meals and juices prepared daily. There were mountains nearby so I could alternate between long hikes and walks on the beach, and a cactus garden that looked like the perfect spot to take a nap on a lounge chair or read a book. It was just the place my soul needed.

I booked it immediately.

What appealed to me most was how intimate it was. There were only two casitas on the property, and the owner told me I'd be the only one staying there that week besides her. I was so grateful that I wouldn't have to meet anyone new or be "on." I could just come exactly as I was: exhausted.

Before I arrived, the owner emailed me a menu of optional add-ons for my visit. I could go snorkeling and hiking, take a private yoga class, and even get facials and daily massages. At the bottom of the list was something called a "Bufo medicine ceremony." Out of all the choices, she encouraged me to seriously consider the ceremony and to bring cash for the "medicine" just in case. She told me it was wildly popular with her guests and that many claimed it was the highlight of their stay.

I'd never heard of "Bufo" before. Next thing I knew, I was hours deep into an internet-search rabbit hole.

I learned that it's a substance made from the venom of the Sonoran Desert toad. When smoked, the venom contains a powerful compound that can create an intense, short-lived psychedelic experience people often describe as an ego death, spiritual enlightenment, or out-of-body experience. I watched videos online of people sobbing, screaming, laughing, and collapsing onto their backs after smoking it. I listened to podcasts where people claimed it changed their life. I learned that CEOs and executives were flying to places where they could do Bufo, and then returning home feeling more grounded and self-aware, as well as less stressed out and anxious.

I found it all fascinating. I also felt certain I would not be participating. I still enjoyed an occasional glass of nice wine, but altering my consciousness with frog poison? Not really my thing.

When I arrived at the retreat, it measured up to all of my expectations—and then some. The property was breathtaking and completely tucked away from the world. I sank into soft linens and slept without any sense of time. I ate fresh fruit that was replenished on the counter of my casita each day, and I read books with the doors open to welcome the ocean breeze. I felt more relaxed than I had in months. My biggest activity each day was a long walk. The whole week was a lesson in slowing down.

After a few days, the retreat owner brought up the Bufo ceremony again.

"There's no pressure," she said. "But I believe it could be meaningful for you." She reminded me that most guests did it, including people I knew.

I gave it some more thought. I had come to this retreat to let go and do something for myself. It was the first time I had ever taken a solo trip like this, and I already felt brave for being at a retreat in another country where I knew no one. Maybe Bufo was *exactly* the thing I needed. I felt an urge to loosen my grip on the version of me who was always careful, controlled, and high-functioning. I wanted to do something *wild*.

I called Spiros to ask if he thought I was nuts, and he encouraged me to do what I wanted. I figured I only live once, so I said yes.

The next day, a shaman arrived. (Words I never thought I'd write.) Before we got started, he walked me through the ceremony and told me that the medicine would show me what was in my heart. He said my only job was to surrender to it. He encouraged me not to resist the experience and instead to let go and trust the process. I was still nervous, but his gentle and calming energy convinced me to take a leap of faith.

While he set things up, I went back to my casita to change into a dress (because why not?) and give myself a pep talk in the mirror. I couldn't *believe* I was actually doing this.

I met my shaman outside, and when he saw that I was wearing a black dress, he was horrified. (Apparently wearing black isn't recommended in plant-medicine ceremonies because it is thought to attract "dark" or "heavy" energy.) He waited while I changed into a yellow one, and this time, when I walked out of my casita, he smiled. I followed him to a beautiful, covered space surrounded by bright pink flowers and string lights that overlooked the ocean. He directed me to meet him in the center of it. Beyond the roof's edge, I could see the moody sky and deep orange clouds lit by the setting sun. The air was warm, and I was growing increasingly anxious. My heart was already racing, and I hadn't even touched Bufo yet.

The shaman prepared a pipe and instructed me to inhale as he held it up to my lips. I took a hit and immediately started coughing as acrid smoke hit the back of my throat. I still remember the taste; it was equal parts harsh, bitter, and earthy.

Within seconds, I was gone. I vaguely remember the shaman helping me lie back on the ground before everything around me dissolved. It felt as if my body disappeared while my awareness remained. I was nowhere and everywhere. Someone and no one. Bright white lights were all I could see. I recall laughing and feeling an overwhelming sense of peace. I wiggled my fingers and toes and found it hilarious that I still had them.

And then I felt terror.

My heart pounded violently. Something started to rise in me, like it was trying to get out—it felt like rage, maybe, or some other painful, long-buried emotion. I wanted to scream at the top of my lungs. I wanted to sob. I wanted to let out whatever was trapped inside.

But I remember feeling like I shouldn't. I told myself to stay composed and pleasant and forced myself to smile, fighting for control while ignoring the thing inside me begging to be released. (Even while I was in another dimension, I was *still* trying to keep people happy.)

Then I slowly came back to my body.

I felt the retreat owner's dog licking my face and heard the shaman playing a wooden flute. When I opened my eyes, he told me I had been gone maybe 15 minutes, but to me it felt like centuries.

I sat up cautiously, stunned and grateful to be alive. Everything around me looked brighter and more beautiful than I'd remembered. I was so relieved to be back on Earth.

After witnessing my experience, the shaman smiled and said, "However you are living your life, keep living it. You are at peace."

I wanted to believe him. But I also wondered why peace had felt so much like panic. Still, I accepted his blessing and moved on. I was proud of myself for stepping so far outside my comfort zone.

The rest of the week was soul-stirring. Now that I'd done Bufo, I felt a new level of courage. I went snorkeling in the ocean and swam in caves—two things I would have normally avoided out of fear. I spent each day journaling, often about the Bufo experience and everything I thought it meant. I took a photo of myself on the last day of the retreat and compared it to the one I'd taken when I arrived, and I looked like a different person. My eyes were smiling. I had never seen myself look so restored.

I promised I would hold on to this version of me when I got back to the busy pace of work, and that I would protect this feeling of rejuvenation. But right after I left Mexico, I flew straight into 17 more nights away from home.

I landed back in the US close to midnight and slept only a few hours before a full week of in-person meetings with my team. From there I flew to another city for a keynote. Then another. Then more virtual events stacked between travel days. My schedule was relentless. The steady stream of work felt more like a firehose, and it was all I could do to keep up. Whatever renewal had happened in Mexico faded almost immediately. I forgot all about the retreat until a couple of months later, when my heart began randomly racing. Then came the ER visit, the heart monitor, and episode after episode.

The night I finally connected the dots, I researched trauma responses to psychedelic trips. I'd scoured every book, article, and Reddit thread I could find on the topic before I found an answer that seemed to fit: I likely had PTSD from doing Bufo.

I hadn't considered the experience to be traumatic, but the body stores experiences differently than the mind. It remembers how it feels to be scared and helpless. It knows when we cross our own limits while pretending we're fine.

Mine had remembered everything:

- The bright, white lights I saw in my ceremony
- The heat as I sat under the pavilion
- The spike in my heart rate
- The feeling of being trapped

Stages were lit with bright lights. Speaking spiked my adrenaline. Airports with their crowds and noise were overstimulating. And my packed calendar left me with no room to breathe. My life had become a giant trigger loop, and I was having panic attacks everywhere I went.

I'd flown to Mexico for rest and self-care and come back with PTSD.

I later learned that because they're so intense, Bufo ceremonies are supposed to include a full integration and grounding process after the fact. It's recommended to talk through the experience with a therapist or guide, journal about it, and make intentional life changes based on what you learn. The shaman had hinted at that, but because it was my first time doing Bufo—or any psychedelic, for that matter—I didn't really know what he meant. I had journaled, and that was about it.

My Bufo experience held up a mirror to the life I was living. The real issue wasn't what happened in those 15 minutes when I was in another realm; it was the schedule I returned to afterward.

At the time, I was doing more than 200 speaking engagements a year. I was taking multiple flights a week for in-person events, and sometimes multiple in a day. When I wasn't traveling, I was glued to my desk for meetings and virtual speeches. I think Bufo was trying to show me what my heart already knew: If I didn't slow down and take care of myself, I was headed straight for a breakdown. And because I had been ignoring those signs, I had one. Isn't that how it goes? If you don't listen to your body, your body will eventually force you to listen.

Or maybe Bufo wasn't trying to show me anything at all. Maybe I simply had panic attacks after an intense psychedelic experience I wasn't prepared for.

Either way, it landed me in the ER. And if I didn't have my health, then what did I have?

My whole business depended on my ability to keep going. My team knew that, and it scared them. They had just watched me go from healthy and unstoppable to sitting in hospitals with a heart monitor stuck to my chest and dealing with debilitating panic attacks. One of them even asked if I had life insurance through the business.

Morbid? Yeah.

Fair? Absolutely.

Because if something happened to me, what would happen to our company?

Chapter 42

Break Week

How did I get here?

That was the question I couldn't stop asking myself in the middle of my Bufo breakdown. It was confusing because, in many ways, I thought I'd grown in my ability to take care of myself. My life was nothing like it used to be.

In the earliest days of Student Maid, I took pride in running myself into the ground. I saw it as a badge of honor and idolized the entrepreneurs who pulled all-nighters and slept in their offices. I worked most nights, nearly every weekend, and rarely took vacations.

At first, working at that pace felt exciting. I was building something from scratch, and seeing it grow and become successful made it all feel worth it. But eventually, I came to resent it.

I was never *not* working. I was always the friend who couldn't go on the trip, and if I did go, I brought my work with me. My heart still breaks when I think about the time my dad drove two hours to be my guest at a formal gala. I still hadn't finished making the cleaning schedule for the following week, so he sat in my office in his tuxedo while I spent hours in front of my computer. We made it to the gala just before it ended.

The way I worked in those days became the culture of our company. No one unplugged because I didn't unplug. The leadership team rarely took more than a few days off, and if they did, no one was ever far from their phones or laptops just in case something came up. During our busiest apartment-cleaning seasons, 16-hour days weren't uncommon for us.

Our first noticeable shift away from hustle culture came in 2019, when I took the leadership team on a retreat to Riviera Maya in Mexico. (Remember the one where I wanted to rent a yacht and Monique helped me keep it on budget? That one.) We were in a grueling season of the business. Student Maid's numbers were far behind where we needed them to be, and the debt haunted us. I was trying to keep the gaps covered with speaking fees, and we were working as hard as we could to grow revenue.

Shortly before the retreat, I read a book called *Dying for a Paycheck* by Jeffrey Pfeffer. It explores the connection between work stress and health, and one statistic in it stopped me cold: Heart attacks are more common on Mondays, especially among working people.

I could already see the toll that stress was taking on me. At this point in 2019, I had been neglecting my health for a long time. I'd stopped exercising, I was drinking wine to escape, and I wasn't prioritizing my sleep or nutrition. A huge part of that came from how unhappy I was in my life because of Student Maid, but it was also because I was constantly working. If stress was affecting me, I wondered what it might be doing to my team. I asked everyone to read the book before our trip so that we could discuss it over dinner one night during our retreat.

Our conversation didn't move the needle much, but it was still important because it was the first time we ever talked about our culture through the lens of health. We spoke openly about the impact of leading a business that operated seven days a week and how we felt like we could never disconnect.

Though nothing changed overnight in our culture, something changed in me.

Not long after that is when I started to get serious about exercise, hired my nutritionist, and fell in love with running. I stopped taking meetings first thing in the morning so that I could begin my day by pouring into my own cup with a workout. I was vocal about protecting that time for myself and encouraged my team to do the same. I hoped that seeing me do it would give them permission to put themselves first every day, too.

I also began reading more books about health and well-being. That's how I found another book that would mark a more meaningful turning point in our culture: *It Doesn't Have to Be Crazy at Work* by Jason Fried and David Heinemeier Hansson. I read it toward the end of 2020, when work felt absolutely crazy. The speaking business had exploded with virtual events, and back then we still believed that Katie was taking over Student Maid, so we were working double-time to get the company back on solid footing.

It Doesn't Have to Be Crazy at Work is about building a "calm" company, which is an organization that respects boundaries, holds people accountable to taking time off to unplug and recharge, and chooses sustainable growth over the endless pursuit of more. As I read the book, I felt a pit in my stomach. I had just set a revenue goal for that quarter that was 43% higher than the previous one. Amazingly, we were on track to hit it, but I started to think about the human cost of that goal.

How could I build a calm company while asking everyone to push that hard? How much stress would it add for us? How many late nights and weekends would it require? How much presence would it steal from our families? And if we hit 43% growth, what would our next goal look like? I realized that even if we landed exactly where we had the previous quarter, we would still have strong results. I didn't need 43% growth to feel like we were doing well.

I asked my leadership team to read *It Doesn't Have to Be Crazy at Work*, and it struck a nerve with them, too. Growth was the first topic to come up when we talked about it as a group.

The team felt the same way about our goals as I now did. They said the company felt like the opposite of calm. In that conversation, we decided to do something I never thought I'd be okay with as a business owner: We lowered our revenue goal. We chose a number that was still ambitious but not nearly as far out of reach. As soon as we did, we each took the biggest sigh of relief. (We ended up surpassing that lower goal, but getting there didn't feel nearly as stressful.)

We discussed several other eye-opening topics from the book. One was the danger of calling your work team a "family." We did that all the time, and only with the best intentions. But the book helped us see how it can blur the line between work and home, leaving people conflicted about which one should come first. (And also, not everyone has happy thoughts when they think about family.) You've likely noticed that my team and I say that we "love" each other, and that's because it feels right to us: We do love and care for each other. But after that discussion, we stopped calling ourselves a family—because we're not.

The biggest thing we talked about was taking time off. We'd had an unlimited paid time-off policy for years, but we acknowledged that because we were a small leadership team, many of us felt guilty about using it. We didn't want to burden others with more work in our absence. For me, that feeling was magnified because when I took time off from speaking, it slowed down our revenue. But if I wanted our company to have a calm culture, it needed to start with me. Taking time off was the area I had been neglecting most, and I realized that if I wasn't doing it, my team wouldn't feel like they could, either.

The one time I usually did take off was at the end of the year when things naturally slowed down in the business. I normally took two weeks, but the year before that one, I'd added a third week for myself. I decided to do it again and encouraged my team to take three weeks off, too.

Little did I know that my break at the end of 2020 would come right after Monique confronted me about closing Student Maid, so it wasn't exactly restorative. I spent it wrestling with one of the hardest decisions of my life. But still, I took it, proving to myself and my team that my longer breaks were becoming a regular thing.

After I came back, I decided to make another bold move: I blocked two separate weeks on my calendar later in 2021 to take off completely. These weren't during our slow season; they were during prime time. I told my team that I was going to protect them at all costs and planned not to work at all, though I think they had their doubts about whether I'd actually follow through.

I kept my promise. During one of the weeks, I had a staycation at home. During the other, I took a trip to see the venue in Mexico where Spiros and I were going to get married. I used it to relax and do a little wedding planning. Both times, I noticed that I came back invigorated, inspired, and a lot calmer—and my team noticed, too.

Toward the end of my second break, I had an idea. I loved what those weeks off were doing for me. They were helping me become a healthier, less-stressed version of myself. What would happen if I gave the leadership team the same opportunity?

That's what prompted me to introduce a company-wide "Break Week." I decided that I'd close the company to allow the whole team to take off an entire week simultaneously. That way, it wouldn't be optional.

We tried one Break Week as an experiment that summer, which was much easier to do without Student Maid in the picture. We informed our clients well in advance, blocked off the calendar from speeches, and turned on our autoresponders when the week arrived.

When we returned, it was unanimous: Break Week was a smashing success.

With the business closed, no one had the guilt of adding extra work to anyone else's plate, and no one felt like they were falling behind. Taking the break together is what allowed us to truly disconnect in a way we hadn't before. After that, I decided to make Break Week a regular thing. I committed to closing the company for six weeks throughout the year: one week at the end of each of the first three quarters, plus three weeks at the end of the last one. I realized that simply offering unlimited paid time off wouldn't guarantee that anyone would actually use it, but this way I could be certain that each person was taking at least six weeks off annually.

I had fears about implementing Break Weeks. I worried that clients might be turned off by it and that the revenue we'd lose would seriously impact the business. But none of that happened. Our clients supported the idea, and many shared that they wanted to implement versions of Break Week within their own organizations. We did have to turn down speaking events, but we made up for that revenue in other quarters, and when we couldn't, the small dip felt like a reasonable tradeoff.

We had our first Break Week in the summer of 2021, and now here I was in 2023, in the middle of my Bufo breakdown. Break Weeks were still going strong. In fact, I had used one to take the retreat in Mexico.

Can you see why I was confused?

I had come a long way from hustle culture. I was taking restorative time off, and I was prioritizing self-care. I thought I was doing everything right. But everyone around me could see that I was still running myself into the ground.

I had an incredible dilemma ahead: Our entire business was built around my speaking work. If I didn't give a speech, we didn't earn revenue, and no one got paid. But if I didn't take better care of myself physically, emotionally, and mentally, none of it would matter because we wouldn't have a business at all. And I didn't know how much longer I could give speeches while having rolling panic attacks onstage.

I think I know what was trapped inside of me during my Bufo ceremony: a voice trying to get my attention, telling me that you can't out-spa, out-massage, or out-vacation a life that is exhausting you.

No amount of self-care can compensate for self-abandonment.

Chapter 43

Mad, Sad, Scared, or Glad

No matter what I tried, the episodes wouldn't stop.

I ordered stacks of books on PTSD and panic attacks. I listened to guided meditations. I even met with a plant-medicine specialist who suggested I do Bufo again to "neutralize" the experience. (Yeah, *right.*)

Feeling helpless, I started looking for a local therapist who treated people with PTSD. After scrolling through dozens of bios and lists of credentials, I chose a woman (also named Kristen) who offered a therapy called EMDR (Eye Movement Desensitization and Reprocessing).

Each virtual session began with me closing my eyes and thinking back to the moment when I was lying on the ground after inhaling Bufo, panicking and feeling like something was trapped in my chest. From there, I would let my mind drift as alternating tones played through my headphones. EMDR works by stimulating either side of the brain with sounds, taps, or eye movement to help it process memories that feel stuck. The goal is to get to a place where you can recall the traumatic memory without reliving the intense emotions associated with it.

Every so often, my therapist would pause the sounds and interrupt to ask where I was in my mind. I'd tell her I was remembering the sweat on my skin, the hard ground beneath me, or something totally disconnected that the experience made me think of. At times, I'd cry out of nowhere. I had forgotten what it was like to let myself feel that much.

After a few months, the memory stopped affecting me so strongly. The panic attacks that had once ruled my life became less frequent, and I reached a point where I felt neutral about the Bufo experience. I was so grateful to close that terrifying chapter.

But I didn't want to stop seeing my therapist. She was exceptional at what she did, so I asked if we could keep meeting. I wanted to do walk-and-talk sessions on the phone once or twice a month, which was my dream format for therapy. I loved being able to stroll down the tree-lined boulevards of my neighborhood while I talked with her.

I didn't realize it then, but my therapist had become my new Jamil.

By this point, my sessions with Jamil had become less frequent. He had seen me through some of the hardest and most formative seasons of my life and career, and I know our paths crossed for a reason. I may have given him that workshop in Phoenix for free, but I could never repay him for what he gave me in return: the courage to face what I would rather have avoided and to rise up and build the future of my dreams. We stay in touch to this day.

Now I wanted a different kind of guide who could help me turn my focus inward. Though my panic attacks had greatly subsided, I still got them from time to time. I wanted to strengthen my nervous system and feel safer in my body.

Every time my therapist and I talked, I'd start by telling her about something that happened in my day, and she would follow it with the same question:

"Does that make you mad, sad, scared, or glad?"

The first several times she asked, I didn't know how to answer. I was highly skilled at talking about what needed to get done and what problem needed to be solved, and I was great at asking other people how *they* felt. But identify my own feelings? I didn't even know where to start. How could I be this accomplished, capable, and responsible and still feel so disconnected from myself?

I decided to start journaling more with the hope that it would help me hear my own voice.

Usually, I found myself staring at a blank page, unsure of what to say. So I'd just start with that: "It's Tuesday and I don't know what to write." After a little while, the words would start coming. I was often surprised by what I wrote when I allowed my thoughts to flow freely without judgment. I'd write that I felt crushed by my workload, that I was exhausted, and that I wished I had the courage to say "no" more. I wrote that I wanted to travel less for work, but I feared how it would affect revenue. I often described conflicting emotions, like being frustrated by and resentful of the business and how much energy it required of me, while also having gratitude for my team's support and the impact I got to make on people every day. I wrote about my dreams for a slower pace, more time with my loved ones, and more time with me. I would remind myself that I could make my life anything I wanted it to be. I didn't *do* anything with what I'd written down. I didn't try to fix any of it. I just focused on being more in touch with my feelings, which felt like huge progress.

My therapist taught me a way to make my journaling even more impactful. One time on a call, I told her I was anxious about a melanoma scare. Skin cancer runs in my family, and because I grew up on a beach in Florida, I get my skin checked religiously. My dermatologist had been monitoring one spot in particular and had already biopsied it a couple of times, but it kept coming back. To be safe, she wanted to biopsy it again and go a few layers deeper, which would leave me with several stitches and a decent chance I'd find out I had cancer.

Waiting for the results was excruciating. It took several days, and I was drowning in worry the whole time. To help, my therapist suggested that I journal about my fear—but use my nondominant hand. She warned me that it would probably feel impossibly frustrating, and that was the point: Being angry would activate my emotions and help me feel their intensity more fully. She told me that the more I felt my feelings, the quicker I'd be able to move through them.

Sure enough, as I was attempting to write with my left hand, I became so frustrated that I started crying. I even screamed into a pillow. I remember yelling louder and louder, being amazed at what it felt like to give myself permission to feel such rage. By the time I was done, it felt like 50 pounds had been lifted off my chest. I was still anxious and worried, but right next to those emotions was a feeling of peace. No matter what the results were, I told myself, I'd figure it out.

Everything came back normal, which was a relief, but that journaling experience left a mark on me. I had always viewed emotions like anger, sadness, fear, and frustration as "dark" feelings that I should try to either smother or transform into positive ones. Instead, my therapist was teaching me that the healthiest thing I could do was invite them to come to the surface.

Many of my journal entries from around that time became topics for my therapy calls. Stress was a theme on nearly every page. I knew I needed to take a hard look at everything in my life that was keeping my nervous system on high alert.

My calendar was the most obvious place to begin.

At the time, I hardly had a break in the day for lunch or to go to the bathroom. Every minute was accounted for from morning until night. If my time wasn't taken up with work, it was self-care appointments or rare moments with Spiros and my family. As an entrepreneur, I had learned how to squeeze the juice out of every second.

First, my therapist and I explored my so-called self-care appointments. I told her about the massages I had to race across town to make and the hair blowouts and facials I sandwiched between meetings. We discussed the early morning workout classes that left me with little time to shower, make breakfast, and get ready for the day.

"If self-care is stressful, it's not self-care," my therapist wisely told me. She said that sometimes, the most caring thing I could do for myself was cancel an appointment.

So I tried it. I had an evening pedicure scheduled after a long day of meetings, but the thought of getting in my car and driving over there was exhausting. All I wanted to do was lie on my couch and watch a true-crime documentary. (Anyone else?) I debated with myself for a few minutes before finally calling to cancel. As soon as I hung up, I melted into the couch with relief.

My therapist helped me see that I'd created all of these "rules" for myself in the name of self-care that were actually keeping me in fight-or-flight.

One of the biggest ones was about morning workouts. No matter where I was traveling, how early it was, or how little sleep I'd gotten the night before, I told myself I *had* to work out first thing. The only exception was if I was deathly ill.

My therapist encouraged me to think about breaking that rule when I was pressed for time or it felt out of sync with what I needed. Instead of getting out of bed at the sound of my alarm, I started asking myself, "Is a workout the best way to serve my body this morning?" Most of the time, the answer was yes. But if I hadn't had a restful night or was starting to feel run down, I slept in. If there was a busy morning ahead of me and working out would cause me to feel rushed, I skipped it. I noticed that every time I chose to do the thing that felt more caring, I had a better day. I had always feared that if I broke that rule even once, breaking it would become a habit, and then I'd stop working out altogether. But if anything, it left me more motivated to get back on the horse the next morning. I proved that I could trust myself.

That realization also changed how I thought about rest in general. I used to bargain with myself all day long: If I could just finish *one* more thing—answer a text message, check something off my list, straighten up the house—*then* I could relax. Rest was something I believed I had to earn.

Breaking my rules meant sitting and reading a book when there were dishes in the sink. Or letting errands wait until the next day when I wanted to disconnect and spend the evening with Spiros instead. I was learning that rest wasn't a reward for productivity; it was something I was allowed to need and deserved to have. As my therapist often reminded me, "You are worthy even when you are doing absolutely nothing."

My definition of self-care had totally changed. Now I saw it as feeling safe in my body and in tune with what I needed most.

The more in sync I felt with myself, the less frequent my now-rare panic attacks became. When one started, instead of resisting, I'd welcome it. I'd decided to give my panic attacks a name: Polly.

Hey Polly, I'd think. *Thanks for being here. I know you're trying to protect me. I'm okay. You can stay here as long as you need to.*

The more I talked to Polly and embraced her, the less often she seemed to need to appear.

Bit by bit, I was moving closer to the kind of life I'd written about wanting in my journal. I wanted more stillness, more margin, more time with myself, and more room to feel like a human instead of a machine that constantly performed and produced.

But arriving there meant focusing on the one part of my life I hadn't touched yet.

The biggest part: my work.

Chapter 44

What Would You Tell a Friend?

One theme kept coming up in my journaling: I wanted to spend more time at home. After my Bufo breakdown I'd reduced my in-person speaking a little, but I was still living out of suitcases.

In one of our calls, I told my therapist I wanted to take on fewer in-person events.

"Does wanting that make you feel mad, sad, scared, or glad?" she asked, as always.

"Scared," I said. There was no question about my feelings there.

Fewer speaking events would mean less revenue, I told her, which would also mean less earning potential for the team. I wasn't worried about how that decision would affect me—I was worried about how it would affect *them*.

My therapist then asked a question that has become one of my favorites. "What would you tell a friend who was in your position?"

The answer came easily. "I'd tell her that if she keeps running herself into the ground, eventually there won't be a business anyway."

"I like that," she said. "Anything else?"

"I'd also tell her that her health is more important than revenue and not to think twice about it."

"Well, then," she said. "I think you just found your answer."

Like I used to do with Jamil, I resisted.

"But I can't just take on less," I said. "It will affect my team's livelihood. That feels so selfish."

"Think about it this way," she said. "By being honest about what *you* need, you're empowering them to consider what *they* need."

I looked up at the gnarled oak tree branches reaching for each other from either side of the street as I walked. "What do you mean?"

"You're giving them reality," she said. "And then they get to decide what they want to do about it. If someone needs more income, they can tell you. If someone decides this no longer works for them, they are capable of getting another job. You don't have to manage everyone's life for them."

It was my limiting belief showing up to make sure no one felt the negative impact of my decisions. My therapist was reminding me that protecting my team from discomfort wasn't my job. My job was to trust that they could meet their own needs.

"If anyone on the team was in your position, they would likely choose themselves, too," she said. "And that wouldn't make them bad people, right? *Everyone* is selfish. That's not a bad word. We all want to do what is necessary to protect and take care of ourselves. It's our human instinct."

I frantically typed her words into the notes app on my phone so I would always remember them.

"Can you think of a time when the team chose what was best for them?" she asked.

I had the perfect example. A few quarters back we had missed a revenue goal because I took a break when my panic attacks were at their worst. That meant we didn't unlock bonuses, so I gave everyone a choice: We could either take the team retreat we had budgeted for, or we could skip it and I'd redistribute the money as bonuses to them instead. They voted for the bonuses.

I loved that they did. They chose what they needed and wanted most without apology.

"Why wouldn't they want you to do the same?" she asked.

It made me think about how easily I gave others permission to choose what was best for them and how hard it was for me to extend that permission to myself. But even though I'd seen my team prioritize themselves before, I was still worried about how they might react when I told them I wanted to cut back on my speaking. I decided to run it by Monique first.

"I have something I want to talk to you about that came up in my therapy call," I warned her in a voice note. Voice messages had become our favorite way to communicate. With me traveling so much, it allowed us to stay connected and respond at the time that worked best for each of us. We also liked that it gave us space to process our thoughts and feelings while still hearing each other's voices. Sometimes our messages were more like podcasts, reaching up to 30 minutes (which we learned is the app's built-in limit). Other people might cringe at that, but we loved it.

"I want to do fewer in-person events so that I can stay home more and focus on my health, but I'm really worried about what it will do to our revenue and the team," I said.

She almost laughed in her reply.

"That's it?" she said. "I'm so happy that you want to do less. *Finally!*"

Monique had been watching me overwork myself for years, but she knew as well as I did: You can't help someone who doesn't want to help herself.

"What do we do about the revenue issue?" I asked.

"Who cares about the revenue?" she said. "Your health is number one. If you don't stay healthy, we'll have a much bigger problem on our hands."

Still, I couldn't ignore that my doing less would have a negative impact. I wanted a successful business—I just didn't want a company that slowed down every time *I* chose to slow down. Monique and I revisited something we'd talked about casually over the years: building revenue streams that didn't rely on my physical presence, like online courses and other ideas. That was a long-term goal, though. In the short term, we focused on strategically selling more virtual events that I could do from home and being more selective with the in-person ones I said yes to, only committing when I genuinely wanted to do them and when the travel felt manageable.

Making those changes would mean a dip in revenue, at least for a little while, so our next step was discussing it with Cheyenne and Rachel. I wanted to be transparent about how they and the business could be affected.

Just like my therapist suspected, they were relieved to hear that I wanted to take on less. They had been worried about me for years, just like Monique was, and assured me it was okay with them if revenue went down. Because that would primarily affect bonuses, they reminded me they never counted on bonuses as guaranteed income anyway. In quarters without them, they had adjusted fine.

Despite all the open conversations we'd had about money, we had never talked directly about what a slower season would mean financially or how the team actually felt about it. I had made up so many stories in my mind about how everyone would react, and none of them were true.

Here's what I wrote about that team meeting later in my journal: "I shared my truth, and I appreciated how I did it. I put it all out there—my desires, my fears, and the solution. It sparked a meaningful conversation. Better yet, it only took 20 minutes. It feels good." I was learning how freeing it was to share my needs out loud.

For the first time, I felt like I could choose whether I wanted to take on a speaking event without guilt. And while that was liberating, having that much latitude felt unfamiliar. Sometimes I didn't know how to decide. I'd heard people say you should feel in your gut if something is a "heck yes" or a "heck no," but that didn't always work for me. I usually felt torn.

My therapist told me that my favorite question—"What would you tell a friend?"—was one of the best ways to find my authentic answer. She explained that your authentic voice is often what you would use with someone you love. It's gentle, and it never comes from a place of pressure. But fear, ego, and guilt can overpower it. Asking that question helps bring forward the part of you that already knows your answer.

I gave it a try. When a new speaking opportunity came along, I'd start by asking myself, *Should I take this on?* If I didn't feel strongly one way or another, I'd follow up with *What would I tell a friend?* And then I'd respond as if I were talking to someone else I cared about.

I heard things like:

- *That seems like a lot of travel and sounds pretty stressful.* That's a no.

- *That's already a tight week. Another opportunity will come around.* Another no.
- *That sounds fun and the travel looks doable.* A wholehearted yes.

Any time I said no, clients understood. Even more surprising, the event requests kept coming. It was almost as if the more serious I became about holding my boundaries, the more people wanted to work with me. I started getting bigger offers, and many of them were for virtual speeches I could do from home. I still did plenty of in-person events, but because they were all genuine yeses, I found more fulfillment in doing them, and I did a better job.

Soon I became more comfortable making choices that were best for me but that risked disappointing my team.

If you can't tell by now, I love going for walks. I do *not* love sitting at a desk all day feeling cooped up inside. Our weekly team meeting was two hours long and always in the middle of the day. When I would log on, I'd often look out the window and wish I could go for a walk while we met. I never did because I feared the team would think I wasn't taking the meeting seriously.

Eventually, I decided to test that assumption. I told them I'd be calling into our meetings while walking outside and invited them to do the same. Not only did no one mind, but some joined me. After that, it became common for someone to log on while taking a walk of their own. I found that when I followed my desire to walk, I showed up to those meetings more present, more engaged, and happier. The same was true for my team.

Then came a harder test.

I had signed up for a multi-day workshop designed for speakers who wanted to elevate their brands, but the closer it got, the more dread I felt about going because of how much energy it would take. Not only would the workshop keep me away from home for multiple days, but it would also come with a major time-zone change and several long flights. The problem was that Cheyenne had already arranged all the travel for it, and it had been complicated, to say the least. We'd changed the flights more than once. If I backed out now, it would create even more work for her and make me feel like a terrible diva of a boss.

I brought it to therapy.

In response, my therapist told me about the *Bill of Assertive Rights*, which includes "You have the right to change your mind." She told me it was an act of respect to trust that the person on the other side of my decision could handle disappointment or inconvenience rather than trying to manage their emotions for them.

I called Cheyenne and told her I wasn't going to go and asked for her help reworking the travel. I apologized and said I understood if she felt frustrated. She said, "It does feel frustrating. But I'm happy to do it." The world didn't fall apart, and neither did our relationship.

That experience with Cheyenne gave me the confidence to start testing my learnings with clients.

Anytime there was a social gathering the night before an in-person event, I used to arrive when it started, stay until it ended, and then drag myself to bed later than I would have liked. I worried that if I didn't go or if I left early, my client would be disappointed. But then I started to think about it differently. Didn't my client want me to be at my best for the main event? Wasn't that the reason they'd hired me in the first place?

I started to see that getting enough rest was a part of doing my job well, and that my energy was my most important asset. I stopped feeling guilty about leaving social events early and simply told my clients I needed to get to bed. Not one person got upset. Eventually, I felt confident enough to skip gatherings altogether if I knew I'd be better served by a night in after a long travel day. It always turned out fine.

It amazes me that by this point—early 2024, nearly two decades into my journey as a leader—I was only just beginning to learn lessons like these. I know I said it before, but this time it really did feel like everything was falling into place. When I put myself first and it went well, it became the evidence I needed to feel like I could do it again. I was healthier, calmer, and choosing myself in ways I never had before.

Little did I know that choosing myself would mean that I was about to spill my ugliest truth yet.

Chapter 45

Resentment Is a Gift

In the summer of 2024, I finally did something I'd been dreaming about for years: I took a sabbatical. I was off for five weeks, which was the longest amount of time I had ever spent away from my work at once.

I spent the first two weeks in Portugal with Spiros, Evie, and my sister, Lauren. We explored the cobblestone streets of Porto, stayed at an enchanting vineyard tucked into the winding hills of the Douro Valley, ate our weight in pastel de natas, took Evie to her first concert in Lisbon (Olivia Rodrigo; it was epic), discovered hidden beaches along the Lagos coast, and ended in the fairytale town of Sintra, where Spiros had a work conference just steps away from historic castles. The trip was every bit as magical as it sounds.

When I got home, I still had *three weeks* off.

I stayed home for all of it. I napped, read fiction for the first time in years, and went on long walks in the sun. I went to workout classes in the middle of the day. I took slow trips to the grocery store, only buying ingredients for what I felt like cooking that night. I ran across town for "boring" errands just because I could and enjoyed the feeling of having all the time in the world to do them. I swam in my own pool for once, went on impromptu dates with Spiros, met friends for dinner. I also hosted my parents, Monique, and her family for the Fourth of July.

I hardly thought about work the whole time. My team handled everything while I was off: They answered my emails, kept sales moving, and texted me if there was something critical (which only happened once or twice).

Their support made it possible for me to completely unplug, and I needed it. Even though I'd cut back on the number of speaking events I said yes to, my calendar still felt full. Too full.

My sabbatical showed me what a different version of my life could feel like, and I *loved* that version. So much so that the closer I got to my first Monday back to work, I felt a creeping sense of resentment. These weren't typical post-vacation blues. My mood darkened with each passing day.

Thank goodness I'd thought to schedule a therapy call a few days before going back to work. I knew I might need it. I walked around my neighborhood that evening, trying to untangle my thoughts before the call.

"I just don't get it," I told my therapist an hour later. "It's the longest break I've ever taken from work. I did everything I wanted, and my team was incredible. Where is this resentment coming from?"

I didn't wait for a response.

"Am I depressed?" I asked. "I have a great job, a great business, a great team. I make great money and have a great life. I've made so much progress in creating better boundaries. What the heck is going on with me?"

You already know what she asked me next:

"Kristen, do you feel mad, sad, scared, or glad?"

"I'm sad," I said. "Sad I feel like this after my sabbatical when I expected to feel grateful."

But I knew that wasn't all of it, and I'm pretty sure she did, too. I also knew how much I was paying for this call, and it was too much to spend 50 minutes skirting the truth.

"I think I'm also mad," I said. Better, but still not true enough.

Finally, I let it rip. "I'm *jealous*." Now we were getting somewhere.

I told her about our culture, which I'd rooted in freedom. I wanted work to *work with* my team's lives instead of their jobs being an obstacle. It started in the Student Maid days: Instead of dictating their schedules, I allowed our students to tell *us* when they wanted to work. I wanted their jobs to support their education, not compete with it. Each semester, we empowered them to choose the days and hours that best accommodated their class schedules. It was a level of flexibility that was practically unheard of at the time, especially in an industry like ours.

That philosophy stuck with me after I closed Student Maid. I let the team design their own schedules and told them they could do their jobs from anywhere they wanted. I valued results over hours worked and kept meetings to a minimum. No one had to ask me to take time off; they just blocked off days on a shared calendar. Not long before I left for Portugal, I had even implemented a four-day workweek to further encourage them to invest in their lives outside of our company. We still had six Break Weeks throughout the year, too.

To me, this was what it meant to build a human culture, and it was one of the things I was most proud of. But my sabbatical had highlighted the fact that there was one person who rarely got to benefit from that culture: me.

When I looked at my schedule for my first week back at work, I could already feel the stress in my body. It started with meetings on Monday, a flight that afternoon, prepping for a workshop, facilitating that workshop the next day. Meetings from a hotel room, landing late, virtual keynote the next morning. Five more meetings, another flight the day after that, then back home on Sunday. The rest of my work would spill into nights and the little weekend time I had. And then I'd do a version of that all over again the next week.

Even *that* was an improvement from how it was before. I had taken on less, but there was a limit to how much I could scale back while keeping the business healthy and continuing to support myself and the team.

Suddenly, the emotions that had been rising inside me for days broke free.

"I'm jealous of what they have," I said, more passionately than I'd ever spoken during a therapy call. "They get to live like I've been living on my sabbatical *every day*."

The words were flying out of me.

"I'm proud that I've made it possible for my team to have so much freedom," I continued, "but it feels like it's come at my expense. They can live their lives however they want to, but I can't."

I was almost crying now. "I give *all* of my energy to my work and my team, but there are other areas of my life that need it, too. My marriage, for one thing. My family. My friends. When I have free time during the week, I have no energy left to do anything with it. I don't want to keep living like this. If I don't make a change, I'm worried I'll regret it one day."

What I wanted to say next felt ugly. I said it anyway.

"You know," I told her, "sometimes I wonder if I even want a team anymore."

I couldn't believe that had just come out of my mouth.

"I don't actually want that," I said quickly. "I *love* my team. But I feel so stuck. Growing the business means traveling more, sacrificing more, and living less of my own life while theirs continue to expand. It's not fair. Plus, a big part of why I work so much is to be able to afford my team's salaries. Sometimes I think about what it would look like if I took on only enough work to make my own ends meet."

I felt so ashamed. My whole job was teaching people how to be more caring and compassionate leaders, and here I was fantasizing about ditching my team. That's not what I *really* wanted, of course. I cared about each person on my team so deeply. It's just that I felt trapped by my responsibility to provide for them.

"Is this my purpose in life?" I asked her. "To build a company where everyone gets to build the lives they want and I don't?"

Then my jealousy got specific.

I told her I was jealous of Monique, who'd had two babies by this point. She built her work schedule around the kind of present, hands-on mom she wanted to be. I couldn't see how anything like that would ever be possible for me. Spiros and I hoped to have a baby one day, but I couldn't even get pregnant if I wanted to because I was apart from him during most of my ovulation windows.

I was jealous of Rachel, who could travel to spend a week with her parents whenever she wanted and often did. I loved that she could do that, but I was sad that I couldn't. I saw my parents multiple times a year, but I had to schedule our visits months in advance, and I could rarely give them 100% of my focus. I made the time we did have together count: I interviewed them about their lives and recorded their answers so I could keep them forever. I spent a week with them to celebrate my dad's 75th birthday and planned a family and friend reunion for my mom's 70th. I took them with me on some of my less-demanding speaking trips. And while all of that was great, it broke my heart that I couldn't just visit them whenever I wanted to.

I was jealous of Cheyenne, who had countless hobbies and interests outside of work. Almost every week, she'd tell us about a new instrument she'd taught herself to play, or a pottery class she signed up for, or a camping trip she was planning. I admired how fully she lived her life. I wanted hobbies, too, but I didn't have time for any. I couldn't remember the last time I'd gone for a run.

In our team meetings when the rest of the team gave their personal updates, they almost always talked about spending time with their friends. It struck me once that it had been literal years since I'd seen some of my closest friends in person, so I did what I called a "friend tour." I blocked a week, traveled to where they each lived, and spent a day with them one by one. I loved it. But the fact that I needed to plan a friend tour probably said everything. Spiros and I had lived in our new home for months, and I hadn't even had time to meet our neighbors.

My sabbatical gave me the chance to do so many of these things: I spent quality time with my parents and Spiros, connected with friends, finally met my neighbors, and got to be spontaneous. I had the energy to show up as my best in the relationships that mattered most to me. I wanted that to be the norm, not the exception. But now that my sabbatical was almost over, I could feel that version of me slipping through my fingers.

What I shared with my therapist that day were the worst things I had ever said about my team out loud. Thankfully, she knew exactly what to say.

"Resentment is a symptom of an unmet need," she said.

That made me stop in the middle of the street. I asked her to repeat it.

"Resentment is a symptom of an *unmet need*."

I had never heard something so powerful. It helped me understand what I had really been feeling all the times before when I sacrificed my own needs in service of someone else's.

She went on to say that resentment is a gift. It often feels like anger or jealousy aimed at other people, but it's really a signal that we are neglecting something within us. If we can learn to look at it this way, our resentment can reveal what we need and want in our own lives. It has the power to show us all the places where we've abandoned ourselves.

It's the kind of perspective that can change your life if you let it. It forever changed mine. If only I had known it the day I looked at my reflection in my high-rise window and saw a stranger all those years ago.

"So," my therapist continued, "Which need of yours is being neglected?"

"Freedom," I said immediately. "I just want to have the freedom to live the life I want outside of work."

"Sounds like you're clear," she said. "And now that you know what's missing, you can figure out what has to change so you can meet that need."

Easier said than done. I knew the drill by now: Acknowledging my feelings alone never changed much. If I wanted more freedom, I'd have to actually do something about it—and that meant my first step was talking things out with my thought partner.

But how was I supposed to tell someone on my team that I was questioning whether I wanted a team at all?

Chapter 46

Magic Wand

On my walk home after my therapy call, I circled the block a couple of times. I was trying to record a voice note to Monique, but I kept stopping, deleting it, and rerecording. I couldn't do it.

Once I told her how I was feeling—especially the part about considering a future without a team—there would be no unsaying it. I didn't actually *want* that future, but I wanted to be honest with Monique so she understood how much my resentment was affecting me. I knew we could find a better way forward together if I could just work up the courage to let her in.

Hours passed, and I still hadn't sent the message. I finally accepted that it wasn't going to get any easier, so I got out my phone and hit record one more time. "I'm really nervous to tell you this," I began in my voice note, "but it's important that I do."

Over the next few minutes, I told her everything I'd shared with my therapist. Even the part about being jealous of the team, including her.

She sent me a voice note back almost immediately.

"I'm so glad you shared this with me," she said. "It makes sense why you feel the way you do. It's hard being the only person on the team who can deliver speeches. I want you to have more freedom in your life. I know how much you want to grow your family with Spiros, and I want that for you, too."

I let out a breath I hadn't realized I'd been holding in as I listened.

"I think a lot of this is due to the natural tension that comes with being a business owner," she continued. "Let's explore all of the options, like those other revenue streams we've talked about that don't rely on you actually being there. Or what if you delegated more of your work to the team? We could also see what it might look like for you to not have a team at all and only work with speaking agents. I'm not going to judge you if that's what you decide, even if it means I don't have a job anymore. You deserve to build the life you want."

Tears rolled down my face. I wasn't surprised by what she said, but it still filled me with relief to hear her say it. I could feel, once again, how much she cared about me. Not Kristen the boss. *Me.*

After that, we continued to exchange voice notes where we explored ways to address everything I was feeling. We didn't seriously consider a path without a team; I already knew that wasn't really what I wanted, so we didn't even entertain the idea.

"Let's give ourselves permission to dream," Monique said, sounding just like Jamil and his "Blue Sky" conversations. "If you could wave a magic wand and change anything instantly, where would you start?"

"Well," I said, "there are two things I wouldn't do anymore."

One was my mastermind group. Out of the five I'd started at the height of the pandemic, I was now facilitating just one, but it took up three precious hours every month. The other was my one-on-one work. Every month, I met with several clients for 90 minutes each.

I loved my clients, but letting go of those two things would free up 12 hours every month, not to mention all the communication and prep that happened in between.

"That would be a great place to start," Monique said after I'd done the math. "What else could free up your time?"

Aside from turning down speaking events, I was at a loss.

"Is there more that Rachel, Cheyenne, and I can do?" she asked. "Can we reduce what's on your plate?"

I wasn't sure. We'd tried this before: I'd had the team create sales proposals, lead calls with prospective clients, and outline speeches without me. But each time, we had decided it was better for me to stay involved.

Part of it was that those things were in my sweet spot; I enjoyed doing them, and they came naturally to me. But the other part was that our brand was literally my name. Every interaction with our clients was a reflection of me, and I wanted my personal touch on every level of their experience.

"What's taking more of your time than it should be?" Monique asked.

Client meetings, I thought. For every speaking engagement, I had multiple content-planning and logistics calls. I had always thought there was no reason to pull the team in for those because I had to be there anyway. I figured I could just handle them myself and relay the information afterward. But that meant that after every client call, I had to send two separate messages: one to Cheyenne about event logistics and one to Rachel about how she could support me with content. Because I spent all of my time between meetings catching everyone up, I had no time left to do my actual work. That was why so much of it crept into my evenings and weekends.

"Why don't we ask Cheyenne and Rachel to be in those meetings with you?" she suggested. "That would save a ton of steps."

My limiting belief wasn't a fan of that idea. "There are *so* many meetings," I said. "They won't like that."

"First of all, you don't know if that's true," Monique said. "But also, imagine how it would feel to leave a meeting and not have to send a single follow-up message. I think they would totally understand and love to support you."

Just imagining it made me feel lighter. I told her I was willing to give it a try.

"I think we have a solid plan here," she said. "We get rid of some things on your calendar to create more space. We get Cheyenne and Rachel involved in client meetings. And then I can focus on building more revenue streams so that speaking becomes something you can scale up or down depending on the season of life you're in."

Now we were dreaming. And then I had an idea of my own.

"Speaking of revenue streams," I said, "there's one I'm really excited about that I've been wanting to do for a long time. I want to host retreats for other speakers. I've met so many people who want to build speaking careers and who already have incredible messages aligned with human leadership. I want to bring them together and spend a few days helping them elevate their speaking and stage presence. And I want to do it in Houston so that I don't have to leave home. A win-win."

Within a week, we were reaching out to people for our first speakers retreat.

Those conversations were another example of Monique and me thriving in our thought partnership. She had helped me get from questioning whether I wanted a team to feeling totally reenergized about the path ahead of us. Somehow, Monique could help me turn almost any challenge into a reason to dream.

Now, all I had to do was ask Cheyenne and Rachel to join a dozen meetings a month.

Will there ever be a time I *don't* have to have a difficult conversation?

Chapter 47

Good Enough

In our next team meeting, I shared the ideas that Monique and I had come up with and asked Cheyenne and Rachel for their help.

"I'd be so happy to join client meetings," Cheyenne said. "It'd be much more efficient."

"Same," Rachel said. "I love this idea. It would take a ton off your plate."

In case you're keeping track, Monique is *always* right. What I'd assumed would feel like a burden to them didn't at all. I expected our conversation to end there, but it turned into a bigger one about how the team viewed the way I used my time.

"You know, Kristen," Rachel said, "sometimes, I think you get back to us too quickly."

Huh? How could that ever be a bad thing?

"You don't need to reply right away when I send you something," she continued. "Like when I'm working on blogs and I tell you my edits are ready, I don't need or expect you to get back to me immediately. That actually stresses me out. It's like I finally cross something off my list, and then it's right back on my plate a couple hours later."

Never thought about it like that.

"I agree," Monique chimed in. "You're so quick to get back to us, but I know it usually means you work late. Most of the time we don't need a response that fast. If something is urgent, we'll say so."

"That makes me think of something else," Cheyenne said. "I don't think you need to attend team meetings when you're traveling. I mean, if you want to, of course. But you don't need to call in from the airport or hotel. That seems like a lot. We can have our meetings without you when you're on the road."

Wow. This just keeps getting better.

"Yeah," Monique added. "I think sometimes you worry about our connection as a team and feel like it all depends on you. But when you have a busy week, we can commit to keeping our connection strong ourselves."

I have the best team in the world.

"I have another idea," Cheyenne said. "I think I could help you more on the client side if we had a better process. I'd like to look at software that can help us manage more of the details so that you aren't the one keeping track of them. I've already looked into a few options, and there's one I think would be great."

"I'd love to partner with you on that," Monique said. "I can already see so many ways that could save a ton of time."

"Okay, I have a fun idea," Rachel said. "What if I traveled with you sometimes, Kristen? I love traveling. I could keep you company on the road and make it so that all you have to focus on is giving your speech."

I would absolutely love that.

How could I have ever questioned having a team? They were the people who made my life so meaningful. I thought I was there to support them, but whenever I had the courage to open up about how I was feeling, they always reminded me that the support went both ways.

"Let's make a promise," I said to them. "If any of this ever feels like too much, tell me and we'll make a change. I still want you to enjoy your freedom and your four-day workweek. I'll trust that if the workload gets overwhelming or takes away from your flexibility, you'll tell me."

"You have our word," Monique said.

"For sure," Cheyenne agreed.

"Absolutely," Rachel said.

And then Monique delivered the zinger: "We can handle a lot more than you think we can."

Touché.

Once again, none of the assumptions I'd made about how my team felt or the stories I'd told myself matched reality. My team helped me see that I *could* still offer flexibility while asking for more support.

Within weeks, we'd purchased a custom software to help us keep track of speaking content and event logistics. It cost $10,000, and I wasn't involved in a single meeting or decision about it. Once the software was up and running, the team removed a surprising number of details from my brain and put them into systems they could manage on their own.

Cheyenne and Rachel began joining the majority of my meetings, and it only improved the client experience. Rachel traveled with me during especially busy weeks when she was up for it (which was every time). I allowed myself to opt out of team meetings while on the road if I was too tired, and I left their messages unread some evenings. The time I got back allowed for proper lunch breaks and several more uninterrupted hours each week to complete my work.

The team promised they'd tell me if it ever became too much. It never did. If anything, they kept seeking out more ways to help.

We even implemented something called a "capacity check-in" during our team meetings, where everyone scored how full their plate felt. A score of 10 meant work was coming out of your eyeballs, and a 1 meant you were lounging by the pool sipping a margarita with nothing to do.

Each week, everyone reported honestly where they were on the scale. If someone scored in the 8 to 10 range, we'd have a conversation about how to help. If I scored in that range, we talked about what the team could do to support me. Our capacity check-ins were so effective that we still do them to this day.

My revelations continued outside of our team: When I phased out the mastermind group and my one-on-one client work, every person understood. I was honest with them about the fact that I didn't have the capacity to do it anymore. I gave them plenty of notice so they could make other plans, and instead of being upset, they were encouraging. Several told me they wondered what had taken me so long; they couldn't imagine how I'd been fitting it all into my schedule.

I felt proud every time I saw an empty white space on my color-coded calendar. I'd made so much progress—but I still had more to make.

On a therapy call a month or so later, I remember telling my therapist I was overwhelmed by my to-do list. Now that I'd brought the team in to help in so many areas, everything left was something only I could do, and that week it was just too much. I knew I'd be spending the whole weekend trying to get to everything.

My most pressing task was creating detailed content outlines for my upcoming keynotes so that my clients could review my message in advance. Though they rarely asked for anything other than a high-level summary, I wanted them to feel good about what they were paying me to deliver. I thought it was a nice touch that showed them I cared.

"Have you ever considered that going above and beyond like that stresses people out?" my therapist asked me.

I hadn't. But it made sense when I thought about it: Expecting someone to find time to read a multi-page document they didn't ask for probably *did* stress some people out. And in creating one, I was holding myself to a caliber of work that no client was calling for.

"Let's look at a different example," she said. "Do you know someone in your life who sends really long and thoughtful texts? Doesn't it make you feel like you need to respond with a text just as long and thoughtful?"

I knew exactly what she meant. Those were the texts I guiltily left unread because of the energy it would take to respond.

My therapist encouraged me to stop overdelivering in my client work and allow "good" to be good enough. I tried it that weekend and sent high-level outlines instead of detailed ones. It took me a couple of hours instead of several, and what do you know—my clients got their feedback to me faster. I brought it up as a learning in our next team meeting and Cheyenne said something that really helped me internalize the lesson.

"I notice that you put in so much extra time on things, Kristen," she said. "I know you want our clients to feel special, but they already do. Your bare minimum is above and beyond for most people.

Sometimes I think you put in 30% more effort than you need to, and it only makes a 3% difference in the end. I don't think spending that extra energy is worth it."

Her feedback struck a chord with me, so I decided to experiment. I still put my heart into every aspect of my work, but I focused on making it good enough (with sometimes a little, *tiny* extra). I got just as many referrals. I had just as much repeat business. All signs pointed to the fact that my clients didn't care about the difference—and probably didn't even notice it.

Already, I felt more free.

My team wasn't just helping me share the workload. They were helping me build a bigger and brighter life.

Chapter 48

True Self

"What makes you happy?"

It was December 2024, and I was at an event with a client and friend of mine. Her question caught me by surprise.

"Long walks in the sun and being with people I love," I said without thinking much about it. It came out so naturally.

I asked her the same question.

"Well, my work . . . "

As I listened to her response, it dawned on me that I hadn't even thought about work. At first, I felt a bit embarrassed by that, especially considering she was my *client* and was asking me this question during *our work* together. But I realized that's not how I saw my life anymore.

The way I answered her question that day was the opposite of how I would have answered it years earlier. For as long as I could remember, my work and I had felt like one and the same. It was all I thought and talked about. My business felt like my baby, and I'm not using that as a figure of speech. In the Student Maid days and beyond, I'd think about what grade or life milestone my child was reaching now. Sixteen years old? My baby's getting a driver's license. My company was my greatest accomplishment, the thing that challenged me more than anything, and what taught me the most about myself, much like a child would.

My self-worth and mood were directly tied to the performance of my business. If the company was doing well and revenue was strong, then I was happy and felt successful. If the company was struggling and we weren't hitting our numbers, then I was stressed and felt like a failure. I used to know our revenue down to the *penny* and tracked it in real time. My emotions rose and fell with our P&L. I could start the day anxious because we were behind on our goals, and then end it on cloud nine if we closed a new contract.

They say that work won't love you back, but mine sure did. I was good at it, and people praised and recognized me for doing it well. It provided for me and other people. It was my biggest source of both stress and pride.

It wasn't until I started meeting with my therapist that I realized just how unhealthy my relationship with my work had become. I was determined to change it—and I was on the right track.

There were times when the team would ask for an update on our quarterly revenue total, and I'd realize I didn't know it. I had to check the spreadsheet to give the exact number. We all celebrated those moments because they felt like proof of how far I'd come. Instead of controlling our numbers and allowing them to dictate how I felt about myself, I decided to surrender and trust that it would all work out. And it did. What went down would eventually come back up again. My measure of success was how *happy* something made me instead of how much money it would bring in. By then, we'd hosted the first speaking retreat at my home in Houston, and it brought me so much joy and fulfillment, the profit hardly mattered.

"Is this what peace feels like?" I asked my therapist one day. "It feels kind of . . . boring. Not in a bad way. There just aren't high highs or low lows anymore, and I'm not used to that."

"Surprising, isn't it?" she chuckled. "Yes. Peace feels calm. And predictable."

"It's so strange," I said. "I care about the business, and I'm still ambitious, but the fire that used to push me to work so hard is gone. I don't want to hustle like that anymore. Does that seem normal?"

"It seems like you know who you really are," she said.

She then began explaining the difference between what she called the true self and the false self.

"You are born as your true self," she said. "When you're a baby, you don't do anything to earn love. You don't have any concept of how you 'should' be, so you don't try to prove your worth or perform. You are alive, and that's enough."

"But then you grow up," she continued, "and little by little, you learn to build a false self. You pick up on cues from others that make you believe that if you achieve more, you matter more. Or that if you make people happy, you're lovable. Or if you have something to offer, you're valuable."

I wrote every word I could in my notes.

"Work is especially connected to the false self," she continued. "It's easy to confuse *what* we do with *who* we are. Our work gives us praise, control, and a sense of competence, even more so when we're good at it. And when your identity is built around helping others with your work, it can go even deeper. You start to believe you're only worthy when you're giving something to someone else."

I'd never heard anything more true. I'd built so much of my life around being someone who served others. It wasn't just what I did; it was who I believed I was.

"But here's the real test of your growth," she said. "How would you feel if all your work went away? If you no longer had the business? The title? The team? The clients? If that idea feels devastating, it probably means your identity is tied to the false self instead of the true self."

Years earlier, thinking about losing all of that *would* have devastated me. But now, it didn't.

"When your identity lives in the false self," she continued, "you become attached to whatever gives you that feeling of value. You cling to it. You defend it. You overwork for it. You fear losing it because losing it feels like losing yourself."

"The true self, on the other hand, is the part of you that knows what truly makes you happy," she said. "It knows what matters when everything else is stripped away. Most people don't discover their true self until life gives them no choice. It usually takes a crisis or loss for people to realize what actually matters to them."

I felt the tears welling. She was describing the journey I'd been on to return to myself since that day I saw my unrecognizable reflection in the high-rise window.

She stopped, then asked, "Kristen, what matters more to you than anything in the world?"

"Love," I said without a second thought. "Love for myself. Love in my relationships. Finding love in everything I do."

I had never been more sure about something.

"At my core," I said, "I am love."

"And that's why your feelings about work have changed," she said. "Because you realize that work is not *you*. Work is something you do. But it's not your identity."

This time, there was no pushback from me. I knew she was right. It's why I answered my client's question the way I did that day. When she asked what made me happy, I had a simple answer: Nothing mattered to me more than spending time with people I love.

I answered her question as my true self.

Once I stopped equating my work with my identity and self-worth, I opened up space for the rest of me. I poured love into all the parts I had neglected that had been waiting patiently for years.

I spent more time traveling the world with Spiros. I flew to surprise Evie at her band concert. I rescheduled meetings and events to visit my parents and offer help when they needed it. I called my sister in the evenings to catch up instead of getting ahead on emails. I hosted parties and cultivated new friendships. I took as many walks in the sun as I could and became my favorite person in the world to hang out with. I started imagining what my life might be like with a baby in it.

All of a sudden, it hit me: I was living the eulogy Paul had asked me to write all those years ago.

For the first time ever, I was living for *me*.

Chapter 49

Just for Me

It's April 2025. I'm standing in a crowd of runners before sunrise with a bib pinned to my sports bra.

I jump up and down to wake up my calves as hip-hop blasts in my headphones. Around me, strangers are also bouncing in place and checking their watches, all of us united in our anxious pre-race energy.

No one here knows I'm a speaker.

No one here knows I own a business.

No one cares.

When the starting gun goes off, I feel like I'm gliding more than running. My body knows exactly what to do. It's everything we've trained for over the past few months.

With each passing mile, I think about the journey that brought me here. After not running for a couple of years, I'd signed up for my first-ever race to motivate me to get back into it. Just a few months ago, I could barely run a mile without wanting to throw up, but I stuck with it. I've been training four days a week, sometimes in the middle of a workday if that's what it takes to keep this promise to myself. And now, here I am, running my longest distance yet—a 15K, 9.3 miles—and preparing for my ultimate goal of doing a half-marathon in the fall.

Running is where I go to reconnect with myself. To believe in myself. To push myself in ways that have nothing to do with my work. To reach for goals that are just mine. It's where I have conversations with my heart.

Around mile three, I start crying. I can't help it. I'm so proud of myself. Life feels so beautiful. I feel so free. And I know it's because of all the hard conversations I've had and the decisions I've made to make it feel this way. I'm proud that I've kept this commitment to myself. That even when life and work get busy, I have the courage to keep my focus on me.

I keep running, the Houston sun beating on my shoulders just like I like it. When I turn the corner and see the finish line, more tears come. It doesn't matter where I place. It's not about that. The fact that I'm doing this for myself is all that I need.

As I cross it, I look up at the sky and let the tears fall down my cheeks.

I did it! I did it! I did it!

I'm smiling wide and gasping for air.

Then, to my surprise, a race volunteer hands me my participation medal and tells me I've won first place in my age group. (Later, I'll learn I was the *only* person in my age group. Details, details.)

I call Spiros to share the news. He isn't there because I didn't ask him to be. This is my thing, just for me.

I don't know it yet, but I'll go on to run more races that year, including three half-marathons.

I used to run to pound out my stress, but now running feels like an actual hobby instead of an escape from my life. I don't feel desperate for vacations. When I look at my days, they feel sustainable. I have breaks. I have time for the people I love most in my life. I have time for me in the middle of the day. And when I lose my way or overschedule myself—which still happens—I know what to do.

I've learned that balance isn't possible, but harmony is. My goal is to make sure that all the parts of my life work together instead of against each other, and what that looks like changes in every season. When I approach my life this way, the business benefits, too.

I used to measure success by how fast I moved, how much revenue my company brought in, and how full my calendar was. But the only place those metrics ever got me was burnout. Now I measure success by how peaceful I feel inside.

The more calm I become, the more calm my company becomes. The more I set boundaries and advocate for what I need, the more my team does, too. The more I make decisions from my true self, the more fulfilled I feel, and the more love I bring into everything I do.

Peace, it turns out, is contagious.

Part IV

Human

Chapter 50

Dreams

I heard my phone buzz while I was in the kitchen. It was a voice note from Monique.

"So, Tim and I had a really nice conversation last night about the future," she began. "We talked about moving to another country and living abroad for a season within the next few years. We also talked about having another baby. It's been a long time since we've dreamed like that, and I just wanted to share because I'm excited."

By April 2025, messages like these weren't uncommon between us. We talked just as much about personal things—dreams, fears, marriages, finances, friendships, family, personal goals, you name it—as we did about work. There were few lines between us.

I thought hearing an update like that would fill me only with happiness. Monique and Tim had talked for years about how much they wanted to live abroad and have more children. I wanted all of that for them, too.

But as I listened to Monique's message, my first feeling wasn't a positive one.

Snap out of it! I said to myself. *Be excited for your friend!*

I pushed the other feeling aside and sent her a reply.

"I'm so happy that you and Tim had that conversation," I said. "I love that you're dreaming together. Thanks for sharing it with me."

A few days later, I brought up my unexpected reaction on a therapy call.

"Why wouldn't I feel only happiness when Monique shared that with me?" I asked her, genuinely wanting to know.

"Did her message make you feel mad, sad, scared, or glad?" my therapist asked. (Of course.)

For a moment, I was stumped. It wasn't really any of those.

"I guess it made me feel . . ."

I searched my heart for words, unsure of how to describe what was happening inside. I clung to the closest ones I could find.

". . . taken advantage of?"

When I said it, it didn't feel quite right. But I couldn't come up with a better way to articulate it.

"Tell me more about that," she said.

I told my therapist that I wanted to celebrate with Monique, but something was stopping me.

"It feels like she just expects that I'll continue to adjust," I said. "Even though I know these aren't definite plans, it seems like she's making an assumption that there are no limits to our culture of flexibility and that I'll always say yes."

I went on to explain that I had already adapted in multiple ways to support Monique through different seasons of motherhood.

Monique had two kids under four at the time, and whenever her schedule needed to change, I embraced it. She'd had a few difficult experiences with childcare and no longer felt she could trust outside help, so she wanted to be home full-time with her children.

It meant an unconventional schedule: Monique worked early mornings, evenings, during naptime, on Fridays when her husband was off, and sometimes on the weekends. I adjusted our team meeting times to whatever she needed because nothing made me happier than watching Monique be the parent she had always wanted to be. She's one of the most present, incredible moms I've ever known.

But now we were talking about even bigger life changes that would require even more flexibility on my part.

"So, are you going to tell Monique how you feel?" my therapist asked.

"No way," I said. "I don't see the point. She was just sharing a dream with me, and it's not happening anytime soon. There's nothing to solve right now."

"You know, Kristen," my therapist said, "Sometimes the point isn't to solve anything. Sometimes a conversation can simply look like sharing your feelings and asking to be seen in them. And being curious about what your honesty brings up in the other person. If you don't tell her how you feel, the resentment will only build."

Resentment. Here we are again.

Chapter 51

Unlike Her

The truth was that, for the first time, I was feeling let down by Monique's performance in her role.

I'd told myself it was the amount of flexibility I'd given her that was bothering me, but really, that only amplified how let down I was feeling.

Monique was our Chief of Growth. We had been talking for years about implementing additional revenue streams that would allow the business to grow while continuing to reduce my time spent away from home. These conversations got more serious after I shared the messy feelings my summer sabbatical had brought up in me the year before, and yet I hadn't seen much progress. She seemed to have stopped taking initiative and running with ideas, which was unlike her.

I had only ever known Monique to be proactive and a self-starter. I never needed to follow up with her about anything; she was always two steps ahead of me. But now I seemed to be the one asking for updates and taking the lead on growth-focused projects to keep things on track.

The strangest part was that she was still doing the rest of her job well: being my thought partner, managing our monthly accounting, helping the team improve their systems. When it came to the future of the business, though, her work was stagnant.

I couldn't pinpoint any other reason for the lack of progress, so I assumed it was that Monique didn't have the bandwidth to focus on it, considering how full her life had become with her two young kids at home.

When I got her voice note about her dream of moving abroad and having another baby, it touched a deeper wound: All I could hear was that she expected me to adapt to more life changes when we hadn't even talked about how her most recent ones were affecting her role and the business.

I knew my therapist was right and that I needed to tell Monique how I was feeling. I was already noticing a little resentment leaking into our conversations anytime we talked about the future. If I didn't address it now, I feared it would only get worse.

I'd been working with my therapist on naming my unpleasant emotions, owning them without guilt, and sharing them honestly with others. But facing an emotion *this* unpleasant that was directed at someone I cared about *this* much would easily be the hardest conversation I'd had in my life so far. How could I possibly tell *Monique*, who'd been there for me every step of the way and was one of my closest friends, that she'd made me feel taken advantage of? I didn't even want to hear *myself* say it out loud.

But the feeling was real. So, with a shaking hand, I hit record on a voice note.

"I need to tell you something that came up in therapy today," I started. "And I'm really scared and embarrassed to share it with you."

I kept going, my stomach twisting tighter with every word.

"When I got your message the other day about moving abroad and having another baby, I wanted to feel happy for you. But what I really felt was something I can only describe as being taken advantage of. It feels like you assume I'll always work around what you need and I'll always say yes. It also made me scared for the future. I want to have a baby, too, and I worry that the business isn't evolving enough to allow both of us to build the lives we want while still supporting the team. I don't want a solution. I'm just interested in what my feelings bring up for you."

My hands were shaking so hard that it took two tries to hit send, but I was proud of myself for recording that message. Besides saying I might not want a team anymore, this was the most vulnerable thing I had ever said out loud. But I didn't say anything about my disappointment in Monique's performance or my assumptions about her lack of capacity for her role. You'd think that if I could tell her that I felt taken advantage of, I could tell her all of *that*. And after the lessons I learned with Amanda about speaking up and addressing feedback promptly, you'd think I would have shared all of my feelings with Monique when I first felt them. But we didn't have the traditional boss-employee relationship. We barely used those words. Our thought partnership had naturally created a different kind of closeness and friendship between us than I had with Cheyenne and Rachel, and I didn't know how to have a conversation with Monique about her role. I was afraid to. I didn't believe her lack of progress was intentional, and I hoped that what I had already said might naturally address it.

Before I went to bed, I noticed that Monique had listened to my voice note but hadn't sent a reply.

Then the next afternoon came. Nothing. By that evening, still no reply.

Finally, late that night, I heard the familiar buzz.

"It took me some time to process what you sent me," Monique's voice note began.

A stab of anxiety shot through me. I could hear it in her voice: She was hurt, and it seemed worse than I expected.

As I listened, she shared that sometimes she struggled to know if she was talking to Kristen her friend or Kristen her boss. She admitted that she'd almost deleted the message about living abroad and having another baby because she couldn't be sure which version of me would receive it. She wished that my first thought had been about what that dream meant for her as a person, not what it meant for her work. She was sad that my reaction hadn't been only happiness for her.

Understandably, she said what had hurt most was me saying I felt taken advantage of. She couldn't understand why I would ever feel that way, especially with the level of ownership she had for the business and the care she had for me.

I felt awful and questioned if I should fire my therapist.

I sent Monique a reply immediately, apologizing for the hurt I had caused and saying I completely understood her feelings.

We talked briefly about how future babies and changing seasons were things we'd need to navigate, but not crises, and she calmed my fears by reminding me we weren't unprepared to handle them: We were taking all of the right steps.

Talking it out with her gave me some temporary reassurance and made me think we'd never have to have the real conversation about her performance. By the end of our back-and-forth, we both thought we'd made it to the other side.

But a couple months later, in a team meeting, I could sense that Monique was frustrated. We were discussing some of her projects, and she was short with her words and visibly agitated—and there was no doubt it was directed at me.

After the meeting, I sent her a voice note and asked if she could help me understand what was bothering her. I assured her that I could handle it, no matter what it was.

"I struggle with sharing difficult emotions," Monique said in her response. "My natural instinct is to keep them to myself. In other areas of my life, I've learned that those feelings get shut down or dismissed, so I don't share them."

She kept going.

"As your thought partner, I struggle to know if I should speak up when we see things differently in a project, which is what happened in our meeting. I'm not sure if I should just follow your vision or challenge you when I disagree. Sometimes, when I get frustrated, I can't tell if it's coming from my own need to control or if it's a sign that something is off and I need to speak up. I'm working on it, and I'd appreciate your grace as I do."

I felt grateful Monique shared that with me. She could be so direct when it came to the business, but her own vulnerability didn't come as easily. Her words made me feel closer to her, and now that I understood what she was struggling with, I could help her work through it.

I thanked her and reminded her that she could tell me *anything*. No matter how difficult it was, I always wanted to hear it.

When I didn't get another response, I thought that was that.

By then, I was walking into a salon to get my hair done. That night, Spiros and I were attending a graduation for his neurosurgery residents, and he was the emcee.

When I left the salon, I was surprised to see another message from Monique. I sat in my car in the parking garage and pressed play.

"Okay," she said. "If you want me to tell you everything, I will."

I straightened in my seat. I could tell by her tone that this message was going to be different.

"When you came back from your sabbatical last year," she began, "and you told me you weren't sure if you wanted to have a team anymore, that really affected me. I felt insulted. It came across like you think you can do all of this yourself without us, and I don't think you can. It made me feel like you aren't grateful for the team or me. Why would I want to put my heart into my job if you feel like you can just do it yourself? I haven't felt as motivated lately because of it."

I closed my eyes and thought back to that season and how trapped I felt. Not having a team was never what I truly wanted, and I hadn't meant it that way. But it didn't matter; I'd said it, and my words were still living inside her, causing pain.

"And when you shared that you might not want a team anymore," she said, "I was completely supportive, even though it would affect my job. I took off my work hat and thought about you as a person. But when I sent you that message about wanting to move abroad, you didn't respond the same way to me. You say you support me, but you made the conversation about you and the business instead."

Her message got quiet. Then I realized she was crying.

My heart broke in the front seat of my car.

"I'm not sure how that conversation turned into me taking advantage of you," she went on through tears. "I've given you *thirteen years* of my life and have done nothing but help you. I care so much that I planned my pregnancies around what was best for the business. How could I take advantage of you? It felt like an attack on my character."

Now tears were running down my face, too. I hadn't realized how much those words were still hurting her.

"I think we avoid the elephant in the room. Would you be okay if I came to you and said that *I* wanted to leave my job to follow a dream? I know you say you would, but I don't know if that's true. And if I did, would we still be friends?"

Every word made it harder to breathe.

"Since day one, I've helped you make nearly every dream you've had come true. But it doesn't feel like that support goes both ways. Was it all a lie? I'm not sure what I believe anymore."

A sledgehammer to my heart would've hurt less. I had to hold the phone closer to my ear to hear her words over my sobs.

"You want me to be 100% vulnerable with you," she said. "But if I'm being honest, I don't feel like I can. Because when I came to you as a friend, it became an entirely different conversation. I don't want to share my feelings and be severely misunderstood. I guess I'm still really hurt."

The message ended.

I just sat there, phone in my lap, tears pouring down my face, unable to move.

Chapter 52

Frozen

As soon as I could catch my breath, I hit record.

"Thank you for opening up to me," I said through my tears. "I'm *so* sorry, Monique. If I were with you right now, I'd give you the biggest hug."

My body was shaking as I tried to collect my thoughts.

"It was never my intention to make you feel any of that. But I did. And I am so deeply sorry."

I apologized for the comment I had made the year before about questioning whether I wanted a team. I reminded her how grateful I was for her—and for everyone on the team—and that I absolutely knew I couldn't do any of this without them. I regretted how carelessly my words had come across.

I also apologized for making her feel like her dream didn't matter to me. It did. I told her I wished I could take that moment back and that I would absolutely support her if she ever chose to leave the company and pursue her own dreams. How could I not?

But there was one part I just couldn't explain to her: why I had said I felt taken advantage of.

Monique had been so honest and courageous with me. It blew me away. I wanted to meet her there and be just as brave. But every time I tried, the words felt wrong. I didn't know how to say what I felt inside without hurting her more than I already had.

I stayed in my car. Recorded. Deleted. Started again.

I knew why I felt taken advantage of. But when I tried to say it out loud, I shut down. I second-guessed every sentence before I could even finish it. I knew how important it was to get this right; the stakes had never felt higher.

An hour and a half later, I was still in the parking garage, updo and all, recording another message without success.

I wanted to give Monique more. She *deserved* more. But no matter how hard I tried, I remained utterly and completely frozen.

Feeling at a loss, I sent her a text.

"I can't record the rest," I wrote. "I have some things I haven't been clear or courageous about, and I want to tell you, but for some reason I can't."

"Do you want to just call me instead?" she wrote.

"I think I might need that," I wrote back. "Are you sure?"

"Yeah," she wrote. "The kids are in the bath."

I told her I'd call in a few minutes and drove home.

When I walked in the door, Spiros was in his tux. We were supposed to leave for the graduation in a few minutes, but he took one look at my red, puffy face and the mascara smudged around my eyes and knew my afternoon had taken a turn. When I told him it was about Monique, he understood immediately.

"Don't worry about the graduation," he said. "Do what you need to do."

I walked upstairs to my office and FaceTimed Monique.

When she answered, we just looked at each other. Then I started crying.

"I'm so sorry I hurt you," I said.

"I know you are," she said.

"I have some things I haven't said. And I'm really scared to say them."

"You can tell me," she said.

"When I said that I felt taken advantage of," I began, "that comes from something deeper."

My throat tightened as I tried to get the words to leave my mouth, but they wouldn't. It was like there was a physical barrier they couldn't break through. I'd never had so much trouble sharing my feelings with someone.

I looked down at the floor, trying to pull myself together.

"I . . ."

My tears fell harder while Monique waited patiently.

"I just—" I started again. "I just feel like I've given you so much flexibility with the kids."

"You have," she said gently. "And I'm really grateful for that."

"No matter what you need," I continued, "the answer has always been yes. Your schedule has changed a lot and I've always made it work. No questions asked."

I took a breath. "I think . . . I think part of it is . . ."

And then I just froze.

"I'm not explaining this well," I said quickly. "I'm really sorry."

"It's okay," she said. "Just take your time."

"I don't know how to say this," I said. I looked down, shaking my head. "I've never felt this stuck trying to explain something."

Monique stayed quiet, giving me space to put my thoughts together.

"There was one time that really hurt me," I said finally. "Two years ago, I came to your house to visit you for a week. I felt so stretched thin and overwhelmed, and I was working almost the entire time."

She listened patiently while I wiped away tears.

"I didn't see you working at all," I said. "You were with the kids the whole time. I loved that you could do that, but it felt unfair."

"I don't remember that," she said. "I'm sorry that hurt you."

"It's not really about that," I said. "It's just that sometimes I worry you don't have the time for everything on your plate. I see how full your life is."

"You don't have to worry about that," she said. "I know it looks like a lot, but I've got it figured out."

"Would you tell me if you ever felt like you didn't have the capacity for your work?" I asked.

"Of course I would," she said.

"I'm so sorry I made you feel like I was judging your character," I said. "I trust you with everything I have. I wouldn't give you the kind of flexibility I do if I didn't. And I want to say this again: When you told me about your dream, I should have been there for you as a friend. You've always shown up for me that way, and I'm so sorry I didn't do the same for you."

"I forgive you," she said.

After a few minutes, we hung up.

I showed up to the graduation an hour late, but I would have missed it completely if it meant repairing my relationship with Monique.

As I sat in a room full of people in tuxedos and evening gowns, I replayed the conversation over and over in my head.

Why had I frozen up like that? Why had I not been able to get my words out? Why had I been such a jumbled mess? Why couldn't I just say the one thing that was underneath it all: that the areas of the business Monique was in charge of weren't moving forward like I expected them to be, and that was the reason for *everything*?

Monique and I texted a few times that evening. Though the pain of our conversation was still fresh, it seemed like things between us were on their way back to normal.

But my heart was still in pieces.

Chapter 53

Lightbulb Moment

Two days later, I woke up in Mexico with a mission.

Spiros had a conference in Punta Mita, and Evie and I had tagged along to enjoy a week together at the beach. When I woke up, they were already down by the pool.

I stepped onto our hotel balcony and looked out at the ocean, soaking in the view. I'd done a lot of thinking over the last couple of days, and I now felt more clear-headed, grounded, and ready to meet Monique's courageous honesty with my own. I felt like I could use my words again.

When I felt ready, I sat down on a patio chair, pulled out some notes I'd taken, opened the app on my phone, and hit record.

"I'd love to try this again," I began, the sound of kids playing on the beach below coming through in the background. "What I've been so afraid to talk to you about is that I want to have an open conversation about your role. I haven't brought it up because we've never had to do that before. I'm not used to having these kinds of discussions with you."

I checked my notes and went on.

"I want to know: Does your current role fit your life? Do you have the capacity, desire, and the passion to be Chief of Growth full-time? Would something else work better? We haven't talked about what this season of life means for your role and whether the way things are set up still works for both of us."

I owned the fact that I'd made assumptions about her capacity instead of asking her these questions, and I apologized. I explained that when she told me about her dream of moving to another country and having more children, my feelings bubbled over because we hadn't had this conversation.

"I've been scared to bring it up because I don't want to lose you as a friend," I said. "If our working relationship ever had to end, it would make me so sad, but I could make peace with it. I can't make peace with losing your friendship. You are one of the most important people in my life."

I took a final deep breath. "So I want to have this conversation if you're willing to have it with me."

I wouldn't exactly call what I said in that message clear and courageous. That would have looked like telling Monique I felt let down by her performance and that I had started to resent the flexibility I'd given her because of it. But at that point, even admitting I wanted to talk with her about her role felt like starting the conversation I'd been avoiding.

Monique recognized my message for what it was: an invitation.

Her reply was the first of more than a dozen long, heartfelt, and occasionally passionate voice notes we exchanged over the next couple days. With each one, we came closer to understanding each other's perspectives.

"This conversation feels long overdue," she said in one of her replies. "But I think we need to zoom out first."

I nodded as I listened, feeling grateful that she was willing to go there with me.

"I don't think the expectations for my role are clear," she began. "It's hard for me to know what success actually looks like. For the rest of the team, there are clear tasks they can check off, but my work isn't black-and-white like that. It's long-term and strategic, and it shifts based on your vision. Sometimes it feels like the sky is the limit—and lately, it seems like the sky is your expectation."

I saw her point. In all our years of working together, we'd never defined her role. Monique was such a self-starter and always got her work done, so it hadn't even occurred to me.

"That makes sense," I said in my reply. "I'm really glad we're talking about this. You're right: Rachel's and Cheyenne's roles are more straightforward, which makes it easier to have these kinds of conversations with them. I think that's part of why this is harder for us. Let me try to define what I think success looks like."

I walked her through what I saw as the core areas of her role as well as the priority level of each, my expectations, and where I felt the gaps were.

Her reply came quickly.

"I actually really agree with all of that," she said. "I don't think we've ever defined it so clearly before. It has always felt gray to me. What you just described feels exactly like my sweet spot."

For the first time in days, I felt a positive shift between us. The energy was returning to our voices.

We ended the conversation there and went to sleep.

The next morning, another message was waiting for me.

"I had a lightbulb moment," she said. "In almost every part of my role, I can run independently except for the biggest one, which is growth. I know that is the area you care about most and where we need to be aligned. But I think that's where we're struggling to come together."

She went on. "All of our growth projects are based on your vision. And I'm not sure you realize how frustrating it is when that vision changes. I'll start down a path, break it into steps, and make progress, and then you shift the direction completely. We end up back where we started and all that work goes to waste."

I winced as I listened. Here it was again: the "Kristen Confetti."

"You're so right," I said. "I know I do that and I can't imagine how frustrating it is. I really need to work on that."

"It's not just frustrating," she said. "It's demotivating. I know you have strong opinions because this is your brand, and that's okay, but you're letting your fear hold you back. You say you don't want a business that relies solely on you, but you don't seem open to the solutions I think will get us there. You stick to what's comfortable and what you know, and that makes it hard for me to experiment. By the time I'm excited to start something new, you've already poked so many holes in it that I end up changing it back to what you want instead of what I think will help us grow. It makes me pull back and share fewer ideas because what's the point?"

She wasn't wrong. Monique had long believed that one of our best paths forward included scalable content, like prerecorded online courses, but I was attached to delivering everything live to create a more human experience. I was afraid that anything less wouldn't feel personal or authentic. But her candor helped me see it in a different light. If I wanted the business to grow in different ways, I had to be willing to try something new, even if it was uncomfortable. I needed to trust her. She couldn't do her job if I continued to allow my fear to lead me.

"You're right," I said. "I need to be more open, and I'm really going to work on that. I think *I'm* having a lightbulb moment now: I didn't realize you'd pulled back on the growth projects because you were so frustrated with me. I thought it was because you didn't have the capacity for them. So I stepped in more, which probably only made it worse for you, and then I started to feel like I was managing your projects."

"Exactly," she said. "And there's one more thing. I don't think you fully see everything that goes into me being your thought partner. Some days, talking through your ideas and everything that comes along with them takes most of my time and energy. There's not much left to put toward my other work on days like that."

"I'm so glad you told me that," I said. "I don't expect you to drop everything to respond to me. I'm sorry I never made that clear. If something is urgent, I'll tell you. Otherwise, you can respond whenever it works for you."

We let the conversation breathe until the next day.

"I think what I'm hearing," I said after I'd spent time reflecting, "is that what you need from me is trust and space to run. So this is me giving you the green light. I want you to take us where you think we should go. I'll work on stepping back. And if you ever feel like I'm not, tell me."

"I will," she said. "I know this isn't something that can be fixed overnight. We'll probably always have to navigate it, but I commit to letting you know when I need more of your vision and input—and when I need less of it."

And just like that, we found our way to the other side. For real this time.

Following Monique's last voice note, I invested in classes for her to learn more about online courses and scalable content. I got out of her way and challenged myself to be open to new ideas. Our conversations didn't solve everything and we didn't always see eye-to-eye, but there was a renewed passion on both of our parts to build a business that could grow beyond me.

What started as a message about a dream turned into uncovering muddied expectations, assumptions, and critical discussions we'd failed to have. Most importantly, I saw my own role in creating so many of the issues between us.

These conversations with Monique were some of the hardest of my life—which, by now, you know is saying something. I've never been on the giving or receiving end of such raw, emotional feedback.

I've often wondered: Did Monique and I blur the line too much between friendship and work? Did we take our transparency too far? If I could go back, would I still share the feelings that started it all?

There's no way around it: When you're friends with someone you work closely with, things will get messy, especially when one reports to the other. And yet our strong friendship is the reason Monique and I could have these conversations in the first place. Admitting to someone I cared about so much that I felt taken advantage of had felt almost impossible. I only managed to say it because I trusted that our relationship could survive it.

That same trust meant it never felt like Monique was against me or that I was against her. It was always the two of us, side by side, trying to find our way through. Together. There were many moments when either of us could have shut down completely and chosen self-protection over connection. But we didn't. Our friendship is what kept us in it.

We chose to make the other feel heard, even when we were hurting. Even when it took many tries and the words came out wrong or stopped coming altogether. And in doing so, we helped each other move past our limiting beliefs: Monique spoke up even when she was afraid her feelings were too much, and I said things that I knew might not make her happy.

So would I take any of it back?

I wouldn't.

In the end, Monique and I both agreed that these were conversations we needed to have. They weren't pretty, but they created a new level of openness that we maintain to this day. We've since explored other areas in the business where expectations or responsibilities weren't clear, and it all started here.

I believe that to be human at work is to have the courage to build real relationships. On our team, we practice that every week. We begin our team meeting by sharing what's going on in our lives outside of work. Not just a surface-level update—a *real* one. We spend the majority of our time on that and save the business-related agenda items for the end. Sharing about our lives helps us stay connected and reminds us of the humanity of the people we get to work alongside. It also helps us understand what each of us is going through so that we can meet one another with empathy.

How far we decide to take our relationships in our work is up to each of us—and up to you. But if you want them to be real, I've learned that you have to accept it will hurt sometimes. The alternative is less risky, but it comes at the cost of never being fully seen or understood. I will always choose to build deep and meaningful relationships, no matter the risk.

My biggest lesson from my conversations with Monique is that when you're close with the people you work with, it's even *more* important to say what you feel when you feel it. And especially when you're the leader. No matter how uncomfortable or scary it might feel, it's my responsibility to speak up when something needs to be addressed.

My therapist told me once that when two people care deeply about their connection, they carry an equally strong fear of disconnection. In trying to protect the relationship, they avoid the conversations that might threaten it, which is what actually threatens the relationship.

That's exactly what I did with Monique. I thought that by avoiding the conversation, I was preserving our friendship, when in reality I broke her trust and nearly cost us everything. She told me later that what hurt her most wasn't what I said; it was all the times I had withheld my feelings.

Those conversations with Monique changed me. They challenged me to show up with more openness and courage in my other relationships. They inspired me to have greater compassion when I'm on the other side of someone who's having trouble finding their own words.

What a gift it is to have a friend like her.

To have someone you can share the truth of your heart with, even when you're shaking. Someone who sees you, even when they don't like what they see. Someone who gives you permission to be human.

I can only hope that every person gets to experience a friendship—and a working relationship—like that.

I don't know where the future will take us or whether we'll work together forever, but I know this: Monique is my friend before anything else.

She has taught me some of the most important lessons in my life, not just about business, but about courage, honesty, and what it means to be a leader. She has made me braver. She has reminded me who I am. She has given me permission to trust my heart and chase what matters most. She has helped me make my dreams come true.

And I will spend the rest of my days doing the same for her every chance I get.

Chapter 54

With Me All Along

It's 4 p.m. I'm sitting in my office at my home in Houston.

I take another sip of water and catch a glimpse of the oak trees outside my window and the leaves swaying in the breeze. I open my laptop and click the document that holds an early draft of my second book.

And then I begin reading the first portion aloud to my therapist. It's the first time I've ever shared these words with anyone.

With each one I say, I feel lighter and more free.

I'm terrified when I think about sharing this book with the world because it's the most vulnerable thing I've ever written. But I'm also proud when I think about sharing it with the world because it's the truest thing I've ever written.

We reach the end of our session, but I still have pages to go.

"Keep going," she says.

So I do. When I finish, she's quiet.

"How is it?" I ask.

Judging by her silence, if I had to guess, she might have tears in her eyes like me.

"You sound like your true self," she says.

I close my laptop. As I look up, I catch my reflection in the window.

That's when I see her.

Big, brown eyes. A smile on her face.

She looks peaceful. Content. Self-assured.

I smile back.

She is no stranger. She is me.

The person I once hoped I could become.

The person I longed for.

The person I needed most.

And suddenly, I understand: She was with me all along.

I just had to see her. Listen to her. Let her lead.

This is how growth happens.

Not overnight. Not with bells and whistles.

It happens on a random afternoon, when you catch your reflection in a window and realize you really like what you see.

You think about the version of yourself who didn't feel this way, and you feel grateful for every step, every impossible decision, every hard conversation that led you here.

And the best part? You know it's not over.

There's still more to discover. More to learn. More steps to take.

It's only now, years after that night when I barely recognized myself, that I can see it clearly: I had it all backwards.

Leadership didn't cost me myself. It taught me how to find myself.

To lead others is a gift. A privilege. A responsibility. A weight worth carrying.

But to lead yourself?

To face yourself?

To have the courage to become who you already are?

That is the honor of a lifetime. The highest calling I've ever known.

Thank goodness for the night I didn't recognize myself.

Because it led me here.

A Check-In Before We Go

Here we are, friend. Back where we started.

I can't believe it's already time to say goodbye. Can we just hang out forever?

Thank you for still being here with me.

There were so many times when you could have gotten up and left the table, so to speak, but you didn't. Through all my ups and downs, the times when you thought it couldn't possibly get any worse, and even the moments I'm not proud of—you stayed.

Before we go our separate ways, I want to have one last check-in with you. How's your heart? What are you thinking about after taking it all in?

As for what's on my own heart, I'm thinking about the version of me who was sitting in my living room, staring at a shell of myself, and wondering how I'd built a life that looked "perfect" on paper but felt so empty inside. And I'm thinking about the version of me today who is sitting here with you, feeling alive in my life and like my insides finally match my outsides.

If I had to boil it all down to the *one* thing that got me from there to here, it would be this: I faced what I would rather have avoided.

When I reflect on all the stories I've shared with you, I now see that there was only ever one thing I was afraid of:

Words. That's it.

The words I didn't want to say because I thought they would hurt people. The truths I kept inside because I was trying to keep everyone happy. The conversations I resisted having with myself because I didn't want to have to do something with what I found.

For so long, I allowed my fear to keep me stuck. But every time I said the thing I was most afraid to say, something in my life changed. Not always how I expected it would. Definitely not always easily or without pain. Always in a way that caused me to learn, though. *Always* in a way that brought me closer to the person I wanted to be.

Isn't it wild to think that words can be the only thing standing between us and the lives we want? Between us and the deeper connection we crave? Isn't it amazing that the words we *don't* say can hold us back and hurt the people around us most?

Finding the courage to say mine unmasked me.

But courage didn't always feel like I thought it would. It was uncomfortable, and at times heartbreaking. I usually didn't get it right the first time. But I stopped hiding. And every time I chose to face the truth, in myself and with others, I became a better leader. I strengthened my relationships. I created a culture of more openness and trust.

That is human leadership: to be willing to be human out loud, fully, imperfectly, and vulnerably.

But don't mistake "human" for soft.

This is the hardest work I've ever done.

Being a human leader means you *will* hurt people sometimes. You *will* make a compassionate decision and still wish parts of it had gone differently. You *will* love something—or someone—and still choose to say goodbye. The real work is learning to keep your heart open and choosing to turn toward others instead of away, even when it's the toughest thing to do.

Now, I want to ask you: Is there something—or someone—you need to face?

Maybe it's a conversation you've been avoiding or a truth you haven't said out loud. Maybe you are where I once was, looking at your reflection and not recognizing the person staring back at you. You know exactly what you need to do to get to the other side, but the thought of doing it feels terrifying.

What could happen if you found the courage to face it with an open heart?

If we were really sitting together right now, this is the part where I'd reach across the table, take your hands in mine, and tell you: The version of you that you've been searching for isn't somewhere out there.

It's already in you.

It's in the conversations you've been avoiding.

In that thing you've been afraid to say out loud.

In the part of you that's waiting to be seen.

You don't have to do it perfectly. You just have to do it.

When you find the courage to face yourself and others, it will set you free.

So, friend, what on earth are you waiting for?

Afterword by Monique

If you had told me back in 2012 that the summer cleaning job I interviewed for in the middle of an Arby's (yes, you read that right) would turn into my dream job, I probably would have laughed in your face. I never planned for the cleaning company I worked at in college to turn into anything more than a means to pay my way through school—and I know that's true for all of us: me, Cheyenne, and Rachel.

In those early days, I saw Kristen as nothing more than an out-of-reach boss. But the day I met her and she handed me a ring of keys, I felt something that I had craved my entire life: implicit trust. I wanted nothing more than to prove to her I was worthy of it.

While cleaning at Student Maid in college, I realized I'd stumbled upon a gem: a company whose leader not only trusted the people working there but who also deeply cared about them as individuals with dreams for their lives. I experienced what it felt like to be seen. In college, some of my most valuable lessons came not from my classes but from my job cleaning houses: I learned what it felt like to have autonomy, to be heard, and to be supported. I experienced the growth and resilience that came with owning my mistakes, making them right, and taking chances on myself. Once you feel those things and hear that so many people have never experienced them in their jobs, you realize you've found something special.

Even though I saw potential in the company I chose to stick with after college, I would be lying if I said I didn't have moments of doubt. The work was absolutely exhausting. I lived and breathed my job, and when I became Kristen's assistant, I saw firsthand how dedicated and, dare I say, obsessed Kristen was with her work. I felt like I had to keep up and prove once again that I was worthy of the opportunity she had trusted me with.

This new role ushered in an entirely different season in our relationship. I got to know Kristen on a deeper level and, naturally, we started spending a lot more time together. She was no longer the boss at arm's length. She had become my friend.

Right next to all of the good sat all of the bad: an amazing and fun culture with people I loved working with . . . and Student Maid's struggling revenue numbers. The potential for an exciting, fulfilling career . . . and the astronomical amount of debt the business was carrying. Believing with every ounce of my being that the work Kristen was doing to make workplaces more human mattered . . . and watching her abandon her own needs to pour her heart into her people and her work.

It was confusing to watch. But then I started to see Kristen change.

In our weekly team meetings, I heard her talk about taking better care of herself. I didn't know anything about how depressed and resentful she was really feeling at the time, but even without that context, I could see that she was working on herself. She shared things with our team like limiting beliefs and personal values, and every time she did, she invited us to grow with her. For the first time in our company's history, we acknowledged the toll our jobs took on us. We started talking about rest, taking more time off, and challenging the hustle culture that pervades the working world. As our thought-partnership blossomed and the layers started to unfold, I saw a new version of Kristen emerging.

Her growth challenged me to grow. Her excitement made me excited. I wanted to learn to speak up. To work through and untangle my own limiting belief. I wanted to grow both personally and at work.

And it wasn't just me: Our whole team committed to learning about ourselves and each other. Together, we learned how to have hard but productive conversations. We called one another out when we recognized a limiting belief getting in the way. We created space for learning and understanding, which meant creating space for screwups, apologies, and do-overs. We cheered each other on and held each other accountable to showing up as our most authentic, human selves, even when it was messy. And we are still doing those things to this day.

We don't always get it right. Some days, we lean into conversations and choose not to hold back, even if the words we find don't come out exactly how we want them to. But what matters is that we keep trying, keep opening our hearts, and keep our commitment to growing together.

We often reflect on a powerful question: "What is it like to be on the other side of me?" It's a question we not only ask ourselves but challenge each other to ponder as well. We've learned that the best measure of our progress is seeing what is reflected in the mirror that others hold up for us and asking ourselves if we like what we see. I believe that's why doing this work as a team was—and is—so powerful.

Being on a team with this level of transparency, connection, and care is an incredible gift. And it's a privilege to have a leader who wants to see us grow and become our best selves right alongside her.

Being human at work is far from easy—but it's absolutely worth it. When we all choose to do the hard work, I can tell you from experience, something beautiful happens.

Each person on our team has the freedom to dream, to build, to grow, to change, and to have a role that evolves with us. But we know that only works when we're honest about what we need. I'm grateful that those conversations are ones we can have and grow through, and that when we speak up, we are met by a leader who not only hears those needs, but is willing to be flexible and support them. Because of that, each of us has been able to create our dream job around the things we value most in life. For me, that is my family and raising my kids. For Rachel, that is family, friends, and freedom. And for Cheyenne, that is time for adventures and creative pursuits.

We have helped each other become people we are proud to be, and everyone around us benefits: our partners, our children, our families and friends. When I think about where we started, I'm so grateful for how far we've come.

Human leadership isn't something any of us is owed. It's something we renew our commitment to over and over again: when we bravely look in the mirror and heal the past. When we advocate for our needs, set boundaries, and take ownership of showing up at our best. When we own where we've messed up, lean in, and have painful but honest conversations.

This work is a daily choice. But if you are willing to be human, to be vulnerable, and to reveal your true self, you might be pleasantly surprised by what is waiting for you on the other side.

Acknowledgments

From the outside, this looks like a book. But on the inside is a whole village of people who held me, challenged me, and believed in me through the final page. Without them, my story really would be in a locked drawer instead of out in the world. I don't think it's possible to ever find the words to properly thank them, but I'm going to try.

From the depths of my heart, thank you . . .

To Monique: For always seeing me, for making me believe I can do anything, for your courage and confidence that has rubbed off on me, for your grace and love as I've learned how to be human, and for helping me create the company and life of my dreams. I know that technically my title says I am the boss, but it is you who has led me. I would not be the person I am, or the leader I've become, without you. Thank you for being the one I can always trust with the keys, and for a thought partnership that has grown into one of the most meaningful relationships in my life.

To Rachel: For sticking with me the longest, for helping me find the words in my heart in a way that no one else can, for your positivity and love that has lifted me up in some of the darkest moments, and for always being along for the ride, even though we never know where it will take us. Thank goodness you hired yourself when I forgot. You are my dream editor, teammate, and friend. I'm so grateful for two books together—and for the way you've been a part of so many of the stories inside of them.

To Cheyenne: For being someone I can always count on, for your consistent and calm presence, for being the kind of friend and teammate who stayed by my side during one of the scariest weeks of my life, and for helping me see the world in a different way. You have inspired me to think deeper, live more fully, get out of my comfort zone, have more fun, and stand up for what I believe in. I'm so grateful you raised your hand in our meeting that day and chose to give your talents here when you could have given them anywhere. Thank you for holding down our entire company while we brought this book to life—and for being our favorite early reader.

To Amanda: For teaching me that two things can be true, for the hardest and most loving goodbye I've ever had, and for your love and compassion that lights up the world around you. Thank you for the conversations we had as I wrote this book—I will treasure them for the rest of my life.

To Katie: For being the one I could trust with Student Maid, for allowing me to be human when I realized I wanted something different, and for being a part of the Student Maid journey from the beginning to the very end.

To Abby: For standing by my side for so many years, for the impact you had on my life and on Student Maid, and for making the decision I didn't have the courage to make. The lessons I learned from our time together will live in me forever.

To the Student Maid team members: For teaching me my purpose, for giving me permission to screw up as I learned how to lead, and for helping me transform a cleaning company into a place where we could all grow into who we were meant to be.

To Paul: For reaching back when I reached out on that lonely night, and for helping me begin to see myself and the limiting belief that ultimately changed my life.

To Jamil: For asking me to lead that workshop in Phoenix, for becoming my role model, for lighting a fire in me to create the life I wanted, and for teaching me what real leadership looks like.

To Kristen: For being my safe space, for always reminding me that my feelings make sense, and for helping me become the truest version of myself. I hit the therapist jackpot.

To Richard: For championing me and my ideas, for your endless wisdom, and for challenging me to write the most generous book I could. I am so grateful to do this again with you—and the entire Inkwell team.

To Brian: For believing in this book since the beginning, for giving me the complete freedom to write what was in my heart, and for making the process of bringing a book into the world feel delightful and fun every step of the way. Working with you and Wiley was the best book decision I could have ever made.

To Debbie S: For giving me time and grace in the production process and for allowing me to be human in it. Your flexibility made it possible for me to write the book I most wanted to bring into the world.

To Adaobi: For seeing what this book could be, for helping me stay true to my vision for it, for your honesty and care in your edits, for making my words shine brighter, and for your ability to see what this book needed often before I did.

To Mark F: For our brainstorming sessions about the title, for helping me uncover the truth of this book, and for empowering me to boldly step into a new season of my life and my story.

To Isabel: For your artistic genius, next-level patience, many iterations, and for creating the cover I saw in my dreams.

To Bryn: For inviting me to dig deeper into my heart than I knew I could, for teaching me that the only way I can help others feel seen is by seeing myself, for helping me unlock my creative expression, and for reminding me often that this book could be anything I wanted it to be.

To Jenn: For our many conversations about this book years ago, for sparking the ideas that started it all, and for teaching me the lesson I carried with me through every page: "Clear thinking is clear writing, and clear writing is clear thinking."

To Debbie W: For walking alongside me and helping me claim the language that was already in my heart, for showing me how to stand in these pages, and for teaching me what a true yes feels like. Our 2/2 conversation will always be imprinted on my heart.

To Charlie: For sketching covers, brainstorming titles, polling your family, and offering some of the most valuable feedback I received. You treated this book like it was your own and have been such an inspiration throughout this story.

To Cindy: For the texts that always came right when I needed them, for celebrating me, and for the kind of friendship that reminds me I'm never alone.

To Darlene: For being one of the safest people in my life, for calling me the moment you read it, and for telling me not to change a single word. Your love was louder than my fear and helped me keep going.

To Amanda G: For the early morning workouts that turned into book strategy sessions, for helping me keep my mind and body strong, and for reading this book and seeing me so clearly.

To Mark B: For coming back with bookmarks and Post-its to help me see every place this book mattered, and for helping me believe in it more. You are simply the best.

To Nicole: For our conversations about the joys and struggles of owning a business and for being someone I've always trusted with my true feelings.

To Anatolia: For checking on me, for the pep talks, for allowing me to stay in my writing bubble without guilt, and for beginning our friendship by ringing the doorbell.

To my friends (you know who you are): For your constant belief in me, this book, and anything I set my mind to, even when it means I drop off the face of the earth for a little bit.

To Coach Enoch: For teaching me the running mindset that allowed me to finish this race strong.

To the team at Hotel St. Augustine: For making me feel at home and becoming a sanctuary for me to write this book.

To Jazmyne: For bringing me daisies when I needed them most.

To Reina: For your healing hands that brought me back to life when I spent too many hours hunched over my laptop.

To our amazing clients: For your love, grace, and patience when my focus had to stretch to make space for writing.

To Brad, my seatmate on the flight to Denver: For helping me make the final decision on the book cover at 30,000 feet.

To Aunt Terry: For believing in me since I was a curly-headed little kid, for reading every page of this book and the first one, and for being my favorite person to call when I take a walk. I love being your niece.

To Mom: For being the reason I'm here in the first place, for teaching me how to be giving and compassionate, for calling me after every chapter and crying with me, and for your unconditional love. I am the world's luckiest daughter and I love you.

To Dad: For being the second reason I'm here in the first place, for teaching me how to live with courage, for being the one I can always call when I screw up, and for your hugs that make everything better. I love you and am so grateful you are my daddy.

To Lauren: For reminding me to be me, for always answering the phone, for believing in my dreams as if they were your own, for the tough love when I need it, and for being the best sister I could ever hope for. I love you and feel so lucky to share this life with you.

To Evie: For being the light of my life, my greatest teacher, and the reason I want to keep growing every day. May you always have the courage to listen to your heart and follow where it leads you. I love you forever.

To Spiros: For encouraging me to be me, for loving me through every high and low, for believing in me when I didn't believe in me, for making my heart feel at home, and for the beautiful life we've built together. I love you so much.

And finally, to the woman I was in Chapter 1 and the woman I am today. I love every version that brought us here.

Recommended Reading

These are the books that had the greatest impact on me as I lived the stories in these pages.

Burnout: The Secret to Unlocking the Stress Cycle by Emily Nagoski, PhD, and Amelia Nagoski, DMA

Dying for a Paycheck: How Modern Management Harms Employee Health and Company Performance—and What We Can Do About It by Jeffrey Pfeffer

Four Thousand Weeks: Time Management for Mortals by Oliver Burkeman

Free the Idea Monkey to Focus on What Matters Most: How the Most Successful People Make Big Ideas Happen by G. Michael Maddock and Raphael Louis Vitón

It Doesn't Have to Be Crazy at Work by Jason Fried and David Heinemeier Hansson

Let Your Mind Run: A Memoir of Thinking My Way to Victory by Deena Kastor

Loving What Is: Four Questions That Can Change Your Life by Byron Katie

Necessary Endings: The Employees, Businesses, and Relationships That All of Us Have to Give Up in Order to Move Forward by Dr. Henry Cloud

The Now Habit: A Strategic Program for Overcoming Procrastination and Enjoying Guilt-Free Play by Neil Fiore, PhD

Profit First: Transform Your Business from a Cash-Eating Monster to a Money-Making Machine by Mike Michalowicz

Real Self-Care: A Transformative Program for Redefining Wellness (Crystals, Cleanses, and Bubble Baths Not Included) by Pooja Lakshmin, MD

Taming Your Gremlin: A Surprisingly Simple Method for Getting Out of Your Own Way by Rick Carson

Traction: Get a Grip on Your Business by Gino Wickman

Untamed by Glennon Doyle

When Things Fall Apart: Heart Advice for Difficult Times by Pema Chödrön

About the Author

Kristen Hadeed believes that authentic, human leadership can change the world.

Today, she spends her time helping leaders and teams around the world build cultures of trust, connection, and courage.

Learn more:

www.kristenhadeed.com

Instagram: @kristenhadeed

LinkedIn: www.linkedin.com/in/kristenhadeed

Beyond the Book

Human leadership is a lifelong journey.

Continue to grow with me at www.kristenhadeed.com/humanleadership.

Index